Lotus

Illustrated DICTIONARY of

PSYCHOLOGY

Complied and Edited by:
Louis Smith

Lotus
PRESS
4735/22, Prakash Deep Building
Ansari Road, Daryaganj,
New Delhi - 110002

Lotus Illustrated

DICTIONARY of PSYCHOLOGY

ISBN 81 89093 56 8

Published by:

Lotus Press Publishers & Distributors

Unit No. 220, 2nd Floor, 4735/22,
Prakash Deep Building, Ansari Road, Darya Ganj,
New Delhi- 110002, Ph.: 32903912, 23280047, 09811838000
• E-mail : lotuspress1984@gmail.com www.lotuspress.co.in

Printed at : Lotus Press Publishers & Distributors, Delhi

PREFACE

The nineteenth century had inherited from the eighteenth, the belief in the rationality of man. Utilitarians and economists as well as other students of man and society believed in the coincidence of reason with action as the key to human existence. Even after Marx had laid bare the connection between group interest and ideology, this mulish insistence on independence of reason did not give way.

But, Sigmund Freud changed the self-perception of man entirely. Writing in the interregnum between the two world wars, Freud discovered the unconscious, repression and libido. His interpretation of dreams and work with neurotic patients convinced him that man was moved not by what he thinks, but that even his thoughts are governed by what his repressed instincts dictate.

It was not a noble picture of man or the civilisation he had created. Freud wrote that civilisation had been bought at a very high price of emasculation of the instinctual life of man.

Freud became a revered 'guru' for many. But, psychology neither begins nor ends with Freud. It has kept evolving. Freud's line of reasoning has been christened psychoanalysis, which many people refuse to accept as a science. Jung, Adler, Erich Fromm have enriched this tradition further. Existential philosophers like Sartre have tried to develop their own kind of psychoanalysis, in which there is no place for the unconscious and repressive censor.

Psychology interests everyone and yet few can claim to have read much of it. A plethora of jargon is one reason for the fear that the study of psychology arouses. This dictionary, we are sure, will help the reader overcome this barrier and enjoy a subject that surely deserves more attention from students, historians, biographers, litterateurs and laymen.

■ **'is' of identity**

the word 'is' expresses the sameness of two things. For example, as in the statement, 'Four things 'is' the same as two things plus two things.'

■ **'is' of predication**

the word 'is' is used to confer a property upon something. For example, as in the statement, 'Her skin is fair.'

■ **a fortiori**

a Latin word and mean 'more so'. If a particular argument is good enough to be accepted, then the same argument, strengthened, provides even more (a fortiori reason to accept it).

■ **a posteriori**

a Latin word, pertaining to truths, which can be known only after observation and experience in the world.

■ **a priori**

a Latin word, pertaining to truths which can be known without prior observation or experience, a form of knowledge that humans may possess which is given to them without experience because it is innate or 'hard-wired' in them. The truths of logic and mathematics are claimed by some to be known a priori. Kant argued that some a priori concepts such as that of a thing or time must be presupposed.

■ **ab design**

it is a single subject research design that contains one baseline (A) and one treatment (B).

■ **a-b-a design**

experimental design in which participants first experience the baseline condition (A), followed by the experimental treatment (B) and then again return to the baseline (A).

■ **a-b-a-b design**

a single subject research design that contains a baseline (A1), treatment (B1), a second baseline (B2) and finally a second treatment phase (B2).

■ **abnormal behaviour**

patterns of emotion, thought and action deemed pathological for one or more of the following reasons: infrequent occurrence, violation of norms, personal distress, disability or dysfunction and unexpectedness.

■ **abnormal psychology**

the area of psychological investigation which deals with the understanding of the nature of individual pathologies of mind, mood and behaviour.

■ **abnormality**

any mental, emotional, or behavioural activity that deviates from culturally or scientifically accepted norms.

■ **abreaction**

in psychoanalysis, the process of reducing emotional tension by reliving (in speech or action or both) the experience that caused the tension.

■ **absolute**

an ideal reality which is completely independent and unconditionally real.

■ absolute refractory period

the period immediately following the discharge of a nerve impulse during which the cell cannot be induced to fire again.

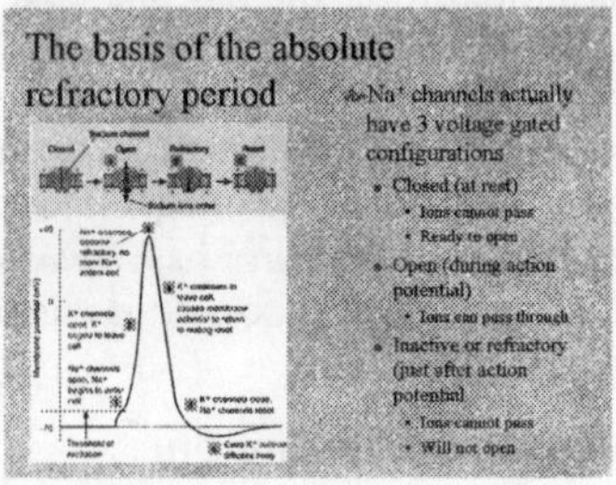

■ absolute threshold

the intensity or frequency at which a stimulus becomes effective or ceases to become effective, as measured under experimental conditions.

■ absolute zero

scale of measurement that contains a point where the scale has no value.

■ absolutism

unrestricted powers of the state.

■ abstinence

foregoing some kind of gratification, in the area of alcohol or drug dependence, being without the substance on which the subject had been dependent.

■ abstinence violation effect

it is the effect when a person attempting to abstain from alcohol use ingests alcohol and then endures conflict and guilt by making an internal attribution to explain why he or she drank, thereby making him or her more likely to continue drinking in order to cope with self-blame and guilt.

■ abstract attitude

a type of cognitive functioning that includes assuming a mental set voluntarily, shifting voluntarily from a specific aspect of a situation to the genera, keeping in mind simultaneously various aspects of a situation, grasping the essentials of a whole and breaking it into its parts and isolating them voluntarily, planning ahead ideationally and/or thinking or performing symbolically. A characteristic of many psychiatric disorders is the person's inability to assume the abstract attitude or to shift readily from the concrete to the abstract and back again according to circumstances.

■ abstract concept

a concept or idea not related to any specific instance or object and which potentially can be applied to different situations. Persons with cognitive deficits often have difficulty understanding abstract concepts.

■ abstract idea

a thought that has eliminated individuating differences between objects and moved from individual cases to a more general, inclusive category, for example, redness, canine, etc. The phrase is associated with empiricists such as Berkeley and Hume who denied that there are such ideas, holding instead that particular ideas or images stand for such abstractions.

■ abstract thinking

being able to apply abstract concepts to new situations.

■ abulia

usually associated with damage to a cerebellar vessel, abulia refers to an inability to make decisions or exercise will. It includes slow reaction and lack of spontaneity.

■ abuse

to misuse, attack, or injure. Abuse may be sexual, physical, or emotional.

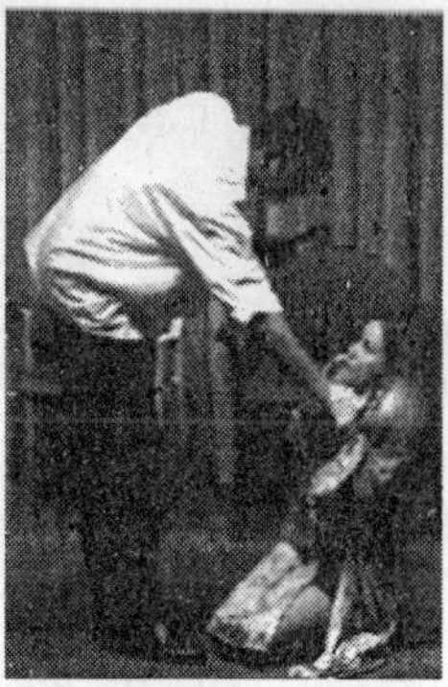

■ abused child

a child or infant who has suffered continuous injuries, which include bone fractures, neurological and psychological damage, or sexual abuse at the hands of an elder. The abuse takes place repeatedly and is often precipitated, in the case of physical abuse, by the child's minor and normally irritating behaviour. Child abuse also includes neglecting the child.

■ academic problem

difficulty arising at the academic life, that is not due to any mental disorder. Examples are failing grades or significant underachievement in a person with adequate intellectual capacity.

■ academic skills disorders

this is a major group of infancy, childhood and adolescence disorders that includes reading disorder, mathematics disorder and disorder of written expression.

■ acalculia

the inability to perform simple problems of arithmetic.

■ acceleration/deceleration

a closed head injury frequently sustained in a car accident, where the brain wrenches forward and backward, hitting the walls of the skull.

■ accident

mean a part which is not the essential nature of a thing. An accident may be added or subtracted to an object without changing its essence. The colour of a person's eyes is an accident, having a mind is not.

■ accident-proneness

vulnerability to accidents based on psychological causes or motivations, usually unconscious.

■ accommodate

to use an alternative means to furnish with something needed or desired.

■ accommodation

(1) the process by which the lens of the eye varies its focus.

(2) in Piaget's theory of cognitive development, the process by which an infant modifies a pre-existing schema in order to include a novel object or event.

■ **accoustics**

deals with the study of the physical characteristics of sound.

■ **acculturation**

extent to which a person identifies with his or her group of origin and its culture or with the mainstream dominant culture.

■ **acculturation difficulty**

a problem in accommodating to or finding an appropriate way to adapt to a different culture or environment. The problem is not based on any coexisting mental disorder.

■ **accurate empathic understanding**

in client-centred therapy, an essential quality of the therapist, referring to the ability to see the world through the client's phenomenology and also from perspectives of which the client may be only dimly aware.

■ **acetylcholine**

the most common of the neurotransmitters. It is found in many synapses in the brain and spinal cord, and is particularly prevalent in an area of the brain called the hippocampus, which plays a key role in the formation of new memories.

■ **achievement**

acquired ability, such as school attainment in spelling.

■ **achievement test**

a test designed to measure what the individual has accomplished, his accomplishment in a particular training programme, course and so on.

■ **achromatic colours**

black, white, and grey.

■ **acid polymer**

in higher organisms the great bulk of DNA incorporating the sugar deoxyribose is located within the chromosomes.

■ **acoustic buffer**

in short-term memory, a hypothesised component of the encoding process which briefly stores information in an acoustic code (i.e., the sound of the digit, letter, or word).

■ **acquaintance rape**

also known as date rape, it is the rape that takes place between two people who know each other, sometimes occurring on a date.

■ **acquisition**

the stage during which a new response is learned and gradually strengthened.

■ **acquisitiveness**

the motive that involves acquiring or collecting material goods for the sake of collecting.

■ **acting out**

expressions of unconscious emotional conflicts or feelings in actions rather than words. The person is not consciously aware of the meaning of such acts. Acting out may be harmful or, in

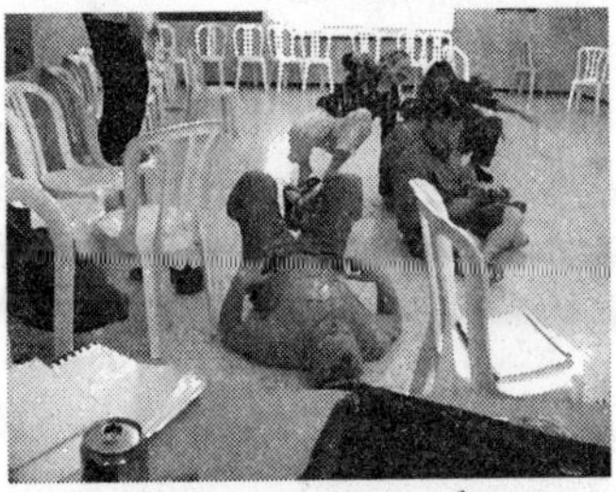

controlled situations, therapeutic (e.g., children's play therapy).

■ **action potential**

synonymous with nerve impulse. The wave of electrical activity that is transmitted down the axon of the neuron when the cell membrane becomes depolarised.

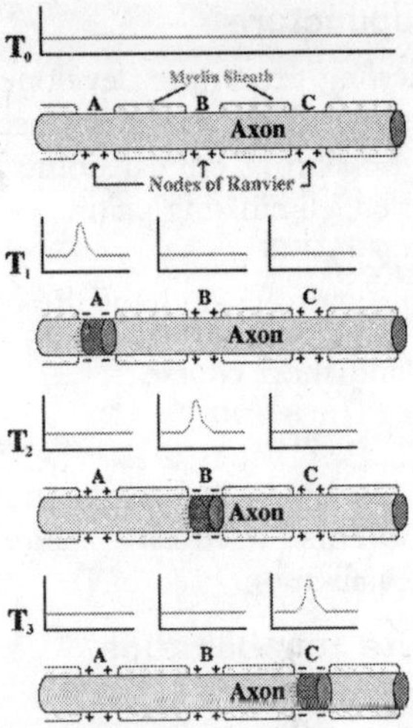

■ **activation model**

in memory, the proposal that retrieval of an item depends on the activation of that item reaching a critical level.

■ **active learning**

the role of the learner in the learning process. Contrasted with passive learning. In active learning, the learner participates in the learning process by making a conscious effort to learn, by taking notes, by outlining, by intensive review, etc.

■ **actor-observer effect**

the tendency for people to attribute their own behaviour to external causes but that of others to internal factors.

■ **actualisation**

realisation of the full potential of an individual.

■ **actuality**

the state of being in reality rather than being in potential.

■ **acupuncture**

a healing procedure developed in China in which needles are inserted in the skin at critical points and twirled, eliminating pain.

■ **acute**

sharp, severe, having sudden onset and short course.

■ **acute care**

the phase of managing health problems which requires hospitalisation.

■ **acute rehabilitation programme**

primary emphasis is on the early phase of rehabilitation which usually begins as soon as the patient is stable. The program is designed to be comprehensive and based in a medical facility with a typical length of stay of one week to several months (short term). Treatment focuses on intensive physical and cognitive restorative services.

■ **acute stress**

a momentary state of arousal with typically clear onset and offset patterns.

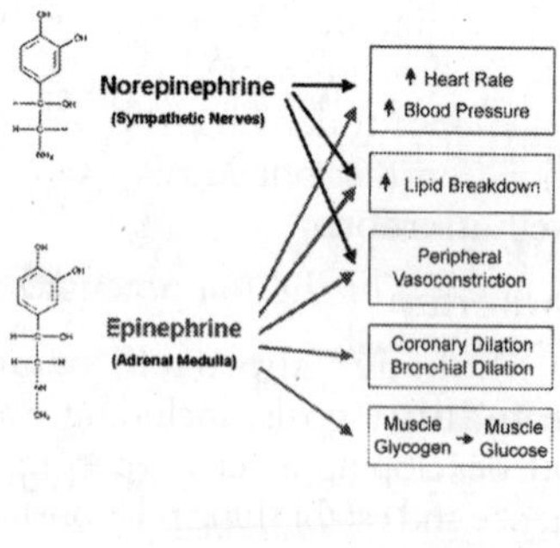

■ **ad hoc**

derived from Latin, it means 'toward this', a statement that may itself have little independent justification, but when added to a theory, saves that theory from rejection, in other words, a temporary fix.

■ **ad infinitum**

Latin word, meaning 'to infinity', without end.

■ **adaptation**

used with regard to the senses, this refers to the fact that after continual stimulation a sense gradually loses its ability to respond. For example, after prolonged exposure to a strong odour, the odour seems to fade away.

■ **adaptive reaction**

a reaction toward a source of frustration that is reality-oriented, that is, oriented toward direct removal of the frustrating situation.

■ **adaptive/assistive equipment**

a special device which assists in the performance of self-care, work or play/leisure activities or physical exercise.

■ **addiction**

dependence on a chemical substance to the extent that a physiological and/or psychological need is established. This may be manifested by any combination of the following symptoms; tolerance, preoccupation with obtaining and using the substance, use of the substance despite anticipation of probable adverse consequences, repeated efforts to cut down or control substance use, and withdrawal symptoms when the substance is unavailable or not used.

■ **Addison's disease**

an endocrine disorder produced by cortisone insufficiency and marked by weight loss, fatigue and a darkening of the skin.

■ **additive mixture**

the mixture of coloured lights, two spotlights of different colours focused on the same spot yield an additive colour mixture.

■ **adiadochokinesia**

inability to stop one movement and follow it immediately with movement in the opposite direction.

■ **adipocytes**

special fat cells in the body. Obese individuals have many more of them and thus, perhaps, a higher body fat base line.

■ **adjustment**

often transitory functional alteration or accommodation by which one can better adapt oneself to the immediate environment and to one's inner self.

■ **adjustment disorder**

refers to emotional or behavioural symptoms that develop in response to an identifiable stressor. The symptoms, which may include anxiety, depressed mood and disturbance of conduct, are clinically significant in that the distress exceeds what would be expected under the circumstances, or significant impairment in social or occupational functioning is produced. Duration of symptoms tends to be self-limited, not persisting more than 6 months after termination of the stressor or its consequences. Sometimes the disorder is designated as 'acute' if duration is 6 months or less, and as 'persistent' or 'chronic' if symptoms endure beyond 6 months.

■ **ADL**

acronym for 'Activities of Daily Living' tasks such as personal hygiene and operating a household.

■ **Adler, Alfred (1870-1937)**

an early associate of Sigmund Freud and founder of the school of individual psychology. Adler rejected Freud's emphasis on sex and maintained that personality difficulties are rooted in a feeling of inferiority deriving from restrictions on the individuals need for self-assertion.

■ **adlerian**

a holistic approach which emphasises goals, including ways of developing a sense of competence and establishing relationships with others.

■ **administrative psychiatry**

the branch of psychiatry that deals with the organisation of clinical practice in a programme, hospital, or other facility. Its focus is on the management process involving interaction of health administration, clinical care or psychiatric patients and the attitudes, values and belief system of the organisation.

■ **adolescence**

the period of transition from childhood to adulthood during which the individual develops to sexual maturity.

■ **adolescent growth spurt**

a period of rapid physical growth that accompanies the onset of puberty.

■ **adoption study**

it is the study of the inheritability of a disorder by finding adopted people with a disorder and then determining the prevalence of the disorder among their biological and adoptive relatives, in order to separate out contributing genetic and environmental factors.

■ **adrenal gland**

one of a pair of endocrine glands located above the kidneys. The medulla of the gland secretes the hormones epinephrine and norepinephrine. The cortex of the gland secretes a number of hormones, collectively called the adrenocortical hormones, which include cortisol.

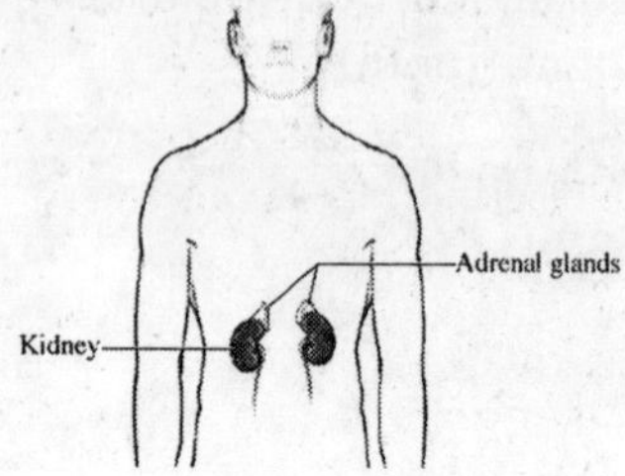

■ **adrenal-cortical-system**

a neuro-endocrine system activated in response to stress. On a signal from the hypothalamus, the pituitary gland secretes a number of hormones. One stimulates the thyroid gland to make more energy available, the other (adrenocorticotropic hormone, ACTH) triggers the outer layer of the adrenal gland (the adrenal cortex) to release some 30 hormones (including cortisol) that play a role in the body's adjustment to emergencies.

■ **adrenaline**

a hormone that is secreted by the adrenal glands. Also called epinerhrine.

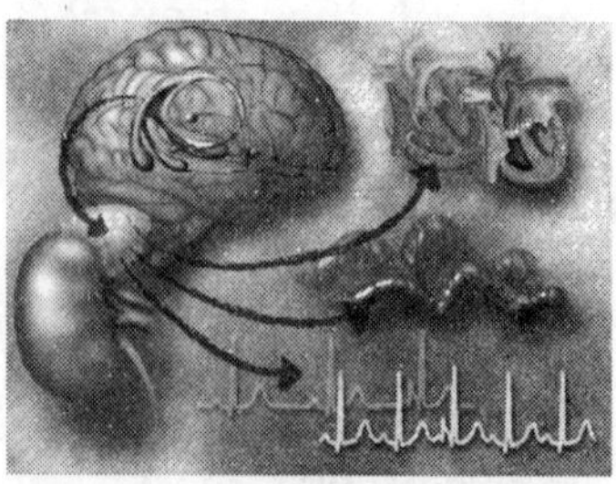

adrenergic

neural activation by catgcholamines, such as epinephrine, norepinephrine and dopamkne.

adrenocorticotropic hormone (acth)

a hormone released by the pituitary gland in response to stress, known as the body's major 'stress' hormone. It is carried by the bloodstream to the adrenal glands and various other organs of the body, causing the release of some 30 hormones, each of which plays a role in the body's adjustment to emergency situations.

advanced accurate empathy

a form of empathy in which the therapist infers concerns and feelings that lie behind what the client is saying. It represents an interpretation.

adverbial theory of sensations

theory which states that the object of one's sensory perception is not an actual object, but an act that is being performed, for example, when viewing an orange sunset, one is seeing 'orange-ly'; thus all perception is active, not passive.

advocacy

support and service, promoting a cause.

advocacy organisation

a group or non-profit entity which provides resource information, support services and/or educational opportunities for individuals or families in need, and makes those needs known to professional care-givers as well as to the general public.

aerobic exercise

any sustained activity that increases oxygen consumption, such as jogging, swimming, cycling, or fast walking.

aesthetics

branch of study that deals with the concepts of art and beauty.

affect

result, implications, consequences of an encounter with a person, place or thing. In the instance of Brain injury, affect often refers to the observable emotional condition of an individual at any point in time.

affect

the experience of (hedonic) pleasure or of (aversive) displeasure or pain.

affective

having to do with emotions.

affective disorders

mental illnesses characterised by abnormalities in mood. The two principal categories are mania and depression.

affective experience

an emotional experience, whether pleasant or unpleasant, mild or intense.

affective flattening

negative symptom of schizophrenia that consists of a severe reduction or complete absence of affective responses to the environment.

affective reaction

refers to a psychotic condition characterised by a severe disturbance in emotion or mood.

affirming the consequent

an error in logic by which, if a person causes another on one occasion, it is assumed that the first person is the cause when the second is observed on any other occasion.

aftercare

post-hospitalisation programme of rehabilitation designed to reinforce the effects of therapy and to help the patient adjust to his or her environment and prevent relapse.

Lecture at a camp for recovered alcoholics and their families.

afterimage

the sensory experience that remains when a stimulus is withdrawn. Usually refers to visual experience. For example, the negative afterimage of a picture or the train of coloured images that results after staring at the sun.

Age Associated Memory Impairment (AAMI)

the mild disturbance in memory function that occurs normally with ageing.

age effects

the consequences of being a given chronological age.

age regression

in hypnosis, the reliving through fantasy of experiences that are based on early memories or that are appropriate to a younger age.

ageing

Changes in life patterns that occur normally in humans, plants and animals as they grow older. Some age changes begin at birth and continue until death, other changes begin at maturity and end at death.

■ **ageism**

prejudice against older people.

■ **aggregated score**

a combination of several measures of the same behaviour or characteristic.

■ **aggression**

physical, verbal or symbolic action that is forceful. May be appropriate and self-protective, including healthy self-assertiveness, or inappropriate as in hostile or destructive behaviour. May also be directed toward the environment, toward another person, or toward the self, as in depression.

■ **aggressive**

an interpersonal style where only the instant needs of the self are considered rather than the needs of others.

■ **aggressive script**

a guide for behaviour and problem solving that is developed and stored in memory, and is characterised by aggression.

■ **agitated depression**

a severe major depressive disorder in which psychomotor agitation is prominent, it was formerly known as involutional melancholia.

■ **agitation**

excessive motor activity, usually non-purposeful and associated with internal tension. Examples include inability to sit still, fidgeting, pacing, wringing of hands, and pulling of the clothes.

■ **agnosia**

1. the brain's loss of ability to recognise objects. Agnosia may occur in any sensory modality and is usually classified according to the sense(s) affected.

2. a perceptual disturbance, resulting from damage to the cerebral cortex, in which the individual has difficulty identifying familiar objects even though visual acuity is normal. People suffering from agnosia appear to perceive but are not capable of understanding the information presented to them.

■ **agnostic**

a person who neither believes nor disbelieves in the existence of God. One for whom the existence of God is a real, continuing, open question. A doubter of God's existence, but not as strong as an atheist.

■ **agnosticism**

the stance of agnostics.

■ **agonist**

in pharmacology, a substance that intensifies or mimics a receptor-mediated biological response by occupying cell receptors.

■ **agoraphobia**

fear of being alone or being in a public place where escape might be difficult or help unavailable should the individual be incapacitated by a panic attack.

■ agraphia

inability to express thoughts in writing.

■ AIDS

acronym for acquired immune deficiency syndrome, a syndrome caused by a virus that damages the immune system and decreases the body's ability to fight infection.

■ akinetic mutism

a condition of silent, yet alert-appearing immobility that characterises certain subacute states of altered consciousness. While sleep-wake cycles have been retained, no observable evidence of mental activity exists. Akinetic mutism is exhibited by persons with high brain stem lesions.

■ akrasia

ancient Greek, incontinence, weakness of will, a condition where one knows a thing is good, desires that thing, yet still does not embrace it.

■ alcohol or drug dependency

a necessary, extreme and regular ingestion of alcohol and/or drugs.

■ alexia

the inability to read.

■ algorithm

a procedure that always provides the right answer for a particular type of problem.

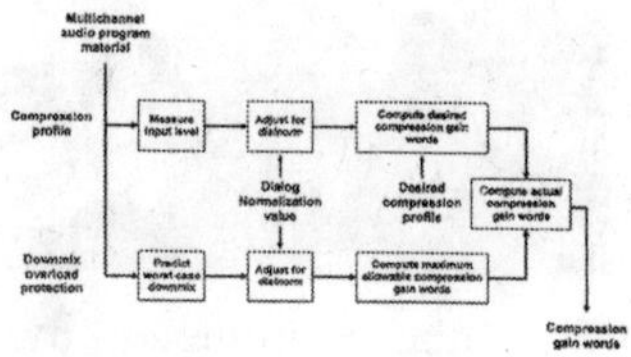

■ alienation

in Marxism, the estrangement imposed by the capitalist between the worker and his/her product, self, community and humanity. In Existentialism, a feeling that the self is never really connected to other selves or the material world.

■ all or none law

the rule that the size of the action potential is unaffected by increases in the force of stimulation beyond the threshold level.

■ all-or-none principle

the rule that the nerve impulse in a single neuron is independent of the strength of stimulation, the neuron either responds completely (fires its action potential) or not at all.

■ alpha

the abbreviation for probability of error in statistical results.

■ alpha waves

see electroencephalogram.

■ alter

to make different without changing altogether.

■ alternate form reliability

the consistency between two or more versions of the same test when given to the same person.

■ alternative hypothesis

It is the hypothesis that states there is a difference between two or more sets of data.

■ altruism

behaviour that is unselfish and benefits others.

■ altruistic helping

a form of helping in which the ultimate goal of the helper is to increase another's welfare without expecting anything in return.

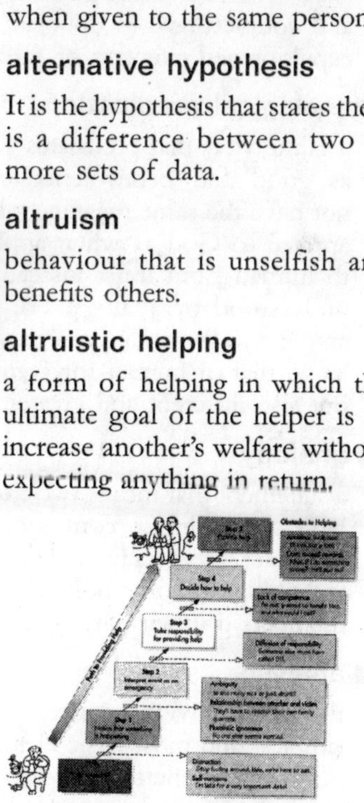

■ Alzheimer's disease

a syndrome characterised by gradual loss of memory, decline in intellectual ability and deterioration of personality.

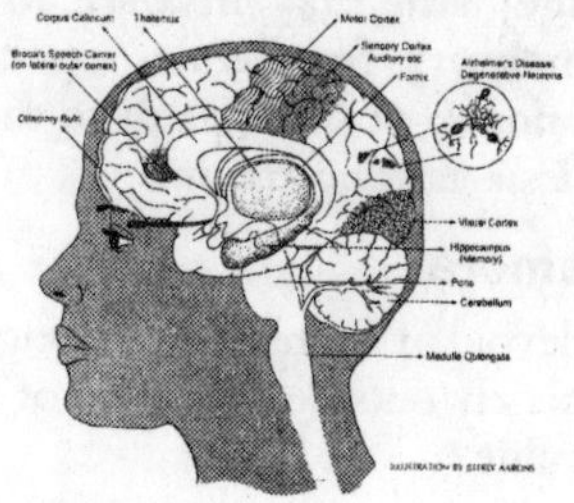

■ amacrine cells

cells that integrate information across the retina rather than sending signals toward the brain. Amacrine cells link bipolar cells to other bipolar cells and ganglion cells to other ganglion cells.

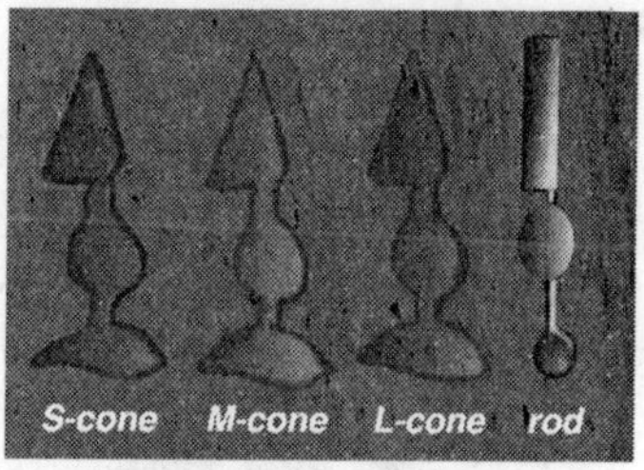

■ ambiguity

an object that may have more than one interpretation.

■ ambulate

to walk.

■ ames room

a perceptual illusion, specifically, a room that when viewed through a peephole leads to distortions in size judgments.

■ amnesia

a partial or complete loss of memory. May be due to psychological factors (for example, emotional trauma) or physiological factors (some form of brain damage) and may involve loss of memory for events occurring prior to or subsequent to the amnesia-causing trauma.

■ **amoral**

devoid of morality, operating completely outside the realm of moral value.

■ **amphetamines**

central nervous system stimulants that produce restlessness, irritability, anxiety, and rapid heart rate. Dexedrine sulfate ('speed') and methamphetamine ('meth') are two types of amphetamines.

■ **amygdala**

a brain structure located below the cerebral cortex that is involved in consolidation of emotional memories.

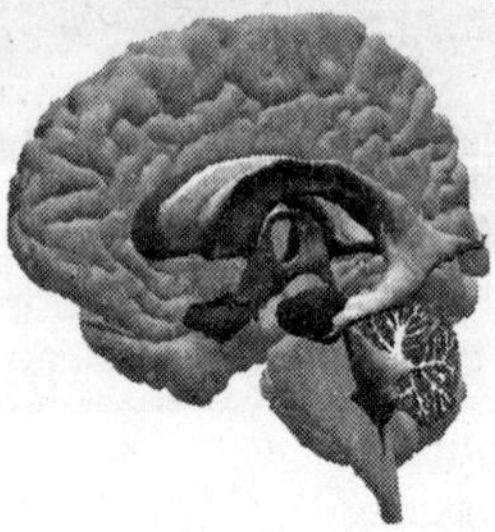

■ **amyloid plaques**

abnormal deposits within the brain tissue of the protein beta-amyloid.

■ **anal expulsive personality**

stemming from the anal stage, a child who becomes fixated due to over control transfers his or her unresolved anal (or control) issues into characteristics such as cruelty, pushiness, messiness, or disorganisation.

■ **anal retentive personality**

stemming from the anal stage, a child who becomes fixated due to under control transfers his or her unresolved anal (or control) issues into characteristics such as compulsivity, stinginess, cleanliness, organisation and obstinacy.

■ **anal stage**

the second stage in Freud's psychoanalytic theory of psychosexual development, following the oral stage. The sources of gratification and conflict have to do with the expulsion and retention of faeces.

■ **analogical predication**

it is the view that predicates such as 'good' and 'benevolence' cannot have the same meaning when applied to God as when applied to humans, but must instead be understood by analogy. For example, God's forgiveness is similar to that of human forgiveness, but also different and greater.

■ **analogy**

a statement that means two things have something in common, for example, 'Democracy is like sailing a ship: it works best when all members do their part.'

■ **analysis**

the act of moving a concept to its simplest and most basic elements in order to understand it better.

■ **analysis of variance**

an inferential statistical procedure used to test whether or not the means of two or more sets of data are equal to each other.

■ **analytic proposition**

a statement that is true or false by virtue of the meaning of its key terms.

■ **analytic psychology**

a branch of psychology that views the person as a constellation of compensatory internal forces in a dynamic balance.

■ **anarchism (anarchy)**

position which holds that governments and laws are unnecessary and that communities should flourish without the coercion of the state.

■ **anchoring heuristic**

an insufficient adjustment up or down from an original starting value when judging the probable value of some event or outcome.

■ **androgen**

a male hormone.

■ **androgens**

the collective name for male sex hormones, of which testosterone, secreted by the testes, is best known.

■ **androgyny**

possessing many traditionally masculine and feminine personality traits.

■ **anecdotal evidence**

based not on scientific inquiry, but on a small sampling and hearsay.

■ **animal cognition**

the cognitive capabilities of nonhuman animals. Researchers trace the development of cognitive capabilities across species and the continuity of capabilities from nonhuman to human animals.

■ **anomia**

inability to recall names of objects. Persons with this disorder can speak fluently but have to use other words to describe familiar objects.

■ **anorexia nervosa**

a pathological desire not to gain weight, distinguished by an extreme, self-imposed weight loss. Dangerous side effects include emaciation, susceptibility to infection, and other symptoms of under nourishment.

■ **anosmia**

loss of the sense of smell.

■ **anoxia**

cells of the brain need oxygen to stay alive. When blood flow to the brain is reduced or when oxygen in the blood is too low, brain cells are damaged. The state of diminished oxygen is called anoxia.

antecedent

within a conditional statement e.g. in the statement, if—, then—, the antecedent is the preceding, 'if' part.

anterior

front.

anterior attentional system

neural structures in the front of the brain that mediate our ability to selectively attend to some attribute of an object (other than its location).

anterograde amnesia

inability to consolidate information about ongoing events. Difficulty with new learning.

anterograde amnesia

loss of memory for events and experiences occurring subsequent to an amnesia-causing trauma, the patient is unable to acquire new information, although recall of information learned prior to the onset may be largely unaffected.

antero-lateral

front and to the side.

antero-posterior

front and to the back.

anthropology

the science that studies chiefly preliterate societies. Its main divisions are archaeology (the study of the physical monuments and remains from earlier civilisations), physical anthropology (concerned with the anatomical differences among people and their evolutionary origins), linguistic anthropology, and social anthropology (concerned with social institutions and behaviour).

anthropomorphism

the representation of nonhuman creatures, as having human characteristics.

anti-anxiety drug

central nervous system depressant (belonging to the family of drugs called benzodiazapines) that reduces anxiety and tension. Causes some drowsiness but less than barbituates. Diazepam (Valium) and alprozolam (Xanax) are examples (syn. tranquilliser).

antibody

a protein produced by the immune system to attack bacteria, viruses or other invading agents. Each antibody has a molecular structure that corresponds to the structure of an antigen, or foreign body.

anticipatory coping

efforts made in advance of a potentially stressful event to overcome, reduce, or tolerate the imbalance between perceived demands and available resources.

anticoagulation

process of slowing down normal blood clotting and thus preventing the formation of blood clots. Sometimes referred to as 'thinning the blood'. Coumadin and Heparin are examples of anticoagulants.

■ **anti-conformity**

opposition to social influence on all occasions, often caused by psychological reactance.

■ **antidepressant**

drug used to elevate the mood of depressed individuals, presumably by increasing the availability of the neurotransmitters norepinephrine and/or serotonin. Examples are imipramine (Tofranil), isocarboxazid (Marplan) and tranylcypromine (Parnate).

■ **antidepressants**

medication used to treat depression.

■ **antidiuretic hormone (adh)**

a hormone that regulates the kidneys so they release water back into the bloodstream and form only very concentrated urine.

■ **antinomy**

the existence of two incompatible statements, each of which, taken on its own, is reasonable.

■ **antipsychotic drug**

a drug that reduces psychotic symptoms, used more frequently in the treatment of schizophrenia. The phenothiazines, such as chlorpromazine (Thorazin) and fluphenazine (Prolixin), are examples (syn. neuroleptic drug).

■ **anti-social behaviour**

behaviour that opposes the customs, mores and taboos of a given society.

■ **antisocial personality**

a type of personality disorder marked by impulsivity, inability to abide by the customs and laws of society, and lack of anxiety or guilt regarding behaviour (syn. sociopathic personality, psychopathic personality).

■ **anxiety**

feelings of apprehension, uneasiness, agitation and fear.

■ **anxiety**

a state of apprehension, tension, and worry. Synonymous with fear for some theorists, although others view the object of anxiety (such as a vague danger or foreboding) as less specific than the object of a fear (such as a vicious animal).

■ **anxiety disorders**

a group of mental disorders characterised by intense anxiety or by maladaptive behaviour designed to relieve anxiety. Includes generalised anxiety and panic disorders, phobic and obsessive-compulsive disorders. Major category of DSM-IV covering most of the disorders formerly called neuroses. See also generalised anxiety disorder, neurosis, obsessive-compulsive disorder, panic disorder, phobic disorder, post-traumatic stress disorder.

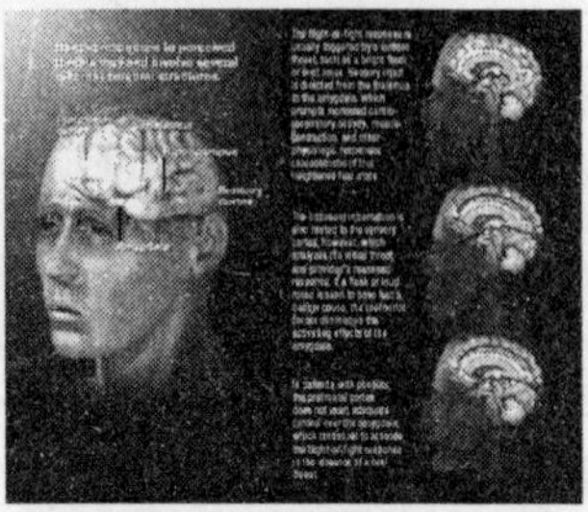

■ **anxiety hierarchy**

a list of situations or stimuli to which a person responds with anxiety ranked in order from the least anxiety-producing to the most fearful. Used by behaviour therapists in systematically desensitising patients to feared stimuli by associating deep relaxation with the situations rather than anxiety.

■ **anxious/ambivalent attachment style**

an expectation in a social relationship characterised by a concern by a person, that others will not return affection.

■ **apallic syndrome**

the behaviour that accompanies diffuse bilateral degeneration of the cerebral cortex. Apallic syndrome, a now obsolete term, occasionally follows anoxic brain injury. It describes patients with absent cortical function but with relatively intact brain stem function.

■ **apathy**

listlessness, indifference, one of the consequences of frustration.

■ **aphagia**

inability to eat.

■ **aphasia**

the inability to communicate either through oral or written discourse as a result of damage in the brain.

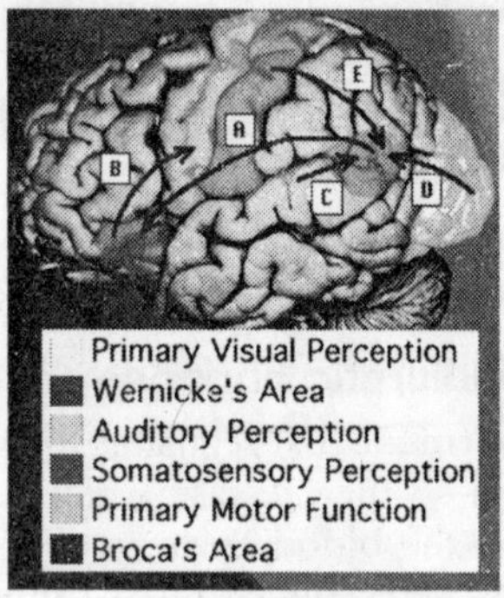

■ **aphasia, expressive**

a condition where the patient understands written and spoken words and know what he wishes to say, but cannot formulate words.

■ **aphasia, fluent**

a condition where the patient's speech is well articulated and grammatically correct, but lacks meaning.

■ **apparent motion**

a movement illusion in which one or more stationary lights going on and off in succession are perceived as a single moving light, the simplest form of apparent motion is the phi phenomenon.

■ **appearance (versus reality)**

the world as known through ever-changing, subjective experience, as opposed to deeper, unchanging reality.

■ **applied research**

research designed to increase the understanding of and solutions to real-world problems by using current social psychological knowledge.

■ **approach-approach conflict**

the conflict presented when two opposite but equally appealing choices are available but can not both be obtained.

■ **approach-avoidance conflict**

the conflict presented when the best positive choice will result in a negative outcome as well as positive.

■ **apraxia**

inability to carry out a complex movement due to an injury of the brain, rather than paralysis or sensory changes.

■ **apraxia, constructional**

impaired ability to assemble, build, draw or copy that is unrelated to apraxia of single movements.

■ **apraxia, ideomotor**

deficit in the execution of a movement due to an inability to access previous motor memory (learned motor skills).

■ **aprosodia**

a condition characterised by a loss of production or comprehension of the meaning of different tones of voice.

■ **aptitude**

the capacity to learn, for instance, a person's typing aptitude prior to practice on a typewriter. Aptitude tests are designed to predict the outcome of training, hence to predict future ability on the basis of present ability.

■ **arachnoid membrane**

the middle of three membranes protecting the brain and spinal cord.

■ **archetype**

an universal, inherited, primitive and symbolic representation of a particular experience or object

■ **aretaic (ethics)**

derived from Greek, arete, means 'virtue'. It proposes that the basis of ethical evaluation should be character rather than actions because good character is the most valuable thing a human can possess.

■ **argument (as a form of reasoning)**

a line of reasoning containing premises that support a conclusion. Philosophers use this term in a technical way that differs from ordinary usage. 'That was a really good argument you just made.' would be a compliment among philosophers, not a sign that you were a trouble-maker.

argument from analogy

a form of reasoning asserting that, given two generally similar things, if one of those things has a particular feature, the other may also contain that feature. Arguments from analogy are strong or weak depending on the degree of similarity between the two things compared.

argument from design

a line of reasoning that argues that the intricate and complex nature of the world could not have existed without a divine designer, God. At the very least, it claims, if the universe shows evidence of intelligent design, then the existence of some intelligent Designer can be inferred as its cause. Also called the teleological argument for God's existence.

argumentum ad . . .

a method of classifying traditional fallacies in reasoning.

argumentum ad baculum

'appeal to force', a fallacy that uses fear of dire consequences, threatening, pressure, etc. to force acceptance of a conclusion that would not otherwise be accepted on rational grounds.

argumentum ad hominem

'appeal to the person', a fallacy of reasoning that attempts to disprove an argument by irrelevantly attacking the person who presents it. Frequently committed in public debates.

argumentum ad ignoranciam

'appeal to ignorance', a fallacy that argues for a conclusion because no evidence is given to the contrary.

argumentum ad misericordiam

'appeal to pity', a fallacy which uses sympathy as a way to redirect attention from relevant evidence in order to gain support for a conclusion that would not otherwise be accepted.

argumentum ad populum

'appeal to the people', a fallacy which exploits the prejudices and widely-held beliefs of the people to gain support for an argument.

argumentum ad verecundiam

'appeal to authority', a fallacy that appeals to an unqualified authority who, although knowledgeable in other areas, is without expertise in the subject area of the argument.

arousal

primitive state of alertness managed by the reticular activating system (extending from medulla to the thalamus in the core of the brain stem) activating the cortex. Cognition is not possible without some degree of arousal.

arousal level

the principle according to which people seek an optimal level of drive or arousal.

■ **arousal theory**

the theory which states that we are motivated by our innate desire to maintain an optimal level of arousal.

■ **arousal: cost-reward model**

a model that says that helping or not helping is a function of emotional arousal and analysis of the costs and rewards of helping

■ **art/expressive arts therapy**

art and various creative processes are used as a means of reconciling emotional conflicts and of fostering self-awareness and personal growth. This approach is applicable to a wide range of issues/populations/ mental health settings. It is particularly useful for individuals who are unable to speak or having trouble expressing verbally.

■ **arterial line**

a catheter inserted into an artery to allow direct measurement of blood pressure or blood gas levels.

■ **Arteriovenous Malformation (AVM)**

a cluster of entwined blood vessels present from birth which may be prone to bleeding.

■ **articulation**

movement of the lips, tongue, teeth and palate into specific patterns for the purpose of speech.

■ **Artificial Intelligence (AI)**

a field of research combining computer science and cognitive psychology, it is concerned with:

1. using computers to simulate human thought processes and
2. devising computer programs that act 'intelligently' and can adapt to changing circumstances. In essence, it is the science of making machines (computers) do things that are normally done by the human mind

■ **aspiration**

'inhaling' fluid or food into the lungs through the trachea.

■ **assertive**

it is a style of interpersonal interaction where both the needs of the self and others are considered.

■ **assertiveness training**

the use of behavioural rehearsal to help an individual learn to express his or her needs in an effective, non-hostile manner.

■ **assessment**

an evaluation of a patient based on the subjective report of the symptoms by the patient, the progress of the condition, and the findings of the examiner based on tests, physical examination and medical history.

■ **assimilation**

in Piaget's theory of cognitive development, the process by which an infant comprehends a novel object or event in terms of a pre-existing schema.

■ **associated reaction**

a non-purposeful movement that accompanies another movement.

■ **association areas**

areas of the cerebral cortex that are not directly concerned with sensory or motor processes, they integrate inputs from various sensory channels and presumably function in learning, memory, and thinking.

■ **association cortex**

the parts of the cerebral cortex in which many high-level brain processes occur.

Large parts of three lobes are association cortex

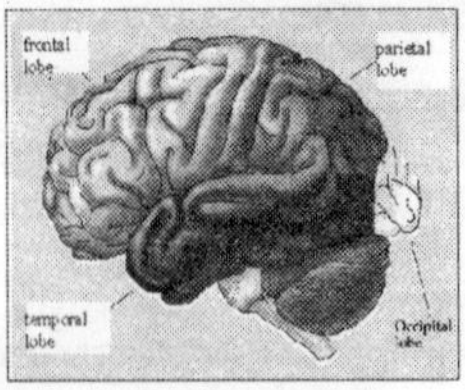

■ **associations**

the phenomenon in learning that states that we are better able to remember information if it is paired with something we are familiar with or which otherwise stands out

■ **associative agnosia**

a perceptual disturbance, resulting from damage to specific areas of the cerebral cortex, in which the individual has difficulty recognising familiar objects presented visually, although he or she can readily name the objects if allowed to touch or hear them.

■ **associative learning**

learning that certain contingencies (or relations) exist between events, learning that one event is associated with another.

■ **assumption**

a principle or proposition that is not argued but taken for granted and that forms the beginning point of an argument. The line of reasoning in an argument flows from these basic assumptions.

■ **astereognosia**

inability to recognise things by touch.

■ **astigmatism**

in vision, an optical defect that prevents horizontal and vertical contours from being in focus simultaneously.

■ **ataxia**

inability to coordinate voluntary muscle movements, resulting in diminished ability to walk, talk, eat or perform other self care tasks, due to a lesion of the cerebellum or basal ganglia.

■ **atheism**

the belief or position that God does not exist.

■ **atheist**

a person who believes that God does not exist.

■ **atrophy**

a wasting away or decrease in size of a cell, tissue, organ, or part of the body caused by lack of nourishment, inactivity or loss of nerve supply.

■ attachment

a strong emotional relationship between two persons.

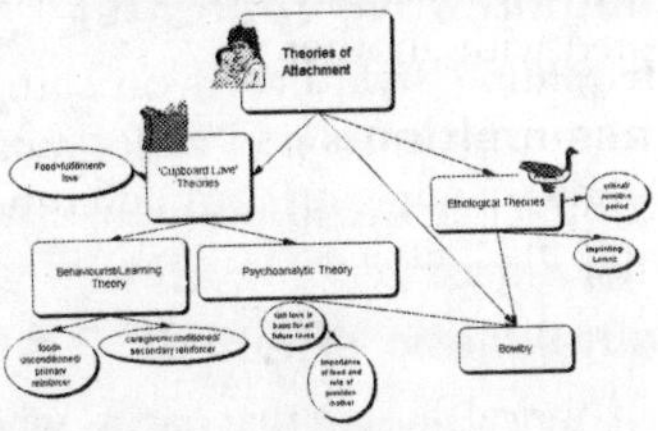

■ attendant care

provision of assistance in activities of daily living for a person with disability. Daily number of hours of required assistance, either physical or supervisory.

■ attention

the focusing of perception leading to heightened awareness of a limited range of stimuli. It has both overt behavioural components and internal components.

■ attention deficit

impaired ability to concentrate.

■ attention span

the length of time one is able to concentrate on a task at hand.

■ attention to task

ability to focus on an activity.

■ attention, alternating

the ability to move attention appropriately from one area to another. It requires directional control, as well as capacity.

■ attention, divided

refers to an intentional task where the performer must attend to two or more inputs or activities at the same time.

■ attention, sustained

refers to a person's ability to work on a particular task or train of thought for an extended time.

■ attention/concentration

the ability to focus on a given task or set of stimuli for an appropriate time.

■ attention/concentration, arousal

the ability to respond consistently to sensory stimulation by eye opening, localising, and tracking with head or eye movement.

■ attention/concentration, distractibility

refers to the patient's inability to sustain attention because of competing internal or external stimuli. The person with a brain injury may have decreased ability to inhibit competing responses.

■ attention/concentration, length

refers to the length of time a patient is able to focus on a given task. Complexity of task and patient fatigability will affect attention span.

■ attitude

a like or dislike, a favourable or unfavourable evaluation of and reaction to an object, person, event, or idea: An attitude comprises a congnitive component, an affective component, and a behavioural component.

■ **attribute**

a quality or characteristic that describes or refers to something.

■ **attribution**

the process by which people use information to make inferences about the causes of behaviour or events.

■ **attribution theory**

the theory that argues people look for explanation of behaviour, associating either dispositional (internal) attributes or situational (external) attributes.

■ **audience design**

the process of moulding a message depending on the audience for which it is intended.

■ **audience inhibition effect**

people are inhibited from helping for fear that other bystanders will evaluate them negatively if they intervene and the situation is not an emergency.

■ **auditory cortex**

the area of the temporal lobes that receives and processes auditory information.

■ **auditory nerve**

the nerve that carries impulses from the cochlea to the cochlear nucleus of the brain.

■ **authoritarian [parents]**

parenting style focused on excessive rules, rigid systems and the expectation of unhindered obedience.

■ **authoritarian personality**

a personality trait characterised by submissiveness to authority, rigid adherence to conventional values and prejudice toward out groups.

■ **authoritative [parents]**

parenting style based on setting reasonable rules and expectations while encouraging communication and independence.

■ **autokinetic effect**

an optical illusion that occurs when someone stares at a stationary point of light in a darkened room where there is no frame of reference. The light appears to move in various directions.

■ **automatic processes**

processes that do not require much attention. They can often be performed along with other tasks without interference.

■ **automatic writing**

writing that the writer is unaware of (does not know that he or she is producing), familiar in hypnosis.

■ **automatism**

automatic actions or behaviour without conscious volition or knowledge. Such episodes might last for a few minutes or a few days. During such episodes, the person appears normal but, is actually in a trance - like state. While in such a state the person is not responsible for his acts and should not be left alone. He may carry out complicated acts without remembering having done so. Such episodes have been associated with severe emotional distress and temporal motor epilepsy.

■ **autonomic nervous system**

part of the nervous system that regulates the involuntary actions of the body (e.g., breathing, heart rate, blood pressure, pupil dilation). It also regulates the Fight or Flight Phenomenon.

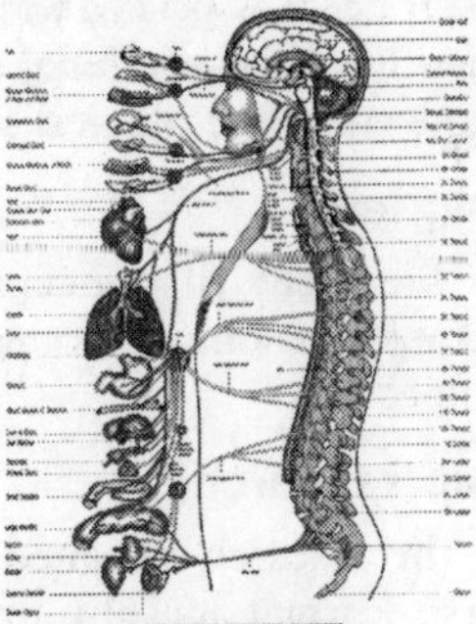

AUTONOMIC NERVOUS SYSTEM

■ **autonomy (autonomous)**

the freedom to act independently of any external rule or authority. In Kant's ethical theory, autonomy of action is a necessary condition for moral choice.

■ **availability heuristic**

a rule of thumb stating that information more readily available in our memory is more important than information not as easily accessible.

■ **aversion therapy**

Refers to a type of behavioural therapy used to treat individuals attracted to harmful stimuli. An attractive stimulus is paired with a noxious stimulus in order to elicit a negative reaction to the target stimulus.

■ **aversive racism**

attitudes toward members of a racial group that incorporate both egalitarian social values and negative emotions, causing one to avoid interaction with members of the group.

■ **avoidance-avoidance conflict**

the argument where both possible choices have an equal negative outcome.

■ **avoidant attachment style**

an expectation about social relationships characterised by a lack of trust and a suppression of attachment needs.

■ **awareness, deficit**

the patient's inability to recognise the problems caused by impaired brain function.

■ **awareness, level of**

rating by a qualified observer of the degree to which a patient perceives internal and external stimuli.

■ **axiology**

the study of value.

■ **axon**

part of the nerve cell that carries outgoing messages from the cell body to other cells.

■ **balance**

the ability to use appropriate righting and equilibrium reactions to maintain an upright position. It is usually tested in sitting and standing positions.

balance theory

a theory that people desire reasonable consistency or balance in their thoughts, feelings and social relationships.

basal ganglia

clusters of neurons located deep in the brain. They include the caudate nucleus and the putamen (corpus striatum), the globus pallidus, the subthalamic nucleus, and the substantia nigra. The basal ganglia appear to be involved in higher-order aspects of motor control, such as planning and execution of complex motor activity and the speed of movements. Lesions of the basal ganglia produce various types of involuntary movements such as athetosis, chorea, cystonia and tremor. The basal ganglia are involved also in the pathophysiology of Parkinson's disease, Huntington's disease, and tardive dyskinesia. The internal capsule, containing all the fibres that ascend to or descend from the cortex, runs through the basal ganglia and separates them from the thalamus.

basal mental age

in individual tests of the Binet type, the highest age level at which, and below which, all tests are passed.

baseline

the state of a phenomenon before the independent variable is manipulated, providing a standard against which the effects of the variable can be measured.

base-rate rule

a rule in probability theory, which states that the probability of something (e.g., a person or object) being a member of a class is greater the more class members there are. People frequently violate this rule when reasoning about real-world situations.

basic human needs

biologic needs associated with maintaining life, food, clothing, shelter, reproduction and physical safety.

basic level

in a hierarchy of concepts, the level at which one first categorises an object.

basic research

it is the research designed to increase knowledge about social behaviour.

basic trust

the infant's sense of security in his or her relationship with the mother (parents, caregiver) that makes it possible for the infant to begin to recognise the parent as other and separate from the self. It is the basis of reality testing, the ability to relate to others and the feeling of self-worth and self-esteem.

basilar membrane

the structure found within the cochlea, or inner ear, that is important in hearing.

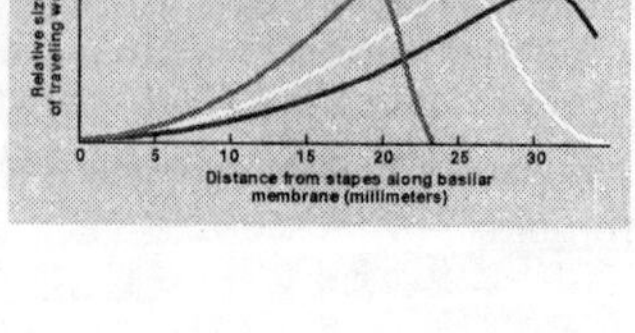

■ **battered child**

see **abused child.**

■ **becoming**

refers to the ever-changing world of experience where all animate and inanimate things are said to come into existence, exist, then pass away. In Plato's universe, it contrasts with the unchanging, eternal world.

■ **begging the question**

the misconception of assuming something to be true rather than proving it to be true, an argument for a conclusion that simply assumes its truth, without any other premises or any other reasoning. To beg the 'question' or conclusion is to assume the very thing you should be trying to prove. Also referred to as circular reasoning.

■ **behaviour**

any observable overt movement of the organism generally taken to include verbal behaviour as well as physical movements.

■ **behaviour analysis**

the area of psychology that focuses on the environmental determinants of learning and behaviour.

■ **behaviour disorders of childhood**

see attention-deficit/hyperactivity disorder; disruptive behaviour disorder.

■ **behaviour genetics**

the study of the inheritance of behavioural characteristics.

■ **behaviour modification**

the systematic use of principles of learning to increase the frequency of required behaviour and/or decrease the frequency of problem behaviours.

■ **behaviour rehearsal**

a behaviour therapy technique in which a client practices new behaviour in the consulting room, often helped by demonstrations by the therapist.

■ **behaviour therapy**

a method of psychotherapy based on learning principles. It uses such techniques as counter conditioning, reinforcement, and shaping to modify behaviour (syn. behaviour modification).

behavioural

uses theories of how people learn to help promote change, usually of a specific troublesome symptom or behaviour.

behavioural assessment

a sampling of cognitions, feeling and overt behaviour in their situational context.

behavioural confirmation

the process by which people behave in ways that evoke from others specific expected reactions and then use those reactions to comply with their beliefs.

behavioural data

observational reports about the behaviour of organisms and the conditions under which the behaviour occurs or changes.

behavioural inflexibility

rigidity in the way an individual behaves or performs tasks.

behavioural measures

apparent actions and reactions that are observed and recorded, restrictive of self-reported behaviour.

behavioural medicine

the study of how social, psychological, and biological factors interact to contribute to physical illness (syn. health psychology).

behavioural neurology

the branch of neurology that concerns itself with functioning, such as language, memory, and purposeful or motivated activity or affect.

behavioural paediatrics

a branch of behavioural medicine which deals with the psychological aspects of childhood medical problems.

behavioural perspective

an approach to psychology that focuses only on observable behaviour, and tries to explain it in terms of its relation to environmental events.

behavioural rehearsal

a technique used by behaviour therapists in which the therapist helps the individual rehearse, or role-play, more adaptive behaviours. Practicing assertive response in situations where a person tends to be timid is an example. See also **assertiveness training**.

behavioural sciences

the science that deals with the study of human development, values, and interpersonal relations. The behavioural sciences encompass such fields as psychiatry, psychology, cultural anthropology, sociology and political science.

behavioural theories of depression

it is the view that depression results from negative life events that represent a reduction in positive reinforcement, sympathetic responses to depressive behaviour then serve as a positive reinforcement for the depression itself.

behaviourism

a school of psychological thought that support the study of observable behaviour rather than unobservable mental processes.

■ behaviourism, metaphysical

it is the branch of materialism that holds that mental activity and the mind are merely another aspect of human behaviour and have no existence apart from it.

■ behaviourism, methodological

a way of investigating in psychology that restricts the data used in analysis to observable and measurable human behaviour, thus excluding mental activity as a proper area of study.

■ behaviourist perspective

the psychological perspective primarily concerned with observable behaviour that can be objectively recorded and with the relationships of observable behaviour to environmental stimuli.

■ being

it is the theory that all that is real and nothing that is unreal is contained in the domain known as 'being'. In Plato's theory, it is a perfect and unchanging world of Forms (ideal essences), after which the changing things of this world's appearances are patterned.

■ belief

the mental acceptance of a statement as true.

■ belief-bias effect

a situation that occurs when a person's prior knowledge, attitudes, or values distort the reasoning process by influencing the person to accept invalid arguments.

■ bell adjustment inventory

a test of personality that estimates the individual's adjustment in different situations - for example, home and health.

■ bell-shaped curve

referred to as a normal distribution or normal curve, a bell-shaped curve is a perfect mesokurtic curve where the mean, median and mode are equal.

■ benevolence principle

it is the belief that the happiness and good of others is desirable and that such happiness should be spread as equally and as widely as possible among the beings affected.

■ bennington study

a study of attitude change carried out at Bennington College by T. M. Newcomb that related the problem of attitude change to the reference group concept.

■ benzodiazepines

a class of drugs with similar chemical structures that are effective in reducing anxiety. Examples are diazepam (Valium) and alprozolam (Xanax).

■ **bereavement**

feelings of deprivation, gloominess and grief at the loss or death of a dear one. The grieving person does not need to seek professional help unless these feelings last for a long period of time or relief is sought for symptoms such as anorexia nervosa or insomnia.

■ **bestiality**

also known as zoophilia, it is the sexual relations between a human being and an animal.

■ **beta (uppercase)**

abbreviation for Power in statistical results.

■ **beta rhythm**

the dominant pattern (14 to 25 cps) of brain waves found in an observant adult responding to a stimulus.

■ **beta-blocker**

an agent that obstructs the action of beta-adrenergic receptors, which modulate cardiac functions, respiratory functions and the dilation of blood vessels. Beta-blockers are of value in the treatment of hypertension, cardiac arrhythmia and migraine. In

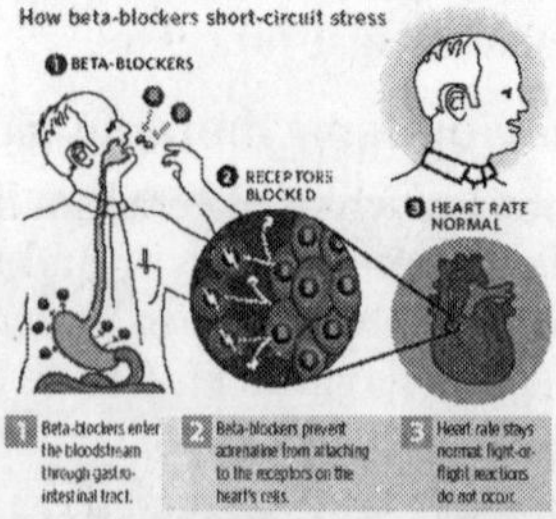

psychiatry, they have been used in the treatment of aggression and violence, anxiety-related tremors and lithium-induced tremors, neuroleptic-induced akathisia, social phobias, panic states and alcohol withdrawal.

■ **between-subjects design**

a research design in which different groups of participants are randomly assigned to experimental conditions or to control conditions.

■ **Big bang theory**

a cosmological model of the evolution of the expanding universe from a huge explosion of highly concentrated matter that occurred between fifteen and twenty billion years ago.

■ **bilateral**

pertaining to both right and left sides.

■ **bilateral (ect)**

an electro convulsive therapy in which electrodes are placed on each side of the forehead and an electrical current is passed between them through both hemispheres of the brain.

■ **binge drinking**

a pattern of heavy alcoholic intake that occurs in bouts of a day or more that are set aside for

drinking. During periods between bouts, the subject may abstain from alcohol.

■ **binge eating**

a period of time of overeating during which a large amount of food is ingested than most people would eat during that time. The person suffering from it feels that he or she cannot stop eating or has no control over what or how much is consumed. During the episode, the person may eat faster than usual, eat until feeling uncomfortably full, eat large amounts of food although not feeling hungry and eat alone because of embarrassment over how much is being eaten. After a bout of overeating, depression, guilt feelings and feelings of disgust with oneself are common. When binge eating is accompanied by compensatory behaviour to control weight, it is termed bulimia nervosa.

■ **binocular cues**

visual cues (convergence and retinal disparity) that require both eyes to perceive distance (as opposed to monocular cues).

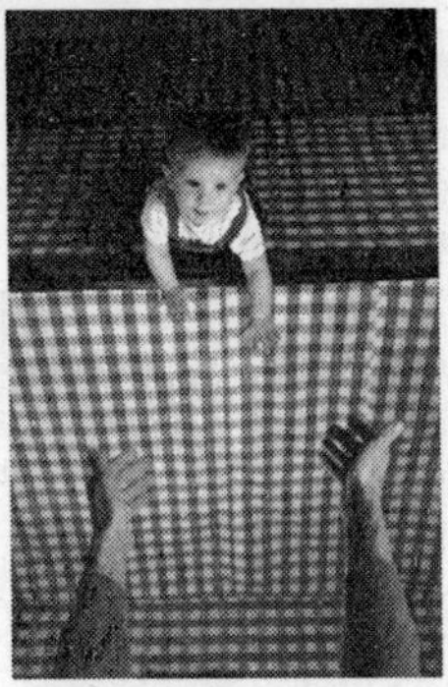

■ **binocular disparity**

a cue to depth perception that arises because an object projects slightly different images on the two retinas (due to the different positions of the right and left eyes).

■ **binocular parallax**

a cue to depth perception that arises because any visible point will differ slightly in its direction to the two eyes.

■ **bio-energetics**

a body-centred therapeutic approach which utilises exercises such as strong expressive movements, stress postures, and breathing techniques to allow the release of repressed emotions and to promote the full experience of feelings.

■ **bioethics**

the branch of ethics that studies moral problems in medicine and biological technology.

■ **biofeedback**

1.a procedure that permits individuals to monitor their own physiological processes (such as heart rate, blood pressure) which they are normally unaware of, to learn to control them.

2. a process that provides sight or sound information about functions

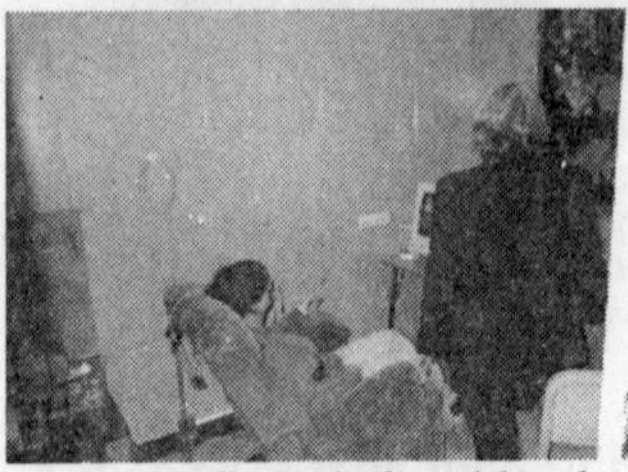

of the body, including blood pressure, muscle tension, etc. By trial and error, one can learn to consciously control these functions.

biofield

an energy field that instils living bodies and extends several inches beyond the body. This concept is employed in therapies such as healing touch, medical qigong, therapeutic touch and reiki. In these therapies, the biofield from a practitioners hands is joined to the recipients biofield in order to cure an illness or to promote health. There is no consensus on what biofield is. Some say it is spiritual energy, others say it is an electromagnetic field.

biogenic amine hypothesis

a concept that abnormalities in the physiology and metabolism of biogenic amines, particularly catecholamines (norepinephrine and dopamine) and an indoleamine (serotonin), are involved in the causes of certain psychiatric illnesses. The concept was derived originally from a serendipitous discovery that monoamine oxidase inhibitors and certain tricyclic drugs had mood-elevating properties, and that these agents exerted dramatic effects on brain monoamine functions. The findings that phenothiazines and other neuroleptics inhibit dopamine activity in the brain further support this theory and suggest that a disorder of dopamine metabolism may be implicated in the etiology of psychosis or of mania. Also, disorders in norepinephrine and serotonin activity have been implicated in the etiology of depression and mania.

biological approach

it is the view which states that biological factors cause and should be used to treat abnormality.

biological constraints on learning

any restraints on an organism's capacity to learn that are caused by the inherited sensory response, or cognitive capabilities of members of a given species.

biological paradigm

a broad theoretical view that holds that mental disorders are caused by some aberrant somatic process or defect.

biological perspective

an approach to psychology that tries to explain behaviour in terms of electrical and chemical events taking place inside the body, particularly within the brain and nervous system.

biological psychiatry

a school of the psychiatric thought that stress on physical, chemical and neurological causes of psychiatric illness and treatment approaches.

■ **biological psychologist**

a psychologist concerned with the relationship between biological processes and behaviour.

■ **biological rhythms**

cyclical changes in physiological and biochemical function, level of activity and emotional state. Circadian rhythms have a cycle of about 24 hours, ultradian rhythms have a cycle that is shorter than 1 day and infradian rhythms have a cycle that may last weeks or months.

■ **biological therapy**

treatment of emotional problems or mental disorders by drugs, electric shock, or other methods directly affecting bodily processes.

■ **biomedical therapies**

treatments for psychological disorders that changes brain functioning with chemical or physical interventions such as drug therapy, surgery, or electro convulsive therapy.

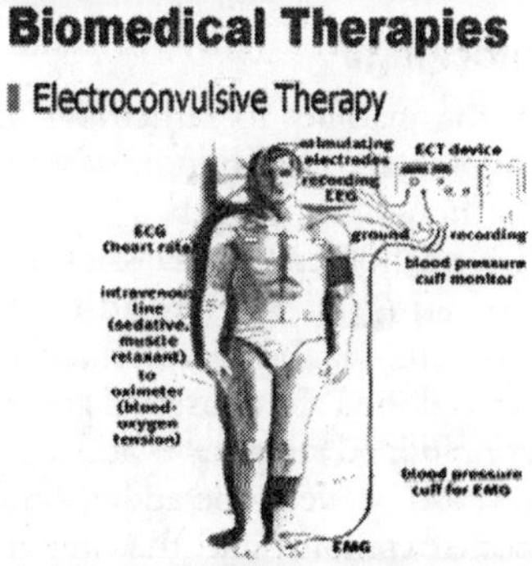

■ **biopsychosocial model**

a model of health and illness which hints at links among the nervous system, the immune system, behavioural styles, cognitive processing and environmental factors can put people at risk for illness.

■ **bipolar cells**

cells in the retina that transmit electrical impulses from photoreceptors to ganglion cells.

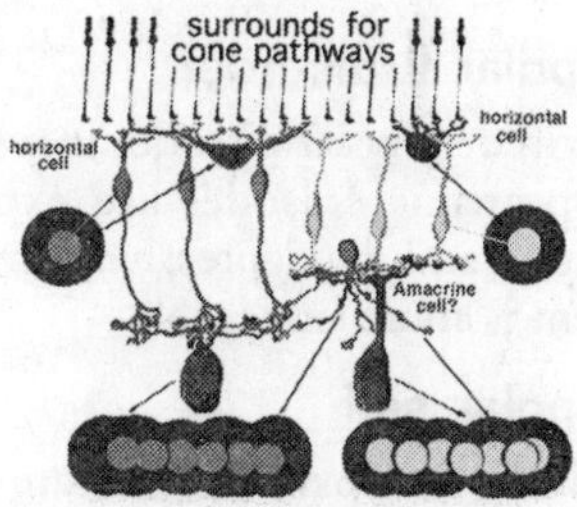

■ **bipolar disorder**

a mood disorder in which people experience episodes of depression and mania (exaggerated excitement) or of mania alone. Typically the individual alternates between the two extremes, often with periods of normal mood in between (syn. manic-depression).

■ **bipolar i disorder**

form of bipolar disorder in which the full symptoms of mania are

experienced while depressive aspects may be irregular or mild.

■ **bipolar ii disorder**

form of bipolar disorder in which hypomanic episodes are experienced, and the depressive component is more noticeable.

■ **bipolar self**

it is the final psychic structure that emerges following successful development and transformations of infantile constellations (equivalent to the mature human psyche of id, ego, and superego) in the self psychology of Heinz Kohut. The structure begins as the nuclear self made up of the grandiose self and the idealised parental imago. In successful development the grandiose self is transformed into self-assertive ambitions at one pole of the bipolar self. At the other pole are the internalised values and ideals that have grown out of the idealised parental imago. Between the two poles are the person's inherent talents and skills.

■ **birth trauma**

term used by Otto Rank to relate his theories of anxiety and neurosis to what he believed to be the unpreventable psychic shock of being born.

■ **bisexuality**

being attracted to or aroused by members of both genders. See

sexual orientation.

■ **blandness**

unperturbed, dull.

■ **blind spot**

an insensitive area of the retina where the nerve fibres from the ganglion cells join to form the optic nerve.

■ **blind study**

way of study which avoid the placebo effect in research, this type of study is designed without the subject's knowledge of the anticipated results and sometimes even the nature of the study. The subjects are said to be 'blind' to the expected results.

■ **blocking**

1. the inability to remember, the involuntary interruption of a train of thought or speech.

2. a phenomenon in classical conditioning: if one conditioned stimulus reliably predicts an unconditioned stimulus, and another conditioned stimulus is added, the relation between the added conditioned stimulus and the unconditioned stimulus will not be learned.

■ **blood alcohol concentration (BAC)**

the concentration, in milligrams, of alcohol per 100 millilitres of blood. The legal definition of intoxication in most states is a blood alcohol concentration of .10 percent (100 milligrams of alcohol per 100 millilitres of blood).

■ **blood pressure**

the pressure of the blood against the walls of the blood vessels. Changes in blood pressure following stimulation serve as one indicator of emotion.

■ **body esteem**

the attitude a person has toward his or her body.

■ **body image**

the subjective experience of the appearance of one's body.

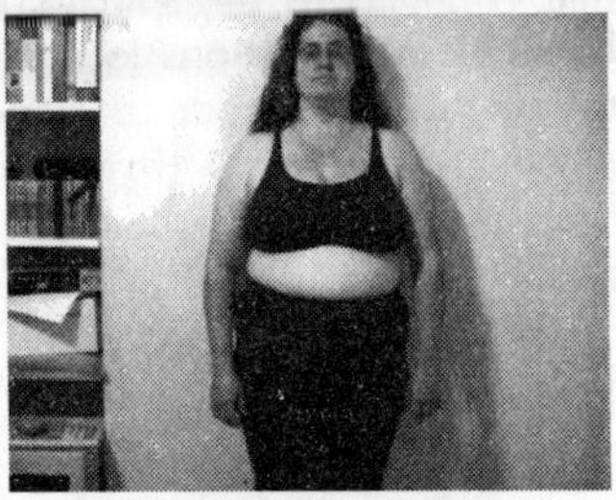

■ **body-mind centring**

a re-education approach that explores how the body's systems contribute to movement and self-awareness. The approach also put stresses on the movement patterns that develop during infancy and childhood. Incorporates guided movement, exercise, imagery and hands-on work.

■ **body-oriented psychotherapy**

seeks to intensify the psychotherapeutic process by incorporating a range of massage, bodywork and movement techniques. Acknowledging the mind-body link, practitioners may use light touch, soft or deep-tissue manipulation, breathing tech niques, movement, exercise or body awareness techniques to help address emotional issues.

■ **borderline personality disorder**

a mental disorder in which the individual has manifested unstable moods, relationships with others, and self-perceptions chronically since adolescence or childhood.

■ **bottom-up processes**

processes in perception, learning, memory, and comprehension that are driven solely by the information input, and that do not involve the organism's prior knowledge and expectations.

■ **bowen natural**

a 'Family Systems' therapy in which healthier family relationships are promoted by encouraging constructive ways of relating in one family member.

■ **brain injury, acquired**

brain injury that is sustained from insult to the brain resulting in impairment of function, rather than congenital brain damage.

■ brain injury, closed

occurs when the head accelerates and then rapidly decelerates or collides with another object (for example the windshield of a car) and brain tissue is damaged, not by the presence of a foreign object within the brain, but by violent smashing, stretching, and twisting, of brain tissue. Closed brain injuries typically cause diffuse tissue damage that results in disabilities that are generalised and highly variable.

■ brain injury, mild

a patient with a mild traumatic brain injury is a person who has had a traumatically-induced physiological disruption of brain function, as manifested by at least one of the following: 1) any period of loss of consciousness, 2) any loss of memory for events immediately before or after the accident, 3) any alteration in mental state at the time of the accident (e.g., feeling dazed, disoriented, or confused), 4) focal neurological deficit(s) which may or may not be transient, but where the severity of the injury does not exceed the following: a) loss of consciousness of approximately 30 minutes or less, b) after 30 minutes, an initial Glasgow Coma Scale score of 13-15, c) Post Traumatic Amnesia not greater than 24 hours.

■ brain injury, traumatic

damage to living brain tissue caused by an external, mechanical force. It is usually characterised by a period of altered consciousness (amnesia or coma) that can be very brief (minutes) or very long (months/indefinitely). The specific disabling condition(s) may be orthopaedic, visual, aural, neurological, perceptive/cognitive, or mental/emotional in nature. The term does not include brain injuries that are caused by insufficient blood supply, toxic substances, malignancy, disease-producing organisms, congenital disorders, birth trauma or degenerative processes.

■ brain plasticity

the brain's ability to employ surviving cells to compensate for damaged one's, thereby taking over their function. This ability diminishes with age.

■ brain scan

an imaging technique in which a radioactive dye (radionuclide) is injected into the blood stream and then pictures of the brain are taken to detect tumours, haemorrhages, blood clots, abscesses or abnormal anatomy.

■ brainstem

the lower extension of the brain that connects to the spinal cord. Neurological functions located in the brain stem include those necessary for survival (breathing, heart rate) and for arousal (being awake and alert).

The Brain Stem

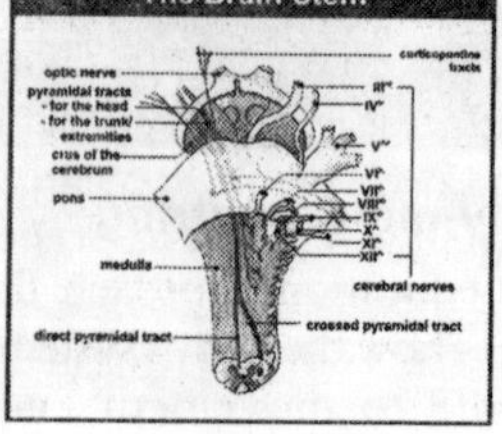

■ breath work

general term for different techniques that use patterned breathing to promote physical, mental and/or spiritual well-being. Some techniques use the breath in a calm, peaceful way to bring about relaxation or manage pain, while others use stronger breathing to stimulate emotions and emotional release.

■ brief therapy

time-limited therapy, usually no more than fifteen sessions, which is goal-oriented, focused and directed toward specific problems and solutions.

■ brightness

it is the dimension of colour space that captures the intensity of light.

■ Broca's aphasia

an aphasia which deal with damage to the Broca's area of the brain, demonstrated by the problems in producing understandable speech.

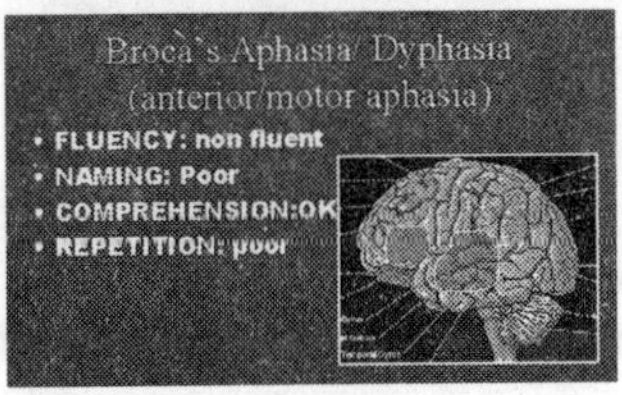

■ broca's area

a portion of the left cerebral hemisphere involved in the control of speech. Individuals with damage in this area have difficulty enunciating words correctly and speak in a slow and laboured way, their speech often makes sense, but it includes only key words.

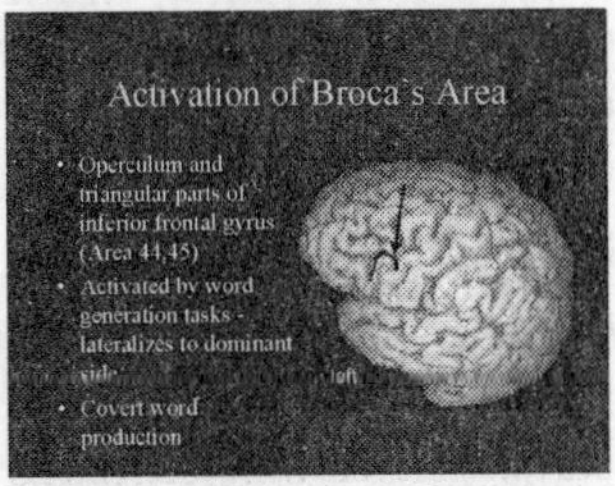

■ bulimia

a pathological desire not to gain weight, characterised by recurrent episodes of binge eating (rapid consumption of a large amount of food in a discrete period of time), followed by attempts to purge the excess eating by means of vomiting and laxatives.

■ bulimia nervosa

an eating disorder characterised by binge eating followed by measures to cleanse the body of the extra calories.

burden of proof

in a two-sided argument, where argument A is appropriately assumed to be true, side B must prove it untrue by proving B in order to win. In American justice, the prosecution has the burden of proof, since the accused is always presumed innocent. One strategy in debate is to try to shift the burden of proof to the opposing side.

burnout

changes in thoughts, emotions and behaviour as a result of extended job stress and repetition of duties. Burnout is seen as extreme dissatisfaction, pessimism, lowered job satisfaction and a desire to quit.

bystander intervention

the willingness to aid a person in need of help.

bystander intervention model

a theory that whether bystanders intervene in an emergency is a function of a 5-step decision making process.

caffeine use disorders

this disorder include caffeine intoxication, caffeine anxiety disorder and caffeine sleep disorder.

calcium channel blockers

name for the treatments for mania.

cannabis

the hemp plant from which marijuana is obtained.

cannabis use disorders

this disorder include cannabis dependence, cannabis abuse, cannabis intoxication, cannabis delirium, cannabis psychotic disorder with delusions or hallucinations, and cannabis anxiety disorder.

Cannon-Bard theory

a classical theory of emotion proposed by Cannon and Bard. The theory states that an emotion-producing stimulus activates the cortex and bodily responses at the same time, bodily changes and the experience of emotion occur simultaneously.

capgras' syndrome

the illusion that others, or the self, have been replaced by impostors. It typically follows the development of negative feelings toward the other person that the subject cannot accept and attributes, instead, to the impostor. The syndrome has been reported in paranoid schizophrenia and, even more frequently, in organic brain disease.

caregiver

any person dealing with the treatment or rehabilitation of a patient including the psychiatrist and other members of the traditional treatment team as well as community workers and other non-professionals.

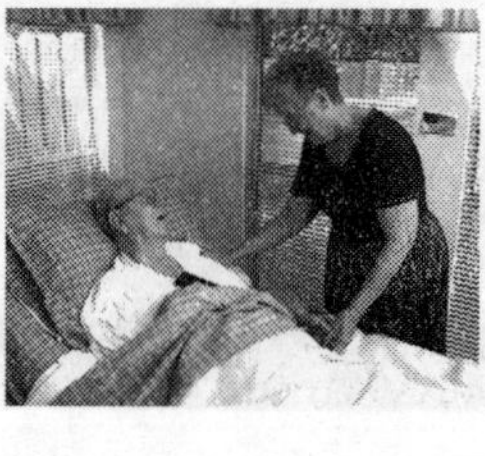

■ **cartesian doubt (method of doubt)**

a process of establishing knowledge based on eliminating any belief that might be false. It is associated with Descartes and advocates suspending belief in any proposition that can be doubted or that has even the barest possibility of being untrue. After all false beliefs are discarded, one builds on the remaining true, indubitable beliefs.

■ **cartesian dualism (interactive dualism)**

a worldview associated with Descartes wherein two independently-existing, ultimate kinds of stuff are assumed to exist. Referring to the mind/body problem, it holds that the mind, although a substance separate from the body nevertheless interacts with the body, a different substance. 'Mind' here is defined very broadly to cover anything mental, including thought, perception and human will. Descartes thought such interaction occurred in the brain's pineal gland.

■ **cartesianism**

the name applied to the philosophy of Rene Descartes.

■ **case history**

a biography obtained for scientific purposes, the material is sometimes supplied by interview, sometimes collected over the years.

■ **case management**

the process of following a patient through various types of treatment and helping with care. A type of health care delivery with emphasis on the development of alternative treatment plans for the patients who have been identified (by preadmission certification, diagnosis, etc.) as potential high-cost cases. Once such a case has been identified, the case manager confers with the patient's physician to develop a cheaper treatment plan and aftercare.

■ **case study**

the collection of historical or biographical information on a single individual, often including experiences in therapy.

■ **case worker**

a professional who facilitates the access of a patient to appropriate medical, rehabilitation and support programs, and coordination of the delivery of services. This role may involve liaison with various professionals and agencies, advocacy on behalf of the patient, and arranging for purchase of services where no appropriate programs are available.

■ **castration**

surgical removal of the gonads, in the male, removal of the testes, in the female, removal of the ovaries.

■ **casual attribution**

the reason for why an event occurred.

■ **casuistry**

a method of evaluating ethical problems situationally, by analysing the circumstances of a case. Casuistry contrasts with applying rules or principles to a problem, and rejects the idea that such application of rules or principles yields real solutions. Practised in Scholastic ethics, it has been revived in modern bioethics.

CAT Scan

Computerised Axial Tomography, a process of diagnosis employing X-rays taken from different angles and then analysed by computer to produce a representation of a specific body area in cross section. Often used on the brain.

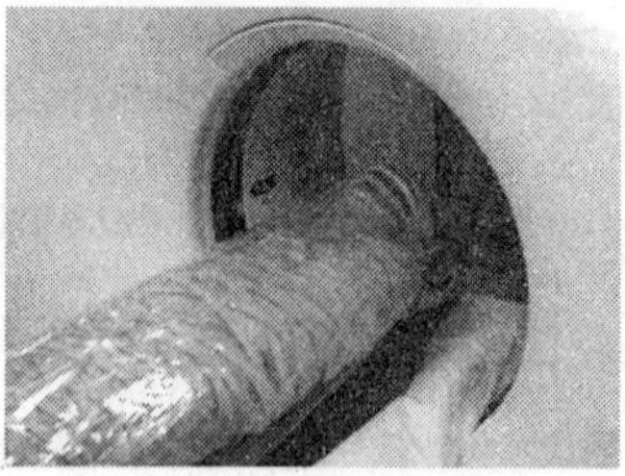

catalepsy

a generalised state of waning responsiveness shown by trance-like states, posturing, or maintenance of physical attitudes for a prolonged period of time. May occur in organic or psychological disorders, or under hypnosis.

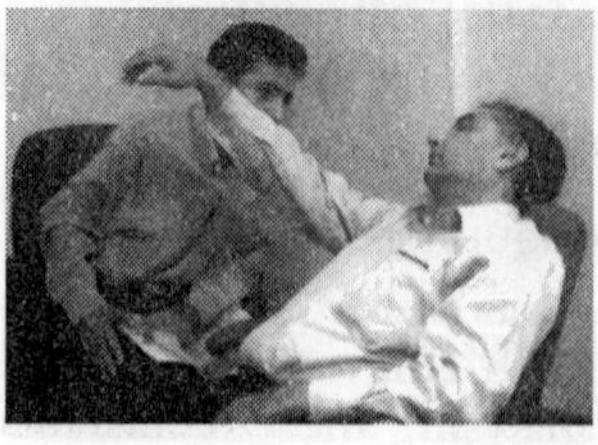

cataonic disorder due to general medical condition

secondary or symptomatic catatonia, catatonic symptoms such as motoric immobility (e.g., catalepsy, cerea flexibilitas), extreme agitation, extreme negativism (e.g., rigidity of posture), and peculiarities of voluntary movement (e.g., inappropriate or bizarre posturing, stereotyped movements, prominent mannerisms) that occur in relation to a general medical condition. This diagnosis emphasises that catatonic symptoms are not confined to schizophrenic disorders.

catatonia

stability with muscular rigidity or inflexibility and at times of excitability.

catatonic behaviour

marked motor abnormalities, generally limited to those occurring as part of a non-organic psychotic disorder. This term includes catatonic excitement (apparently purposeless agitation not influenced by external stimuli), stupor (decreased reactivity and fewer spontaneous movements, often with apparent unawareness of the surroundings), negativism (apparent motiveless resistance to instructions or attempts to be moved), posturing (the person's assuming and maintaining an inappropriate or bizarre stance), rigidity (the person's maintaining a stance or posture against all efforts to be moved), and waxy flexibility, or cerea flexibilitas (the person's limbs can be put into positions that are maintained).

■ catatonic excitement

state of incessant agitation and excitability.

■ catatonic immobility

a fixity of posture maintained for long periods with accompanying muscular rigidity and a trance-like state of consciousness. A symptom in some cases of schizophrenia.

■ catatonic posturing

bizarre, inappropriate bodily position of considerable duration in which a person remains oblivious to the outside world.

■ catatonic stupor

motionless, apathetic state in which one remains oblivious to external stimuli.

■ catchment area

a geographic area for which a mental health programme or facility has responsibility for its residents.

■ catechol-o-methyltransferase

an enzyme that deactivates catecholamines in the synapse.

■ categorical classification

an approach to assessment in which the basic decision is whether a person is or is not a member of a distinct grouping.

■ categorisation

assigning an object to a concept.

■ category mistake

closely associated with the work of Gilbert Ryle, an English philosopher of the mid-20th century, it occurs when a thing of one category is incorrectly presented as if it was in another, for example, 'He wanted to know where he could see the spirit of America.' In this sentence, it is a category mistake to assume that the spirit of America is in the category of things that can be seen.

■ catharsis

1. the reduction in the aggressive drive following an aggressive act. 2. the healthful (therapeutic) release of ideas through 'talking out' conscious material accompanied by an appropriate emotional reaction. Also, the release into awareness of repressed ('forgotten') material from the unconscious.

■ cathartic method

a therapeutic procedure introduced by Breuer and developed further by Freud in the late nineteenth century. In this method, a patient recalls and relives an earlier emotional catastrophe and re-experiences the tension and unhappiness, the goal being to relieve emotional suffering.

■ catheter

a flexible tube for withdrawing fluids from, or introducing fluids into, a cavity of the body. Frequently used to drain the urinary bladder.

■ cathexis

it is the attachment, conscious or unconscious, of emotional feeling and significance to an idea, an object, or, most commonly, a person.

causalgia

a sensation of intense pain of either organic or psychological origin.

causation

it is one of the main philosophical problems examined in the area of metaphysics. It is the relationship that exists between two events where, when one occurs, the other always follows and where the first makes the latter occur.

celiac plexus

a cluster of nerve fibres located in the abdomen that operate in conjunction with the autonomic nervous system and conduct pain sensations of the abdominal organs.

central core

the most central and the evolutionally oldest portion of the brain. It includes structures that regulate basic life processes, including most of the brain stem.

central executive

in short-term memory, a hypothesised component of the encoding process that coordinates the acoustic and visual buffers.

central fissure

a fissure of each cerebral hemisphere that separates the frontal and parietal lobes (syn. fissure of Rolando).

Central Nervous System (CNS)

the CNS includes the brain and spinal cord. The prevailing theory is that CNS cells won't repair themselves. Experiments show, however, that CNS nerves can regrow and reconnect to appropriate targets. A clinical 'fix' for spinal cord injury has not yet been found.

central route to persuasion

persuasion that occurs when people think carefully about a communication and are swayed by the strength of its arguments.

central traits

traits that exert a disproportionate influence on people's overall impressions, causing them to assume the presence of other traits.

centration

a thought pattern common during the beginning of the preoperational stage of cognitive development. It is characterised by the child's inability to take more than one perceptual factor into account at the same time.

cephalgia

headache or head pain.

cephalocaudal axis

refers to the fact that behaviour develops from the head downwards in the foetus.

cerea flexibilitas

the 'waxy flexibility' often present in catatonic schizophrenia in which the patient's arm or leg remains in the same position in which it is placed.

cerebellum

the region of the brain attached to the brain stem that controls motor coordination, posture and balance as well as the ability to learn control of body movements.

■ cerebral contusion

a wounding of neural tissue marked by swelling and haemorrhage and resulting in coma. Can permanently impair intellectual functioning.

■ cerebral cortex

the surface layer of the cerebral hemispheres in higher animals, including humans. It is commonly called grey matter because its many cell bodies give it a gray appearance in cross section, in contrast with the myelinated nerve fibres that make up the white matter in the centre.

■ cerebral embolism

a blocked blood vessel, usually caused by a blood clot that prevents blood flow to the brain.

■ cerebral haemorrhage

bleeding into the brain.

■ cerebral hemisphere

half, or one side of the brain. Typically, the left side of the brain controls language and the right side deals with spatial orientation.

■ Cerebral Vascular Accident (CVA)

an event resulting in diminished or blocked blood flow to an area in the brain. Symptoms of CVA can include paralysis, loss of speech, unconsciousness, and death.

■ Cerebrospinal Fluid (CSF)

liquid that fills the ventricles of the brain and surrounds the brain and spinal cord.

■ cerebrovascular disease

an illness that disrupts blood supply to the brain, such as a stroke.

■ cerebrum

the largest section of the brain that is divided into hemispheres and controls speech, muscles/ movement, vision, personality, and memory.

■ cervical

the upper spine (neck) area of the vertebral column. Cervical injuries often result in quadriplegia (tetraplegia).

■ ceteris paribus

Latin word meaning, 'other things being equal'. Assumed in a context where one is implying something and where one is also holding external causes or variables constant so as to not affect the direct line of what one is implying.

■ character

the sum of a person's relatively fixed personality traits and habitual modes of response.

■ character analysis

psychoanalytic treatment (see psychoanalysis) aimed at the character defences.

■ character defence

any personality trait that serves as an unconscious defensive purpose.

chemical dependence

a generic term for dependence (addiction) on alcohol or other drugs.

chemotherapy

the treatment of mental illness with chemical drugs.

child analysis

employment of modified psychoanalytic methods and goals to problems of children to remove impediments to normal personality development.

child and adolescent psychiatry

it is the diagnosis, prevention and treatment of mental disorders in persons under the age of 18.

child sexual abuse

sexual contact with a person who is below 18 years of age.

child-directed speech

it is a special form of speech with an exaggerated and high-pitched intonation that adults use to speak to infants and young children.

childhood amnesia

the inability to recall events from the first years of one's life.

chlorpromazine

see **antipsychotic drug.**

cholinergic

activated or transmitted by acetylcholine (e.g., parasympathetic nerve fibres).

cholinergic hypothesis

it is the theory that says that the basic defect in Alzheimer's disease is an inadequacy of acetylcholine for neurotransmission.

cholinergic system

all the nerve cells for which acetylcholine is the transmitter substance, in contrast to the adrenergic.

choreiform

referring to the involuntary, spasmodic, jerking movements of the limbs and head found in Huntington's chorea and other nervous disorders.

choroid

a layer in the eye that serves to obstruct light.

chromatic colours

all colours other than black, white, and grey, for instance, red, yellow, blue. See also **achromatic colours.**

chromosome

rodlike structures found in pairs in all the cells of the body, carrying the genetic determiners (genes) that are transmitted from parent to offspring. A human cell has 46 chromosomes, arranged in 23 pairs, one member of each pair deriving from the mother, one from the father.

chromosome 21

the chromosome involved in Down syndrome (21 trisomy), which is most frequently due to nondisjunction of chromosome 21, resulting in 3, rather than 2 chromosomes (and making the total 47 chromosomes, rather than the normal total of 46). In 1987, it was reported that the genetic defect in familial Alzheimer's disease is located on chr^mosome 21, the same chromosome of which there is an extra copy in Down syndrome. This supports the idea that at least one form of Alzheimer's is inherited and that a similar genetic defect may occur on both Down and familial Alzheimer's disorders.

■ chronic

marked by long duration or frequent recurrence.

■ chronic stress

refers to the constant state of arousal in which an individual perceives demands as greater than the inner and outer resources available for dealing with them.

■ chronological age (ca)

age from birth, calendar age.

■ chunk

the largest meaningful unit of information that can be stored in short-term memory, short-term memory holds 762 chunks.

■ chunking

the method of taking single items of information and recoding them on the basis of resemblance or some other organising principle.

■ cilia

hair like structures that are sometimes parts of receptors.

■ circadian rhythm

a cycle or rhythm that is roughly 24 hours long. Sleep-wakefulness, body temperature, and water excretion follow a circadian rhythm, as do a number of behavioural and psychological variables.

■ circumlocution

use of other words to describe a specific word or idea which cannot be remembered.

■ clairvoyance

perception of objects or events that do not provide a stimulus to the known senses (for example, identifying a concealed playing card, the identity of which is unknown).

■ classical concept

a concept where an instance must have every property mentioned in the concept. An example is the concept of bachelor, every instance must have the properties of being adult, male, and unmarried.

■ classical conditioning

a kind of learning in which a behaviour (conditioned response) comes to be discovered by a stimulus (conditioned stimulus) that has acquired its power through an association with a biologically significant stimulus (unconditioned stimulus).

■ claustrophobia

fear of closed places.

■ clear and distinct ideas

a phrase used by Rene Descartes to describe those ideas that are so clear and distinct, so self-evident and so that are impossible to imagine as false, that we must accept them, even when employing Cartesian doubt. The redness of a bright, clean fire truck is an example of a clear idea, the unique design of a fire truck, as opposed to all other trucks, is an example of a distinct idea.

client

a person under the protection of another, one who engages the professional advice or services of another.

client-centred (rogerian)

a humanistic therapy which relies on a safe, non-judgmental relationship between the therapist and the client to help the client realise his/her own values. The client retains the right of choice in the solutions to his/her problems.

client-centred therapy

a method of psychotherapy developed by Carl Rogers in which the therapist is nondirective and reflective and does not interpret or advise. The operating assumption is that the client is the best expert on his or her problems and can work them out in a nonjudgmental, accepting atmosphere. (syn. nondirective counseling).

Clifford W. Beers (1876 - 1943)

he is the author of *A Mind That Found Itself* and founder, in 1909 of the National Committee for Mental Hygiene, now the National Mental Health Association.

clinical ecology

a field of psychology that relates disorders such as anxiety and depression to environmental irritants and sources of crisis.

clinical psychologist

a psychologist, usually with a Ph.D. or Psy.D. degree, trained in the diagnosis and treatment of emotional or behavioural problems and mental disorders.

clinical psychology

one of the largest sub disciplines of psychology. Clinical psychologists usually work in hospitals, clinics and private practice and their main concern is the diagnoses and treatment of learning and emotional problems.

clinical social worker

a professional psychologist whose specialised training prepares him or her to consider the social context of people's problems.

clonus

a sustained series of rhythmic jerks following quick stretch of a muscle.

closed head injury

trauma to the brain in which the skull remains intact.

closure

a tangible organising process that leads one to see incomplete figures as complete.

cocaine

a central nervous system stimulant derived from leaves of the coca plant. Increases energy, produces euphoria, and in large doses causes paranoia.

■ cochlea

the portion of the inner ear containing the receptors for hearing.

■ coding by pattern

coding the quality of a sensation in terms of the pattern of neural firing.

■ coding by specificity

coding the quality of a sensation in terms of the specific neurons involved.

■ coefficient of correlation

a numerical index used to indicate the degree of correspondence between two sets of paired measurements. The most common kind is the product-moment coefficient designated by r.

■ cogito ergo sum

it means, 'I think, therefore I am.' Has been extracted from Descartes' famous Meditations, it refers to his certain, indubitable knowledge of his own existence as a thinking, conscious being.

■ cognition

an individual's thoughts, knowledge, interpretations, understandings, or ideas.

■ cognitive

works on the assumption that feelings and behaviour can be changed if ideas are changed. Cognitive therapy focuses on correcting learned misconceptions.

■ cognitive appraisal

the interpretation of an event or situation with respect to one's goals and well-being. The cognitive appraisal of an event influences both the quality and intensity of the emotion experienced and the degree of perceived threat.

■ cognitive appraisal theory of emotion

a theory stating that the experience of emotion is the joint effect of physiological arousal and cognitive appraisal, which serves to define how an ambiguous inner state of arousal will be labelled.

■ cognitive behaviour modification

a therapeutic approach that combines the cognitive emphasis on the role of thoughts and attitudes influencing motivations and response with the behavioural emphasis on changing performance through modification of reinforcement probabilities.

■ cognitive behaviour therapy

a psychotherapy approach that emphasises the influence of a person's beliefs, thoughts, and self-statements on behaviour. Combines behaviour therapy methods with techniques designed to change the way the individual thinks about self and events.

■ cognitive consistency

the tendency to seek consistency in one's cognitions.

■ cognitive development

the development of methods of knowing, including imagining, perceiving, reasoning, and problem solving.

cognitive dissonance

the theory that the tension-producing effects of incongruous cognitions stimulate individuals to diminish such tension.

cognitive distortions

in Beck's theory of depression, systematic errors in thinking that lead depressed individuals to misperceive reality in a way that contributes to their negative self-schema. Examples are overgeneralisation (drawing a sweeping conclusion on the basis of a single negative event) and selective abstraction (focusing on an insignificant negative detail while ignoring the more important positive features of a situation).

cognitive function

an intellectual process resulting in an understanding, perception, or awareness of one's ideas.

cognitive map

a hypothetical structure in memory that preserves and organises information about the various events that occur in a learning situation, a mental picture of the learning situation.

cognitive map

a mental description of physical space.

cognitive neuroscience

an interdisciplinary approach that combines aspects of cognitive psychology and neuroscience to study how mental activities are executed in the brain.

cognitive perspective

an approach to psychology that focuses on mental processes such as perceiving, remembering, reasoning, deciding, and problem solving, and tries to explain behaviour in terms of these mental processes.

cognitive process

higher mental functioning, learning, memory, imagination, comprehension, decision making. The means by which an individual becomes aware of people, objects and situations in the environment and their subjective, symbolic meaning.

cognitive psychology

a general approach to psychology that stresses the role of mental processes in understanding behaviour. The cognitive psychologist explains behaviour at the level of mental representations and the mental processes that operate on these representations to produce products (including responses). The approach is not restricted to the study of thought and knowledge, its early concerns with these topics led to the label 'cognitive psychology', but in recent years the approach has been generalised to all areas of psychology.

cognitive rehabilitation

therapy programs which aid persons in the management of specific problems in perception, memory, thinking and problem solving. Skills are practiced and strategies are taught to help improve function and/or compensate for remaining deficits. The interventions are based on an assessment and understanding of the person's brain-behaviour deficits and services are provided by qualified practitioners.

cognitive response theory

a theory that proposes that persuasion induced by a communication is actually self-persuasion produced by the thoughts that the individual generates while receiving or even just anticipating the communication.

cognitive science

a term introduced in the 1970s to focus attention on how humans acquire and organise knowledge, a 'new' science dedicated to understanding cognition. In addition to psychology, the disciplines relevant to cognitive science are neuroscience, linguistics, philosophy, mathematics, and computer science (particularly that branch of computer science known as artificial intelligence).

cognitive therapy

cognitive psychology applies to the study of thinking, concept formation and problem solving. This therapy stresses on changing how the client thinks.

cognitive triad

in Beck's theory, the major concomitant, and possibly cause, of depression. Consists of negative thoughts about the self, the present situation, and the future.

cognitive-appraisal theory

a theory of emotion that proposes that the subjective emotional state is a function of the individual's appraisal, or analysis, of the emotion-arousing situation. A state of physiological arousal can produce different emotions (even antithetical ones) depending on how the person appraises the situation.

cognitivism

the view that evaluative expressions, like 'What a beautiful day!' are meaningful statements. Generally, it is the view in ethics that statements involving morality can be true or false.

coherence theory

it is the theory that believes that a belief is true because it is a member of body of a consistent set of beliefs that all hold together and make sense and hence, need not rest on one certain truth.

collective unconscious

the part of a person's unconscious mind that is inherited, evolutionarily developed and common to all members of the species.

colour circle

an arrangement of chromatic colours on the circumference of a circle in the order in which they appear in the spectrum but with the addition of nonspectral reds and purples. The colours are so arranged that those opposite each other are complementariness in additive mixture.

colour constancy

the tendency to see a familiar object as of the same colour, regardless of changes in illumination on it that alter its stimulus properties.

■ **colour solid**

a three-dimensional representation of the psychological dimensions of colour, with hue around the circumference, saturation along each radius, and brightness from top to bottom.

■ **colour-opponent cells**

in colour vision, cells that respond only to their two opponent colours.

■ **coma**

a state of unconsciousness from which the patient cannot be awakened or aroused, even by powerful stimulation, lack of any response to one's environment. Defined clinically as an inability to follow a one-step command consistently.

■ **common sense realism**

see **direct realism.**

■ **communicative disorder**

an impairment in the ability to:
1) receive and/or process a symbol system,
2) represent concepts or symbol systems, and/or
3) transmit and use symbol systems. The impairment may be observed in disorders of hearing, language, and/or speech processes.

■ **community integration programme**

provides services designed to accomplish functional outcomes focused on home and community integration, including productive activity. Services may be provided in residential facilities, day treatment programs, and the consumer's home. They may be of short-term (several weeks) or long-term duration (several months).

■ **community skills**

those abilities needed to function independently in the community. They may include: telephone skills, money management, pedestrian skills, use of public transportation, meal planning and cooking.

■ **comorbidity**

experiencing multiple disorders at the same time.

■ **companionate love**

refers to the affection a person feels for those with whom his life is deeply entwined.

■ **compatibilism (compatibilist)**

a claim that states that both determinism and free will can be true. In other words, every event may have a cause and I am still free to make my own choices.

■ **complementary colours**

refer to the colours opposite each other on the colour circle. When additively mixed, they create the sensation of white light.

■ **complete lesion**

an injury with no motor or sensory function below the zone of cord destruction at the site of primary trauma.

■ **complex cell**

a cell in the visual cortex that responds to a bar of light or straight edge of a particular orientation located anywhere in the visual field.

■ **complex idea**

a concept composed of two or more simple, intransmutable ideas, for example, 'lemon' is a complex idea derived from a combination of 'yellow', 'sour', 'round', etc.

■ **complex learning**

learning that involves more than forming associations, for example, using a strategy to solve a problem or forming a mental map of one's surroundings. Contrasted with habituation and conditioning which are simpler types of learning.

■ **compliance**

publicly conforming to the wishes of an influencing source but not necessarily changing one's private beliefs or attitudes.

■ **comprehension**

understanding of spoken, written, or gestural communication.

■ **compulsion**

a repetitive action that a person feels driven to make and is unable to resist, ritualistic behaviour.

■ **compulsive talking**

unrestrainable, repetitive irrational talking.

■ **compulsive writing**

uncontrollable urge to repetitive irrational writing.

■ **computer simulation**

the use of a computer to simulate a phenomenon or system in order to study its properties. In psychology, the simulation usually involves an attempt to program a computer to mimic how the mind processes information and solves problems. In this sense, the computer program is literally a theory of how the mind functions.

■ **computerised axial tomography (CT scan)**

a series of X-rays taken at different levels of the brain that allows the direct visualisation of the skull and intracranial structures. A scan is often taken soon after the injury to help decide if surgery is needed. The scan may be repeated later to see how the brain is recovering.

■ **concentration**

maintaining attention on a task over a period of time, remaining attentive and not easily diverted.

■ **concept**

the properties or relationships common to a class of objects or ideas. Concepts may be of concrete things (such as the concept poodle referring to a given variety of dog) or of abstract ideas (such as equality, justice, number).

■ **conceptual tracking**

the ability to follow a series of abstract ideas or thoughts.

■ **conclusion**

refers to the concluding point of an argument. In a valid line of reasoning the conclusion should be supported by the principles.

■ **concrete operational stage**

piaget's third stage of cognitive development (ages 7 to 11 years) during which a child becomes capable of logical thought and achieves conservation concepts.

■ **concrete thinking**

a style of thinking in which the individual sees each situation as unique and is unable to generalise from the similarities between situations. Language and perceptions are interpreted literally so that a proverb such as 'a stitch in time saves nine' cannot be readily grasped.

■ **concussion**

the common result of a blow to the head causing a temporary altered mental state.

■ **conditioned emotion**

an emotional response acquired by conditioning: one aroused by a stimulus that did not originally evoke it.

■ **conditioned fear**

a fear acquired by classical conditioning. The object that the organism comes to fear was originally neutral, but when it is repeatedly paired with an aversive stimulus it becomes an object of fear.

■ **conditioned reinforcers**

a stimulus that has become reinforcing through prior association with a reinforcing stimulus (syn. secondary reinforcer).

■ **Conditioned Response (CR)**

in classical conditioning, the learned or acquired response to a conditioned stimulus, in other words, to a stimulus that did not evoke the response originally.

■ **Conditioned Stimulus (CS)**

in classical conditioning, a previously impartial stimulus that comes to bring out a conditioned response.

■ **conditioning**

conditioned response conforming to the pattern of Pavlov's experiment. The main feature is that the originally neutral conditioned stimulus, through repeated pairing with the unconditioned one, becomes associated with the unconditioned stimulus.

■ **cones**

these are the photoreceptors which are concentrated in the centre of the retina that are responsible for visual experience under normal viewing conditions and for all experiences of colour.

■ **confederate**

a companion of an experimenter whom research participants assume is a fellow participant or bystander.

■ **confirmation**

the degree to which evidence, collected through reasonable investigation, supports the conclusion it is meant to support.

■ **conformity**

the inclination for people to adopt the behaviours, attitudes and values of other members of a reference group.

■ **confounding variable**

a stimulus other than the variable an experimenter clearly introduces into a research setting that affects a participant's behaviour.

confusion

a state in which a person is bewildered, perplexed, or unable to self-orient.

conjugate movement

both eyes move simultaneously in the same direction. Convergence of the eyes toward the midline (crossed eyes) is a disconjugate movement.

conjunction rule

a rule in probability theory, which states that the probability of a proposition cannot be less than the probability of that proposition conjoined with another proposition. People frequently violate the rule when reasoning about real-world situations.

connectionist models

models of cognitive processes (like perception) that incorporate a network of nodes, with excitatory and inhibitory connections between them.

connotation

the original, objective meaning of a word, as opposed to its denotation, the objects to which it applies.

connotative meaning

the suggestive and emotional meanings of a word or symbol, beyond its denotative meaning. Thus, naked and nude both refer to an unclothed body (denotative meaning), but they have somewhat different connotations.

conscience

an internal recognition of standards of right and wrong by which the individual judges his or her conduct.

conscious

in Freud's topographic model, the part of the mind containing thoughts and memories of which the individual is currently aware.

conscious processes

events such as perceptions, private thoughts, and dreams, of which only the person is aware. They are accessible to others through verbal report or by way of inference from other behaviour (syn. experience, awareness).

consciousness

we are conscious when we are aware of external events, reflect on past experiences, engage in problem solving, are selective in attending to some stimuli rather than others, and deliberately choose an action in response to environmental conditions and personal goals. In some contexts, the term is used as a synonym for awareness.

consensual validation

the joint authentication of conscious views of reality.

consequentialism

the view that the value of an act should be judged solely on the basis of that act's effects on other beings.

■ **conservation**

Piaget's term for the ability of the child to recognise that certain properties of objects (such as mass, volume, number) do not change despite transformations in the appearance of the objects.

■ **consistency paradox**

the observation that personality ratings across time and among different observers are reliable, while behaviour ratings across situations are not consistent.

■ **construct validity**

the ability of a test or assessment instrument to confirm predictions of the theory underlying some theoretical concept or construct. Confirming results validate both the concept and the assessment instrument simultaneously.

■ **constructive memory**

the memory that results when we use general knowledge construct and elaborate a more complete and detailed account of. some event.

■ **contact comfort**

refers to the comfort of an infant's physical contact with the mother or caregiver.

■ **contact hypothesis**

the theory that under certain conditions, direct contact between antagonistic groups will reduce discrimination.

■ **context of discovery**

the preliminary phase of research, in which observations, beliefs, information and general knowledge lead to a new idea or a variety of ways of thinking about some phenomenon.

■ **context of justification**

the research phase in which evidence is brought to bear on hypotheses.

■ **contextual distinctiveness**

the assumption that the serial position effect can be changed by the context and the distinctiveness of the experience being recalled.

■ **continental philosophy**

it represents a spectrum of philosophical approaches developed in continental Europe in the twentieth century and consists of various theories of phenomenology, existentialism and deconstruction.

■ **contingency management**

a general treatment strategy involving changing behaviour by changing its results.

■ **contingency model of leadership**

the theory that leadership effectiveness depends both on whether leaders are task-oriented or relationship-oriented and on the degree to which they have situational control.

■ **contingent**

the state of relying on something else for existence.

■ **contradiction**

two statements which are mutually restrictive so that if one is true, the other is necessarily false.

■ **contraries**

two statements where only one may be true, but both may be false, for example, 'All Indians eat mangoes', and 'No Indians eat mangoes', are contraries because only one of the statements can be true and it is possible that both are false.

■ **control group**

experimental participants who are not exposed to the independent variable.

■ **control procedures**

steady procedures for giving instructions, scoring responses and holding all other variables constant except those being systematically varied.

■ **control processes**

regulatory processes that serve to establish equilibrium or monitor goal-directed activities.

■ **controlled stimulation**

conditions in which the perceptual experiences of an organism are systematically varied in order to determine the effect on subsequent performance. For example, rearing kittens in an environment where they see only vertical stripes for the first few months of life or having humans wear prism goggles that distort the directions of objects.

■ **convergence**

the degree to which the eyes turn inward to fixate on an object.

■ **converse**

reversed in position. 'A implies B' is the converse of 'B implies C'.

■ **conversion disorder**

a neurosis caused by the patient's conscious or unconscious desire to escape or avoid some unpleasant situation or responsibility or, to obtain sympathy or some other secondary gain.

■ **coping**

the process of dealing with internal or external demands that are supposed to be threatening or overwhelming.

■ **coping strategies**

skills developed through experience for life situations.

■ **core**

the part of a concept that contains the properties that are more essential for determining membership in the concept.

■ **cornea**

the transparent surface of the eye through which light enters and rays are bent inward to begin image formation.

■ **corporeal**

bodily or physical.

■ **corpus callosum**

the mass of nerve fibres linking the two hemispheres of the cerebrum.

■ **correlation coefficient**

a statistical measure of the direction and strength of the linear relationship between two variables, which can range from -1.00 to +1.00.

■ **correlational method**

a research method used to determine whether some difference that is not under the researcher's control is associated, or correlated, with another difference of interest.

correlational studies

research designed to examine the nature of the relationship between two or more naturally occurring variables.

correspondent inference

an inference that the action of an actor corresponds to, or is indicative of, a stable personal characteristic.

cortical blindness

loss of vision resulting from a lesion of the primary visual areas of the occipital lobe. Light reflex is preserved.

Corticotropin-Release Factor (CFR)

a substance secreted by neurons in the hypothalamus in response to stress. It, in turn, is carried through a channel-like structure to the pituitary gland, causing ACTH (the body's major 'stress' hormone) to be released.

cortisol

one of the steroid hormones produced by the adrenal glands. It has many effects on the body, including the formation of glucose, the reduction of inflammation, and the retention of water. Its level in the blood is used as a measure of stress.

cosmogony

see cosmos.

cosmological argument

the argument that uses facts of the known natural universe, i.e. motion, causation and contingency to assume the existence of God as the original cause of these phenomena.

cosmology

study of the origin and the nature of the universe.

cosmos

ancient Greek 'order', it means the organised universe, especially as subject to laws and principles of some kind.

counselling psychologist

a trained psychologist, usually with a Ph.D. or Psy.D. degree, who deals with personal problems not classified as illness, such as academic, social, or vocational problems of students. He or she has skills similar to those of the clinical psychologist but usually works in a non-medical setting.

counter conditioning

in behaviour therapy, the replacement of a particular response to a stimulus by the establishment of another (usually incompatible) response.

counter-example

an example used to disprove a general claim or principle, for example, a pine tree is a counter-example of the claim that all trees shed their leaves in autumn.

counter-factual(s)

a provisional statement which contains an untrue antecedent, for example, if humans had four eyes instead of two, then there would be fewer traffic accidents.

■ **counter-transference**

situation in which a psychoanalyst develops personal feelings about a client because of perceived likeness of the client to significant people in the therapist's life.

■ **coup**

a blow to the head at the site of impact.

■ **covariation principle**

a principle of attribution theory stating that for something to be the cause of a particular behaviour, it must be present when the behaviour occurs and absent when it does not occur.

■ **craniotomy**

surgical removal of the skull in small pieces.

■ **cranium**

the portion of the skull that encapsulates the brain.

■ **creation ex nihilo**

derived from Latin, this phrase mean 'creation from nothing' the proposition that the natural universe was brought into existence from absolutely nothing by an act of God.

■ **creationism**

the doctrine that all species were created by God in one instant. It contrasts with the theory of evolution.

■ **creativity**

the ability to generate ideas or products that are both novel and appropriate to the circumstances.

■ **criterion**

1. a set of scores or other records against which the success of a predictive test is verified.
2. a standard selected as the goal to be achieved in a learning task, for example, the number of runs through a maze to be made without error as an indication that the maze has been mastered.

■ **criterion problem**

the difficulty that arises in validating a test or assessment instrument when there is no criterion behaviour the investigator is willing to accept as the 'true' measure of the concept being evaluated.

■ **criterion validity**

the ability of a test or assessment instrument to predict the behaviour it is designed to predict (syn. empirical validity).

■ **criterion-keyed method of test construction**

selecting items for a test or assessment instrument by comparing the responses of some criterion group (for example, paranoid individuals) with a control group and retaining only those that discriminate between the two groups.

■ **critical legal studies**

a view that the law is best thought about by reference to what actually occurs in courts and among lawyers, the academic side of legal realism.

■ **critical period**

crucial time periods in a person's life during which specific events must occur for development to proceed normally.

■ **critical realism**

any view that admit that our knowledge of the real, objective nature of the world is relived by the mind, on which sensory experience is necessarily dependent.

■ **critical thinking**

the analysis, criticism and appraisal of statements claimed to be true and of arguments claimed to be valid.

■ **cross-pressure**

conflicting social influences on an individual's beliefs, attitudes, or behaviours. Usually arises when a person identifies with more than one reference group.

■ **cross-sectional design**

a research method in which groups of participants of different chronological ages are noted and rated at a given time.

■ **crystallised intelligence**

the facet of intelligence involving the knowledge a person has already obtained and the ability to access that knowledge, measured by vocabulary, arithmetic and general information tests.

■ **cue**

a signal, hint, or direction used to assist a person in remembering, or performing an activity.

■ **cultural perspective**

it is the psychological perspective that focuses on cross-cultural diversity in the causes and consequences of behaviour.

■ **cultural psychology**

an interdisciplinary approach involving psychologists, anthropologists, sociologists, and other social scientists that is concerned with how an individual's culture influences his or her mental representations and psychological processes.

■ **cultural relativism**

the ethical theory that moral evaluation is rooted in and cannot be separated from the experience, beliefs and behaviour of a particular culture and hence, that what is wrong in one culture may not be so in another.

■ **culture**

the total lifestyle of a people from a particular social grouping, including all the ideas, symbols, preferences, and material objects that they share.

■ **cumulative curve**

a graphic record of the responses emitted during an operant conditioning session. The slope of the cumulative curve indicates the rate of response.

■ **cutaneous senses**

the skin senses that register different sensations like pressure, warmth and cold.

■ **cutting off reflected failure (corfing)**

actively misidentifying with and

distancing oneself from the failures or negative evaluations of others.

■ cynicism (cynics)

a school of ancient Greek philosophy associated with Diogenes of Sinope that called for arriving at true happiness by giving up all material desires and praising the self-sufficiency of the desire to be a good person. The Cynics held that by reducing all material wants to the barest minimum, one will not disappointed in life: if one expects nothing, one lacks nothing.

■ cyrenaicism (cyrenaics)

a school of ancient Greek philosophy most closely associated with Aristippus of Cyrene. Its doctrine upheld that the only good was the attainment of happiness, as defined by 'pleasure' defined broadly.

■ dark adaptation

the increased sensitivity to light when the subject has been continuously in the dark or under conditions of reduced illumination.

■ dasein

derived from German, it means 'existence, being'. It is a term made famous by the German philosopher, Martin Heidegger, referring to the relationship of a person to surrounding people and objects.

■ data (singular, datum)

derived from Latin word meaning 'the given', it is that which is put forth as evidence and which serve as the basis for a particular inquiry.

■ data-driven learning

a kind of associative learning in which people have no prior beliefs about the relation that has to be learned, learning is driven only by the input or data.

■ date rape

sexual violation by a known person in the context of a consensual dating situation.

■ daytime sleepiness

the experience of extreme sleepiness during daytime activities, the major complaint of patients at sleep disorder centres.

■ de dicto

a Latin derivative, the word mean 'of what is said', understood in conjunction with de re; something may be true about the statement (de dicto) or properties of the thing the statement refers to (de re). 'The cat has four paws' is a de re statement. The word 'cat' has three letters, is a de dicto statement.

■ debriefing

a procedure at the conclusion of a research session in which participants are given full information about the nature and hypotheses of the study.

■ decay

theory which states that memory weakens and/or vanish over time if it is not used or accessed.

■ deception

a research technique that provides false information to persons participating in a study.

■ decerebrate posture
exaggerated posture of extension as a result of a lesion to the prepontine area of the brain stem, and is rarely seen fully developed in humans.

■ decerebration
removal of the brain or cutting the spinal cord at the level of the brain stem.

■ decibel (db)
a measure of sound intensity. A change of 10 decibels corresponds to a change in sound power of 10 times, 20 decibels, a change of 100 times, and so forth.

■ decision aversion
the leaning to avoid decision making. The tougher the decision, the greater the likelihood of decision repugnance.

■ decision making
the process of selecting between alternatives from available options.

■ declarative memory
the part of long-term memory where factual information is stored, such as mathematical formulas, vocabulary and life events.

■ decubitus
pressure area, bed sore, skin opening, skin breakdown. A discoloured or open area of skin damage caused by pressure. Common areas most prone to breakdown are buttocks or backside, hips, shoulder blades, heels, ankles and elbows.

■ deductive reasoning
reasoning about arguments in which the conclusion cannot be false if the premises are true.

■ deep relaxation
an approach which utilises breathing techniques, muscle relaxation, and/or guided visualisation to create a state of complete relaxation and to allow for the release of physical, emotional, and mental tension.

■ defeasible
that which can be overturned by a stronger and better consideration; it means literally, capable of being defeated.

■ defence mechanisms
in Freud's psychoanalytic theory, the strategies used by the ego to ward off or to reduce anxiety. These consist of adjustments made unconsciously, either through action or the avoidance of action, to keep from recognising personal motives that might threaten self-esteem or heighten anxiety.

■ degradation
the process in which enzymes in the membrane of a receiving neuron react with a neurotransmitter to break it up chemically and make it inactive, one method (in addition to reuptake) of terminating a neurotransmitter's action.

■ degrees of freedom
the number of individual scores that can vary without changing the sample mean. Statistically written as 'N-1' where N represents the number of subjects.

■ deindividuation

1. the loss of a sense of individual identity and a loosening of normal inhibitions against engaging in behaviour that is inconsistent with internal standards.
2. a psychological state in which persons feel that they have lost their personal identities and have merged anonymously into a group. Hypothesised to be the basis for the impulsive, aggressive behaviours sometimes shown by mobs and crowds.

■ delayed conditioning

a classical conditioning procedure in which the CS begins several seconds or more before the onset of the UCS and continues with it until the response occurs.

■ delusion

false beliefs characteristic of some forms of psychotic disorder. They often take the form of delusions of grandeur or delusions of persecution.

■ demand characteristics

cues in an experimental setting that influence the participants' awareness of what is expected of them and that systematically manipulater their behaviour within that setting.

■ dementia

mental deterioration due to an organic cause.

■ demoralised

crushed, overcome, stricken.

■ demyelination

the loss of nerve fibre 'insulation' due to trauma or disease, which reduces the ability of nerves to conduct impulses (as in multiple sclerosis and some types of spinal cord injury). Some intact but non working nerve fibres might be coaxed into remyelination, or refiring, thus restoring function.

■ dendrite

microscopic fibres extending from the axon of a nerve cell (neuron) that serve as receptors of electrochemical impulses. The total length of dendrites within the human brain exceeds several hundred thousand miles.

■ denial

defence mechanism allowing an individual to maintain that a problem has been resolved with an increase in personal competence, although the problem still remains. It protects against physical or emotional conflict or loss.

■ denotative meaning

the primary meaning of a symbol, something specific to which the symbol refers or points.

■ dependent variable

the variable whose measured changes are attributed to (or correspond to) changes in the independent variable. In psychological experiments, the dependent variable is often a response to a stimulus.

■ depolarisation

change in the resting potential of the nerve cell membrane in the direction of the action potential, the inside of the membrane becomes more positive.

■ depressants

psychoactive drugs that tend to reduce arousal. Alcohol, barbiturates, and opiates are examples.

■ depression

1. an abnormal emotional state in which the individual experiences an exaggerated feeling of sadness, worthlessness and hopelessness, inappropriate and out of proportion to some personal loss or tragedy.
2. a mood disorder characterised by sadness and dejection, decreased motivation and interest in life, negative thoughts (for example, feelings of helplessness, inadequacy, and low self-esteem) and such physical symptoms as sleep disturbances, loss of appetite, and fatigue.

■ depressive explanatory style

a habitual tendency to attribute negative events to internal, stable, and global causes, and positive events to external, unstable, and specific causes.

■ depth perception

the perception of the distance of an object from the observer.

■ descriptive statistics

numbers that summarise and describe the behaviour or characteristics of a particular sample of participants in a study.

■ destabilisation

an abnormal emotional response to physical or mental trauma in which the individual is rendered unable to adjust to his or her normal roles. Individuals who become psychologically destabilised can manifest subjective cognitive impairments that mimic brain injury.

■ determinism

an assumption that all behaviour and observable events have causes.

■ deterrence theory (of punishment)

a theory that is realistic in origin, holding that harming a person for a wrong committed is justified only if it serves both to deter the offender from future transgressions and if it deters others tempted to commit the same crime from so doing. In this theory, if there is no deterrent value in punishment, it is unjustified.

■ developmental age

the age at which all normal children show a particular level of physical or mental development.

■ developmental psychologist

a psychologist whose research interest lies in studying the changes that occur as a function of the growth and development of the organism, in particular the relationship between early and later behaviour.

■ developmental psychology

the branch of psychology concerned with interaction between physical and psychological processes and with stages of growth from conception throughout the entire life span.

deviation IQ score

a standard score used for reporting IQ scores where the mean is set to 100 and standard deviation to 15.

diagnosis

identification of a disease or condition by a scientific evaluation of physical signs, symptoms, history, as well as laboratory tests and procedures.

dialectical method

the question-and-answer method used by Socrates to arrive at knowledge by exposing truths already absolutely known and by challenging the contradictions and faulty reasoning of opposing viewpoints.

dialogue

the process between two people of asking questions and giving answers.

diathesis-stress hypothesis

a hypothesis about the cause of certain disorders, such as schizophrenia, that implies that genetic factors predispose an individual to a certain disorder, but that environmental stress factors must interrupt in order for the potential risk to manifest itself.

dichotic listening

an experimental technique in which a various auditory stimulus is concurrently presented to each ear.

dichromatism

colour blindness in which either the red-green or the blue-yellow system is lacking. The red-green form is relatively common, the blue-yellow form is the rarest of all forms of colour blindness.

diencephalon

this area houses the hypothalamus, which regulates appetite, sleep, and body temperature.

difference reduction

a problem-solving strategy in which one sets up sub goals that, when obtained, put one in a state closer to the goal.

difference threshold

the minimum difference between a pair of stimuli that can be perceived under experimental conditions. See also absolute threshold, just noticeable difference, threshold, Weber's law.

differential reinforcement

a procedure in conditioning in which reinforcement is given only in the presence of a certain stimulus. The outcome of this procedure is a conditioned discrimination.

diffuse

widely spread.

Diffuse Axonal Injury (DAI)

a shearing injury of large nerve fibres (axons covered with myelin) in many areas of the brain. It appears to be one of the two primary lesions of brain injury, the other being stretching or shearing of blood vessels from the same forces, producing haemorrhage.

■ **diffuse brain injury**
injury to cells in many areas of the brain rather than in one specific location.

■ **diffusion of responsibility**
the tendency for persons in a group situation to fail to take action (as in an emergency) because others are present, thus diffusing the responsibility for acting. A major factor in inhibiting bystanders from intervening in emergencies.

■ **dilemma**
a problem where one is confronted with two choices, either of which lead to an unwanted situation.

■ **diminished ability to abstract**
lack of flexibility and adaptability to use ideas and generalisations.

■ **diplopia**
double vision.

■ **direct realism**
holds the view that objects in the physical world possess all the characteristics that ordinary people believe they do.

■ **disability**
the loss, absence or impairment of physical or mental fitness that can be seen or measured.

■ **disaster syndrome**
a three-stage behaviour pattern that is a common reaction to a traumatic event. The person is at first dazed and disoriented, then passive but able to respond to instructions, and finally anxious, apprehensive, and unable to concentrate.

■ **discharge planning**
preparation for life after rehab, including insurance and legal issues, home adaptation, and community support issues.

■ **discipline**
when referring to health care or education it means a particular field of study, such as medicine, occupational therapy, nursing, recreation therapy or others.

■ **discounting principle**
a principle of attribution theory stating that whenever there are several possible causal explanations for a particular event, people tend to be much less likely to attribute the effect to any particular cause.

■ **discrimination**
in perception, the detection of differences between two stimuli.
in conditioning, the differential response to the positive (reinforced) stimulus and to the negative (non-reinforced) stimulus.
in social psychology, prejudicial treatment, as in racial discrimination.

■ **discrimination, sensory**
a process requiring differentiation of two or more stimuli.

■ **discriminative stimulus**
a stimulus that becomes an occasion for an operant response, for example, a knock that leads one to open the door. See also operant behaviour.

■ dishabituation

a return in strength of a response following habituation to a repeated stimulus. Indicates renewed attention on the part of the organism to a change in the stimulus situation.

■ disinhibition

inability to suppress (inhibit) impulsive behaviour and emotions.

■ disjunction

in logic, an 'either/or' statement that technically takes the form, 'p or q'.

■ disorientation

not knowing where you are, who you are, or the current date. Health professionals often speak of a normal person as being oriented 'times three' which refers to person, place and time.

■ displaced aggression

aggression against a person or object other than that which was (or is) the source of frustration.

■ displacement

1. a defence mechanism whereby a motive that may not be directly expressed (such as sex or aggression) appears in a more acceptable form.

2. the principle of loss of items from short-term memory as too many new items are added.

■ display rules

a culture's rules for the types of emotions people should experience in certain situations, and the behaviours (including facial expressions) appropriate for each emotion.

■ disposition

a liking to be a certain way under a specific set of circumstances.

■ dispositional attribute

an attribute explained or interpreted as being caused by inner influences.

■ dispositional attribution

attributing a person's actions to internal dispositions (attitudes, traits, motives), as opposed to situational factors.

■ dispositional properties

the properties of a thing that are potential and defined in terms of what would happen if a certain set of situations were to occur; for example, polar ice has the character of solubility if above-freezing temperatures were ever to occur, whether such temperatures ever occur or not.

■ dispositional variables

the organismic variables, or inner determinants of behaviour, that occur within human and non-human animals.

■ dispositions, mental

according to Gilbert Ryle, the observable characteristics of a person by which the mind may be understood, for example, likes and dislikes, habits, temperament, etc.

■ dissociation

the process whereby some ideas, feelings, or activities lose relationship to other aspects of consciousness and personality and operate automatically or independently.

■ **dissociative amnesia**

the failure to remember significant personal experiences, caused by psychological factors in the absence of any organic dysfunction.

■ **dissociative disorder**

a personality disorder marked by a disorder in the integration of identity, memory, or consciousness.

■ **dissociative identity disorder**

the existence of two or more distinct identities or personalities within the same individual. Each identity has its own set of memories and characteristic behaviours. Typically, the attitudes and behaviours of the alternating personalities are markedly different. Formerly called multiple personality disorder.

■ **dissonance**

1. in music, an inharmonious combination of sounds, contrasted with consonance.
2. in social psychology, Festinger's term for discomfort arising from a perceived inconsistency between one's attitudes and one's behaviour.

■ **distal stimulus**

in the methods of perception, the physical object in the world, as opposed to the proximal stimulus, the optical image on the retina.

■ **distance cues**

1. in vision, the monocular cues according to which the distance of objects is perceived such as superposition of objects, perspective, light and shadow, and relative movement and the binocular cues used in stereoscopic vision.
2. in audition, the corresponding cues governing perception of distance and direction, such as intensity and time differences of sound reaching the two ears.

■ **distinctiveness**

the phenomenon in memory that states we are better able to remember information if it is distinctive or different from other information.

■ **distractibility**

inability to maintain attention, over-reaction to stimuli.

■ **distributive justice**

the part of justice which concerns itself with the fair distribution of benefits and difficulties within a society. In medicine, distributive justice covers both allocative ('who-gets-what-and-why') issues that affect all of society, as well as issues of rationing, which affect particular patients or classes of particular patients.

■ **divergent thinking**

the ability to use previously gained information to debate or discuss issues which have no agreed upon definitive resolution.

■ **dizygotic (dz) twins**

twins developed from separate eggs. They are no more alike genetically than ordinary brothers and sisters and can be of the same or different sexes (syn. fraternal twin).

dls

daily living skills.

DNA (deoxyribonucleic acid)

the physical basis for the communication of genetic information.

dominance

the higher status position when social rank is organised according to a dominance-submission hierarchy, commonly found in human societies and in certain animal groups.

dominant gene

a member of a gene pair which, if present, determines that the individual will show the trait controlled by the gene, regardless of whether the other member of the pair is the same or different (that is, recessive).

door-in-the-face technique

a two-step compliance technique in which, after having a large request refused, the influencer counteroffers with a much smaller request.

dopamine

a neurotransmitter of the central nervous system believed to play a role in schizophrenia. It is synthesised from an amino acid by the action of certain body enzymes and, in turn, is converted into norepinephrine.

dopamine hypothesis

the hypothesis that schizophrenia is related to an excess of the neurotransmitter dopamine, either schizophrenics' produce too much dopamine or have an abnormally large number of dopamine receptors.

dorsal root

the collection of nerves entering the dorsal section (on the back) of a spinal cord segment. These roots share central and peripheral nerve connections, and enter the spinal cord in an area called the dorsal root entry zone (DREZ).

dorsiflexion

when applied to the ankle, the ability to bend at the ankle, moving the front of the foot upward.

double aspect theory

the metaphysical principle that mind and matter are but two fundamental aspects of one reality.

double blind

an experimental design, often used in drug research, in which neither the investigator nor the patients know which subjects are in the treatment and which in the non-treatment condition until the experiment has been completed.

double blind control

an experimental technique in which partial expectations of experimenters are removed by keeping both participants and experimental assistants unaware of which participants have received which treatment.

double blind study

research style in which both the subjects and the experimenter are unaware or 'blind' to the anticipated results.

■ **down's syndrome**

a form of mental deficiency produced by a genetic abnormality (an extra chromosome on pair 21). Characteristics include a thick tongue, extra eyelid folds, and short, stubby fingers (syn. mongolism).

■ **dream analysis**

the psychoanalytic interpretation of dreams used to gain insight into a person's unconscious intentions or conflicts.

■ **dream interpretation**

a psychoanalytic technique in which clients report their dreams as accurately as possible and the therapist interprets the elements of the dreams as symbols of desires and conflicts.

■ **dream therapy**

mental activity related to the rapid-eye-movement period of sleep. Generally consists of visual images and may reflect bodily disturbances or external stimuli. In primitive and ancient cultures, dreams played an extensive role in myth and religion. Freud stressed on dreams as keys to the makeup of the individual and distinguished between the experienced content of a dream and the actual meaning of the dream. Jung held that dreams are not limited to the personal unconscious but may also be shaped by archetypes that originate in the collective unconscious of the human species.

■ **dream work**

in Freudian dream analysis, the process by which the internal censor transforms the dormant content of a dream into visible content.

■ **drive**

an internal cause for motivation, which arises independent of events outside the individual. Drive theories of motivation stress the role of physiological states and of homeostasis.

■ **drive-reduction theory**

the theory that a motivated sequence of behaviour can be best explained as moving from an aversive state of heightened tension (or drive) to a goal state in which the drive is reduced. The goal of the sequence, in other words, is drive reduction.

■ **drug abuse**

continued use of a drug despite serious consequences in the absence of signs of dependency (i.e., no symptoms of tolerance, withdrawal, or compulsive craving).

■ **drug dependence**

a pattern of compulsive drug use usually characterised by tolerance (the need to consume more and more of the drug to achieve the same effect) and withdrawal (unpleasant reactions if use is discontinued).

■ **drug therapy**

various drugs are used to ease symptoms of some mental illnesses. Lithium is used in easing symptoms of manic depression. Tranquillisers are used to reduce anxiety. All drugs have side effects, such as Ritalin, which is prescribed for hyperactive children and can hold back physical growth.

■ DSM-IV

the fourth edition of the Diagnostic and Statistical Manual of the American Psychiatric Association, revised.

■ dualism

in philosophy and theology, system that explains all phenomena in terms of two distinct and irreducible principles, e.g., ideas and matter (as in Plato, Aristotle, and modern metaphysics) or mind and matter (as in psychology). In theology the term refers to a concept of contrasting principles, e.g., good and evil.

■ dualism (mind-body)

the most well-known example of dualism, it proposes that mind and body are separate and distinct kinds of stuff that can never be reduced to each other.

■ dual-memory theory

a theory that distinguishes between a short-term memory of limited capacity and a virtually unlimited long-term memory. Information is encoded into long-term memory via short-term memory.

■ dura mater

the outermost of three membranes protecting the brain and spinal cord, it is tough and leather-like.

■ duty

something which ought to be done, either legally or morally.

■ dysarthria

difficulty in forming words or speaking them because of weakness of muscles used in speaking or because of disruption in the neuromotor stimulus patterns required for accuracy and velocity of speech.

■ dysphagia

a swallowing disorder characterised by difficulty in oral preparation for the swallow, or in moving material from the mouth to the stomach. This also includes problems in positioning food in the mouth.

■ eardrum

the membrane at the inner end of the auditory canal, leading to the middle ear.

■ early selection

selective attention that occurs in the early stages of recognition, when the organism is constructing a description of the input and before the meaning of the input has been determined.

■ echoic memory

sensory memory that allows auditory information to be stored for brief periods.

■ echolalia

imitation of sounds or words without comprehension.

■ eclectic

uses/ techniques/concepts/ideas from several different schools. The therapist may use gestalt techniques with particular kinds of issues and/ or transactional analysis concepts with other kinds of issues.

■ **edema**

collection of fluid in the tissue causing swelling.

■ **educational psychologist**

a psychologist whose research interest lies in the application of psychological principles to the education of children and adults in schools.

■ **ego**

in Freud's tripartite division of the personality, the rational part or controlling self. Operates on the reality principle, holding back the impulses of the id until they can be satisfied in socially approved ways.

■ **ego analyst**

a psychoanalyst, who focuses on the integrative, positive functions of the ego (for example, coping with the environment) rather than the functions of the id (for example, gratifying sexual impulses).

■ **ego defence mechanisms**

mental tactics (conscious or unconscious) used by the ego to defend itself against conflicts experienced in the normal course of life.

■ **ego ideal**

in psychoanalytic thought, this is the ideal behaviour of the ego according to the superego.

■ **egocentric**

the thinking in the preoperational stage of cognitive development when children believe everyone sees the world from the same perspective as he or she does.

■ **egocentrism**

in cognitive development, the inability of a young child at the preoperational stage to take the perspective of a person other than him.

■ **egoism, ethical**

an ethical theory claiming that the quest of self-interest is morally correct and rational. Often associated with the Russian-born, American philosopher, Ayn Rand it claims that ethics would be less hypocritical if everyone acknowledged the truth of its claims.

■ **egoism, psychological**

a view in ethics or psychology holding that all human behaviour is stimulated by self-interest. This theory makes a factual claim about human nature, whereas ethical egoism makes a claim about how humans should act, regardless of the truth of psychological egoism. The view arises in ethics because, if true, it renders altruistic theories impossible. Hence defenders of altruistic theories see a need to defeat it.

■ **egoistic helping**

a form of helping in which the ultimate goal of the helper is to increase his or her own welfare.

■ **eidetic imagery**

the ability to retain visual images of pictures that are almost photographic in clarity. Such images can be described in far greater detail than would be possible from memory alone.

elaboration

a memory process wherein one expands verbal material so as to increase the number of ways to retrieve the material.

elaboration likelihood model

a theory that there are two ways in which persuasive messages can cause attitude change, each differing in the amount of cognitive effort or elaboration they require.

elaborative rehearsal

a technique for improving memory by enriching the encoding of information.

electro convulsive therapy (ECT)

a treatment for severe depression in which a mild electric current is applied to the brain, producing a seizure similar to an epileptic convulsion.

electroencephalogram (EEG)

a record obtained by attaching electrodes to the scalp (or occasionally to the exposed brain). Among the brain waves observed are alpha waves (8-13 Hz), characteristic of relaxed wakefulness, delta waves (1-3 Hz), a slower wave of high amplitude that occurs during deep sleep, and theta waves (4-7 Hz), a pattern characteristic of the EEG of the hippocampus and indicative of behavioural arousal.

electromyography (EMG)

an insertion of needle electrodes into muscles to study the electrical activity of muscle and nerve fibres. It may be somewhat painful to the patient.

eliminative materialism

a metaphysical principle that holds that inquiry into concepts of the non-physical mind should be removed, because such psychological inquiries (and their resulting 'explanations') are so infected with error as to make them useless.

Ellis, Albert

a cognitive psychologist who developed the concept of Rational-Emotive Therapy.

embarrassment

an unpleasant emotion experienced when we believe that we cannot perform coherently in a social situation.

emotion

the condition of the organism during affectively toned experience, whether mild or intense.

emotional appropriateness

the correctness or suitability of feelings evaluated from an objective perspective.

emotional blunting

a dulling of emotional response.

emotional intelligence

type of intelligence defined as the abilities to perceive, appraise and express emotions accurately and appropriately, to use emotions to facilitate thinking, to understand and analyse emotions, to use emotional knowledge efficiently and to regulate one's emotions to promote both emotional and intellectual growth.

■ emotional liability

exhibiting rapid and drastic changes in emotional state (laughing, crying, anger) inappropriately without apparent reason.

■ emotion-focused coping

ways of reducing anxiety or stress that do not deal directly with the anxiety-producing situation, defence mechanisms are a form of emotion-focused coping.

■ empathy

a feeling of compassion and tenderness upon viewing a victim's plight.

■ empathy-altruism hypothesis

a theory proposing that experiencing empathy for someone in need produces an altruistic motive for helping.

■ empirical

something which can be proved or disproved by sensory experience.

■ empiricism

the view that behaviour is learned as a result of experience.

■ encephalography

non-invasive use of ultrasound waves to record echoes from brain tissue. Used to detect haematoma, tumour or ventricle problems.

■ encoding

the conversion of information to be stored in memory.

■ encoding specificity

the principle that subsequent retrieval of information is enhanced if cues received at the time of recall are constant with those present at the time of encoding.

■ endocrine system

a system of ductless glands that discharge their secretions (hormones) into the extracellular fluid around capillaries and hence into the bloodstream. The hormones secreted by the endocrine glands are important integrators of bodily functions.

■ endorphins

chemicals produced by our own body that act like morphine to reduce pain.

■ endotracheal tube

a tube that serves as an artificial airway and is inserted through the patient's mouth or nose. It passes through the throat and into the air passages to help breathing. To do this it must also pass through the patient's vocal cords. The patient will be unable to speak as long as the endotracheal tube is in place. It is this tube that connects the respirator to the patient.

■ engineering psychologist

a psychologist who specialises in the relationship between people and machines, seeking, for example, to design machines that minimize human error.

■ engram

the physical memory trace for information in the brain.

enkephalins
a chemical in the brain that naturally inhibits pain messages by attaching to special receptors in the brain and spinal cord.

environmental variables
exterior influences on behaviour.

enzyme
a protein in the body that functions to initiate a specific chemical reaction.

Epicureanism
a view associated with the ancient philosopher Epicurus, which supports the pursuit and enjoyment in moderation of broadly-defined pleasures, for example, friendship, peace and the contemplation of beauty and it decries aspiring for material pursuits.

epidural
referring to an area outside the brain and its fibrous covering, the dura, but under the skull.

epinephrine
the principal hormone secreted by the adrenal medulla in response to stressful situations. Its effects are similar to those brought about by stimulation of the sympathetic division of the autonomic nervous system (for example, arousal, increased heart rate and blood pressure). It is also an excitatory neurotransmitter in the central nervous system (syn. adrenalin).

epiphenomenalism
a view about the mind that states that mental events, such as conscious thought, subjective experience and emotions really do exist but not in any way independent of the brain and body; instead, they are merely the effects of the physical brain. More important, such mental states can have no causal effect on the natural world or the human body.

episodic memory
a type of memory that stores facts about personal episodes. The fact or episode is encoded with respect to the memoriser and often with respect to the specific time and place as well.

EQ
the emotional intelligence counterpart of IQ.

equal intervals
characteristic of a scale of measurement where the individual units possess the qualities of equal intervals. The difference between each unit of measurement is exactly the same.

equilibratory senses
the senses that give discrimination of the position of the body in space and of the movement of the body as a whole. See also **kinesthesis, semicircular canals, vestibular sacs**.

equity theory
the theory that people are most satisfied in a relationship when the ratio between rewards and costs is similar for both partners.

equivocal
a word, statement or phrase with multiple meanings; ambiguous.

■ **erogenous zones**

the areas of the skin surface that are especially sensitive to stimulation and that give rise to erotic or sexual sensations.

■ **error**

the amount of other variables that can influence the observed score

■ **error level**

the level of accepted error within a given set of data. The greater the error level, the wider the confidence interval.

■ **escape conditioning**

operant conditioning based on the idea that a behaviour is more likely to be repeated if it results in the cessation of a negative event.

■ **escape learning**

learning to make a response in order to escape from an aversive event.

■ **eschatological verification**

the term used by John Hick to refer to a method, where the existence of God and other tenets of Christianity could be verified after death or after Armageddon. 'Eschatology' is the study of 'the final days', hence postponed verification in the future.

■ **esse**

Latin derivative meaning 'to be'. It refers to the state or act of being.

■ **essence**

that basic element of a thing, without which it would cease to exist.

■ **essential tremor**

a movement disorder that produces uncontrollable trembling, usually in the hands.

■ **estimate**

an idea about a characteristic of a population based on sample data (e.g., the sample mean IQ was 102 so we estimate that the population mean IQ is also 102)

■ **eta**

a co-relational technique used mainly for non-linear relationships. (Example, income and age are positively correlated until older age at which point the correlation reverses itself to some extent.

■ **ethnic identity**

an individual's sense of personal identification with a particular ethnic group.

■ **ethnocentrism**

a pattern of increased hostility toward out groups accompanied by increased loyalty to one's in-group.

■ **etiology**

the reasons, or factors related to, the development of a disorder.

■ **eudaimonia**

derived from ancient Greek, this word mean 'happiness or well-being', almost always associated with the ethical views of Aristotle, which posit eudaimonia as the meaning and goal of life, defined as honourable happiness among others in a cultivated, proud society that practise science and the arts.

euphoria

an exaggerated or abnormal sense of well-being not based on reality.

euthanasia

derived from ancient Greek, this word mean 'good death or good dying'; bringing about the death of another with the intention of preventing suffering.

evil (problem of)

the view that a benevolent, omnipotent, omniscient God is mismatched with the existence of real evil in the world.

evocative interaction

the interaction between individuals and their environments that arises because the behaviour of different individuals evokes different responses from others.

evoked potential

registration of the electrical responses of active brain cells as detected by electrodes placed on the surface of the head at various places. The evoked potential, unlike the waves on an EEG, is elicited by a specific stimulus applied to the visual, auditory or other sensory receptors of the body. Evoked potentials are used to diagnose a wide variety of central nervous system disorders.

evolutionary psychology

an area of research that studies how psychological processes have evolved by means of natural selection, those behaviours that aided survival or increased the chance of reproduction have tended to persist through the course of evolutionary history.

exacerbate

to increase the seriousness of a condition marked by more intense signs or symptoms.

excitable

emotional, nervous, agitate, sensitive.

excitation transfer

a psychological process in which arousal caused by one stimulus is transferred and added to arousal elicited by a second stimulus.

excitatory inputs

information entering a neuron that signals it to fire.

excitatory synapse

a synapse at which the neurotransmitter changes the membrane permeability of the receiving cell in the direction of depolarisation.

executive functions

the capacity to formulate, plan and carry out plans effectively. These functions are essential for independent, creative and socially constructive behaviour.

exemplar strategy

a categorisation strategy in which (a) old instances of a concept are memorised and (b) a new item is declared a member of that concept if it is sufficiently similar to the memorised instances.

exemplification

eliciting perceptions of integrity and moral worthiness.

existence precedes essence

a central principle of existentialism that holds that the essence of any human being is entirely determined by the free choices made by that already-existing person. It denies that God or anything else created a human nature that makes humans a certain way. For Existentialists, 'human nature' is not something that is inherited but is merely a generalisation is made from millions of ways of acting that people have chosen and hence, could have chosen differently.

existential

a humanist therapeutic orientation that 'takes the unfolding of the client's genuine self as its goal'.

existentialism

a term for the branch of modern philosophy that explores an assortment of questions having to do with the individual's lack of an essential nature, the absolute freedom he or she has to create his or here essence and the modern problems of meaninglessness, alienation, the absurdity of life and the absence of a rational meaning in the universe, etc.

expectancy effects

results that occur when a researcher or observer faintly communicates to participants the kind of behaviour he or she expects to find, thereby creating that expected reaction.

expectancy theory

a cognitive theory of work stimulus that proposes that workers are motivated when they expect their efforts and job performance to result in desired outcomes.

expectation

an anticipation or prediction of future events based on past experience and present stimuli.

experience-sampling method

an experimental method that helps researchers in describing the typical contents of consciousness. Herein, participants are asked to record what they are feeling and thinking whenever signalled to do so.

experimental design

a plan for collecting and treating the data of a proposed experiment. The design is evolved after preliminary exploration, with the aims of economy, precision, and control, so that appropriate inferences and decisions can be made from the data.

experimental group

in an experimental design contrasting two groups, that group of subjects given the treatment whose effect is under investigation.

experimental methods

research designed to test cause-effect relationships between variables.

experimental psychologist

a psychologist who uses experimental methods to study how people (and other animals) react to sensory stimuli, perceive the world, learn and remember, reason and respond emotionally.

■ experimental realism

the degree to which an experiment absorbs and involves those who participate in it.

■ experimenter bias

mistakes in a research study due to the predisposed notions or beliefs of the experimenter.

■ expert power

power derived through advanced knowledge or experience in a particular subject.

■ explicit memory

the kind of memory that underlies a conscious recollection of something in the past.

■ explicit uses of memory

the conscious efforts to recover information through memory processes.

■ ex-post-facto (after the fact) research

research method in which the independent variable is administered prior to the study without the researcher's control and its effects are investigated afterward

■ expressive therapies

this form of therapy uses the arts to promote physical and mental health and personal growth like art therapy, dance therapy, drama therapy, music therapy, poetry and psychodrama.

■ extended care facility-basic

residential facility which supplies 24-hour nursing care and supervision and assistance with activities of daily life.

■ extended care facility-skilled

a residential facility for the patient who requires 24-hour nursing care (IV, intramuscular injections, special feeding tubes, skin care, oxygen) and rehabilitative therapy, such as physical therapy, occupational therapy, or speech therapy on a less intensive basis than as an inpatient in a comprehensive rehabilitation centre.

■ extension

movement which brings the body or limbs into straight position.

■ external attribution

an attribution that locates the cause of an event to factors external to the person, such as luck, or other people, or the situation.

■ external locus of control

it is the belief that the environment has more control over life circumstances than the a person does.

■ external validity

the extent to which a study's findings can be generalised to people beyond those in the study itself.

■ external world

is the exterior which exists around us and is perceived and acted upon by body and mind.

■ extinction

1. the experimental procedure, following classical or operant conditioning, of presenting the conditioned stimulus without the usual reinforcement.

2. the reduction in response that results from this procedure.

■ **extracellular fluid**

fluid, including the blood, outside the cells, one of the critical variables monitored in the control of thirst.

■ **extracellular reservoir**

water outside the body's cells, including blood.

■ **extrasensory perception (ESP)**

response to external stimuli without any known sensory contact.

■ **extremity**

arm or leg.

■ **extrinsic**

a property that an object possesses only because of its relationship with something else, for example, a movie that is number one at the box office has the extrinsic property of being a box-office champion. It only holds that property in relationship to weekly box-office sales, not because there is something inherently within the movie that makes it a box-office champion regardless of ticket sales, or any other factor.

■ **extrinsic motivation**

the desire or internal force to perform a certain behaviour based on the potential external rewards that may be received as a result.

■ **extroversion**

a personality style where the individual prefers external and group activity as opposed to internal and individual activity.

■ **face validity**

the degree to which test items appear to be directly related to the quality the researcher wishes to measure.

■ **facial feedback hypothesis**

the hypothesis that people's subjective experience of an emotion is determined by feedback from the physiological arousal caused by engaging in specific facial expressions.

■ **facticity**

a term associated with Sartre, which deals with the totality of conditions that exist for an individual and which are capable of being known to be true or false.

■ **factor analysis**

a statistical method used in test construction and in interpreting scores from batteries of tests. The method enables the investigator to compute the minimum number of determiners (factors) required to account for the inter correlations among the scores on the tests making up the battery.

■ **factorial ANOVA**

an Analysis of Variance used when there are two or more independent variables. When there are two, the ANOVA is called a Two-Way ANOVA, three independent variables would use a Three-Way ANOVA, etc.

■ **faculty**

one of the abilities of the mind, for example, intelligence, memory, perception, imagination, etc., that allows us to know, feel and act.

■ **faith**

the belief in the truth of a doctrine that may not be capable of being proven true by reason or evidence and which may require suspension of logical judgement through an act of will.

■ **fallacy**

an error in reasoning which traditionally takes two forms: a formal fallacy is an error in the formal structure of a valid argument; an informal fallacy is any other flaw including vagueness of language, irrelevancies, ambiguities, etc.

■ **false consensus bias**

the tendency to exaggerate how common one's own characteristics and opinions are in the general population.

■ **family resemblance**

the idea that objects may be related not just because they share a common essence, but because they share a constellation of loosely-related, overlapping resemblances, like the appearances of people in a large, extended family. This view of concepts explains how a word or concept can refer to a class of similar things without having a common essence.

■ **family systems**

an orientation in which individuals are seen as part of, and affected by, their families. Family history and interaction is made a part of the individual's therapy.

■ **family therapy**

psychotherapy with the family members as a group rather than treatment of the patient alone.

■ **fatalism**

the doctrine that all events are predetermined to happen and that no human action can influence their occurrence. In fatalism, events happen outside of and despite, the choices of humans.

■ **fatigue**

a state of exhaustion, the loss of strength or endurance.

■ **fear**

emotional reaction to the threat of danger, emotional reaction to immediate and evident danger.

■ **feature detector**

a general term for any perceptual mechanism that detects distinctive features in a complex display. An example is a line (or edge) detector in vision. Since anything we see can be approximated by a series of line segments at angles to each other, feature detectors have been postulated to be the building blocks for recognising more complex forms.

■ **Fechner's law**

the assertion that the perceived magnitude of a stimulus increases in proportion to the logarithm of its physical intensity.

■ **femininity**

possession of expressive personality traits.

■ **feminism**

movement that studies the different ways that men and women experience the world politically, ethically, socially and epistemologically, either because of their different natures or because of their different gender socialisations. As a social-political orientation, it seeks to reduce bias based on gender and to value women's achievements, experiences and perspectives.

■ **feminist therapy**

therapy of any orientation, using any technique, which attempts to acknowledge and address the effect of gender roles and societal pressures on personal growth for both sexes.

■ **foetal alcohol syndrome**

abnormal development of the foetus and infant caused by maternal alcohol consumption during pregnancy. Features of the syndrome include retarded growth, small head circumference, a flat nasal bridge, a small midface, shortened eyelids, and mental retardation.

■ **fetish**

a state in which arousal and/or sexual gratification is achieved through inanimate objects (shoes, pantyhose) or non-sexual body parts (feet, hair). It is considered a problem when the object is needed in order to obtain arousal or gratification and the person can not complete a sexual act without the presence of this object.

■ **field experiment**

an experiment conducted in natural, real-life settings, outside the laboratory.

■ **fight-or-flight response**

a pattern of bodily responses that prepares the organism for an emergency. Most of these physiological changes result from activation of the sympathetic system and the adrenalcortical system. Includes increases in pupil size, heart rate, blood pressure, respiration, muscle tension, and the secretion of epinephrine, norepinephrine, ACTH and other hormones, decreases in saliva, mucous, digestive activity, and the size of blood vessels.

■ **figure**

object-like regions of the visual field that are distinguished from background.

■ **figure-ground**

the differentiation between the foreground and the background of a scene, this refers to all sensory systems, including vision, hearing, touch.

■ **figure-ground organisation**

perceiving a pattern as foreground against a background. Patterns are commonly perceived this way even when the stimuli are ambiguous and the foreground-background relationships are reversible.

■ **file-drawer problem**

a problem that arises because studies that fail to obtain positive results are less likely to be published than studies that do obtain positive results.

■ **five-factor model**

a far-reaching descriptive personality system that maps out the relationships among common traits, theoretical concepts, and personality scales; informally called the Big Five.

■ **fixation**

in Freud's psychoanalytic theory, arrested development through failure to pass beyond one of the earlier stages of psychosexual development or to change the objects of attachment.

■ **fixed interval schedule**

a schedule in which the reinforcement is presented after a specific duration.

■ **fixed ratio schedule**

a schedule in which the reinforcement is presented after a specific number of responses.

■ **flaccid**

lacking normal muscle tone, limp.

■ **flaccidity**

a form of paralysis in which muscles are soft and limp.

■ **flashbulb memory**

a vivid and relatively permanent record of the circumstances in which one learned of an emotionally charged, significant event.

■ **flattened affect**

emotionally lacking, listless.

■ **flexion**

bending a joint.

■ **flooding**

a behaviour therapy procedure in which a fearful person exposes himself or herself to what is frightening, in reality or in imagination, for extended periods of time without opportunity to escape.

■ **flower essences**

these are intended to lessen negative emotional states that may contribute to illness or hinder personal growth. Drops of a solution infused with the captured essence of a flower are placed under the tongue or in a beverage. The appropriate essences are chosen, focusing on the client's emotional state rather than on a particular physical condition.

■ **fluid intelligence**

the feature of intelligence that involves the capability to see complex relationships and solve problems.

■ **foley catheter**

a tube inserted into the urinary bladder for drainage of urine. The urine drains through the tube and collects into a plastic bag.

■ **folk psychology**

the set of beliefs and practices of ordinary people which posit mental states such as ideas, wants and desires as reasons for human behaviour.

■ **foot-in-the-door technique**

a two-step compliance technique in which the influencer secures compliance to a small request, and then later follows this with a larger, less desirable request.

■ **formal assessment**

the systematic activities and measurement instruments used by trained professionals to assess a person's functioning, aptitudes, abilities, or mental states.

formal operational stage

Piaget's fourth stage of cognitive development (age 11 and up) in which the child becomes able to use abstract rules.

formalism

in the field of aesthetics, it is a view that a work of art's essential characteristics are the only basis for evaluating it.

foundational theories

these are the frameworks for initial understanding devised by children to explain their experiences of the world.

foundationalism

term for any epistemological view that an adequate theory of knowledge must have a very certain base or foundation.

four noble truths

a Buddhist teaching attributed to Siddhartha which says that:

· existence consists of suffering.
· cravings are the source of suf fering and bind us to existence.
· suffering can be overcome by eliminating cravings.
· suffering can be overcome by means of an 8-step path, resulting in enlightenment.

fovea

in the eye, a small area in the central part of the retina, packed with cones, the most sensitive part of the retina for detail vision and colour vision in daylight.

frame

a particular description of a choice; the perspective from which a choice is described or framed affects how a decision is made and which option is ultimately exercised.

framing

style of presenting information either positively or negatively in order to manipulate the influence it has on an individual or group.

free association

1. the form of word-association experiment in which the subject gives any word he or she thinks of in response to the stimulus word.
2. in psychoanalysis, the effort to report without modification everything that comes into awareness.

free recall

a memory task in which a subject is given a list of items (usually one at a time) and is later asked to recall them in any order.

free will

the capability of human being to make choices free of coercion or compulsion and to choose the important actions of their lives.

freedom

the ability to act in a personal and private sphere without interference, so long as one's actions do not harm others.

frequency distribution

a gist of how frequently each score appears in a set of observations.

■ frequency effect

the phenomenon in memory by which a person tend to remember information better if it is repeated.

■ frequency theory

the theory that a tone produces a rate of vibration in the basilar membrane equal to its frequency, with the result that pitch can be coded by the frequency of the neural response.

■ Freud, Sigmund

often referred to as the father of clinical psychology. His extensive theory of personality development (psychoanalytical theory) is the cornerstone for modern psychological thought and comprises of (1) the psychosexual stages of development, (2) the structural model of personality (id, ego, superego) and (3) levels of consciousness (conscious, subconscious and unconscious).

■ Freudian slip

in psychoanalytic theory, a mistake or substitution of words in speaking or writing that is contrary to the speaker's conscious intention and presumably expresses wishes or thoughts repressed to the unconscious.

■ Fromm, Erich (1900-1980)

an American psychoanalyst who held that the individual is a product of society and that in industrial society, human beings have become estranged from themselves.

■ frontal cortex

front part of the brain involved in planning, organising, problem solving, selective attention, personality and other 'higher cognitive functions.'

■ frontal lobe

a portion of each cerebral hemisphere, in front of the central fissure.

■ frustration

1. as an event, the thwarting circumstances that block or interfere with goal-directed activity.
2. as a state, the annoyance, confusion, or anger engendered by being thwarted, disappointed, defeated.

■ frustration tolerance

the ability to persist in completing a task despite apparent difficulty. Individuals with a poor frustration tolerance will often refuse to complete tasks which are the least bit difficult. Angry behaviour, such as yelling or throwing things while attempting a task is also indicative of poor frustration tolerance.

■ frustration-aggression hypothesis

the theory that frustration causes aggression.

■ functional

the ability to carry out a purposeful activity.

■ functional approach

attitude theories that emphasise that people develop and change their attitudes based on the degree to which they satisfy different psychological needs. To change an attitude, one must understand the underlying function that attitude serves.

■ Functional Electric Stimulation (FES)

the application of low-level, computer-controlled electric current to the neuromuscular system, including paralysed muscle, to enhance or produce functions such as walking or bike exercises.

■ functional fixedness

an inability to perceive a new use for an object previously associated with some other purpose, it badly affects problem solving and creativity.

■ functional MRI (fMRI)

a brain imaging technique that combines benefits of both MRI and PET scans by detecting magnetic changes in the flow of blood to cells in the brain.

■ functionalism

1. it is the perspective on mind and behaviour that focuses on the examination of their functions in an organism's interactions with the environment.
2. the school of thought popular in the 19th century stressing on conscious experiences as a precursor to behaviour.
3. a notion about the mind that proposes that mental states are real but cannot, or should not, be defined by assuming a non-physical mind, but instead by their functions, particularly with respect to the behaviour they cause and produce.

■ fundamental

the frequency being played in a musical note.

■ fundamental attribution error

the tendency to underestimate situational influences on behaviour and assume that some personal characteristic of the individual is responsible, the bias toward dispositional rather than situational attributions.

■ fuzzy concept

a concept in which one primarily relies on prototype properties in determining membership, and hence cannot always be sure of one's decisions.

■ G

the factor of general intelligence underlying all intelligent performance. Typically compared to s, which represents specific intelligences. G is the culmination of all possible s's.

■ GABA (Gamma-Amino Butyric Acid)

a neurotransmitter involved in the inhibition of apprehension and excitation.

■ gainful occupation

includes employment in the competitive labour market, practice of a profession, farm or family work (including work for which payment is 'in kind rather than in cash), sheltered employment, work activity (to the extent that there is net pay), and home industries or other home-bound work.

■ **gait training**

instruction in walking, with or without equipment, also called 'ambulation training.'

■ **Galvanic Skin Response (GSR)**

changes in electrical conductivity of, or activity in, the skin, detected by a sensitive galvanometer. The reactions are commonly used as an emotional indicator.

■ **Gamma-Aminobutyric Acid (GABA)**

an important inhibitory neurotransmitter.

■ **gamma-knife radio surgery**

a surgical application using laser-like beams of radiation to reach obscured areas of the brain.

■ **ganglion**

a mass of nervous tissue composed principally of nerve-cell bodies and lying outside the brain or spinal cord.

■ **ganglion cells**

cells in the visual system that amalgamate impulses from many bipolar cells in a single firing rate.

■ **gate control theory of pain**

according to this theory, the sensation of pain requires not only that pain receptors be activated, but also that a neural gate in the spinal cord allow these signals to continue to the brain. Pressure stimulation tends to close the gate, this is why rubbing a hurt area can relieve pain.

■ **gender**

the meanings that societies and individuals attach to being female and male.

■ **gender constancy**

a child's realisation that a person's sex does not change with age or appearance (e.g., wearing opposite-sex clothes). A direct analogue to Piaget's concept of conservation in the child's understanding of the physical world.

■ **gender differences**

culturally based differences between males and females.

■ **gender identity**

the knowledge that one is a male or a female and the internalisation of this fact into one's self-concept.

■ **gender role**

the accepted behaviour, thoughts and emotions of a specific gender in context with a particular society, culture or country.

■ **gender schema**

a mental structure that organises the person's perceptual and conceptual world into gender categories (male-female, masculine-feminine). Gender schema theory holds that society produces gender identity and sex typing by teaching individuals to use the gender schema as a set of 'lenses' through which to view reality.

■ **gender schema theory**

Bem's theory that children develop schemas containing culturally based gender information which they use to understand themselves and the world.

gender stereotypes

a society's expectations about the characteristics of females as a group and males as a group.

gender typing

the process of developing the behaviour, thoughts and emotions associated with a particular gender.

gene

the basic unit of hereditary transmission, localised within the chromosomes. Each chromosome contains many genes. Genes are typically in pairs, one member of the pair being found in the chromosome from the father, the other in the corresponding chromosome from the mother.

general adaption syndrome (GAS)

the pattern of non-specific adaptational physiological devices that occur in response to continuing hazard by almost any serious stressor.

General Problem Solver (GPS)

a computer program to simulate human problem solving by setting up subgoals and reducing the discrepancies to each subsequent subgoal.

generalisation

1. in concept formation, problem solving, and transfer of learning, the detection by the learner of a characteristic or principle common to a class of objects, events, or problems.
2. in conditioning, the principle that once a conditioned response has been established to a given stimulus, similar stimuli will also evoke that response.

generalised anxiety disorder

an anxiety disorder characterised by persistent tension and apprehension. May be accompanied by such physical symptoms as rapid heart rate, fatigue, disturbed sleep, and dizziness.

generativity

a commitment beyond one's self and one's partner to family, work, society and future generations. Typically, a crucial step in development in one's 30s and 40s.

genetics

that branch of biology concerned with heredity and the means by which hereditary characteristics are transmitted.

genital stage

in Freud's psychoanalytic theory, the final stage of psychosexual development, beginning at puberty and culminating in mature adult sexuality.

genocide

the systematic destruction of one group of people, often an ethnic or racial group, by another.

genotype

in genetics, the characteristics that an individual has inherited and will transmit to his or her descendants, whether or not the individual manifests these characteristics.

geon

in perception, geometric forms (such as cylinders, cones, blocks, and wedges) that comprise the features of objects. Recognition of an object is good to the extent that the geons of the object can be recovered.

gestalt

promotes increased awareness and integration of the self as a whole, including aspects of self that are often feared or misunderstood. The goal is to understand and create a 'working relationship' with these aspects of self.

gestalt psychology

a system of psychological theory concerned primarily with perception that emphasises pattern, organisation, wholes, and field properties.

gestalt therapy

in Gestalt therapy, the analyst persuades the clients to release their emotions and to recognise these emotions for what they are. Emphasises the individual's movement towards wholeness. It tends to be somewhat confrontational and directly challenge the client's defences against coming to grips with their problems. This therapy holds that a person's inability to successfully assimilate the parts of his or her personality into a healthy whole lie at the root of psychological disturbance.

ghost in the machine

a derisive term used by Gilbert Ryle to refer to the common view that the mind is a spiritual substance, or soul-like, a view that Descartes held.

gi tube

a tube inserted through a surgical opening into the stomach. It is used to introduce liquids, food, or medication into the stomach when the patient is unable to take these substances by mouth.

Glasgow coma scale

a standardised system used to assess the degree of brain impairment and to identify the seriousness of injury in relation to outcome. The system involves three determinants: eye opening, verbal responses and motor response all of which are evaluated independently according to a numerical value that indicates the level of consciousness and degree of dysfunction. Scores run from a high of 15 to a low of 3. Persons are considered to have experienced a mild brain injury when their score is 13 to 15. A score of 9 to 12 is considered to reflect a 'moderate' brain injury and a score of 8 or less reflects a 'severe' brain injury.

glia cells

supporting cells (not neurons) composing a substantial portion of brain tissue, recent speculation suggests that they may play a role in neural conduction.

■ **Gloss Pharyngeal Breathing (GPB)**

a means of forcing extra air into the lungs to expand the chest and achieve a functional cough.

■ **glutamate**

an amino acid that serves as an important excitatory neurotransmitter.

■ **goal-directed selection**

a determinant of why people select some parts of sensory input for further processing. It reflects the choices made as a function of one's own goals.

■ **gonads**

sexual organs that secrete sexual hormones and that manufacture reproductive cells. Female gonads, called ovaries, secrete oestrogen and produce egg cells. Male gonads, called testes, secrete androgen (especially testosterone) and produce sperm cells.

■ **graded potentials**

potential changes of varying size induced in a neuron's dendrites or cell body by stimulation from synapses from other neurons. When the graded potentials reach a threshold of depolarisation, an action potential occurs.

■ **grand mal**

a convulsion accompanied by loss of consciousness.

■ **grandiosity**

boastfulness, bragging, self praising.

■ **grief**

the physical and emotional responses to the death, separation or loss of a beloved person or thing.

■ **grief process**

emotional responses to grief which progress from alarm to disbelief and denial, to anger and guilt, to finding a source of comfort, and finally to adjustment.

■ **ground**

the backdrop or background areas of the visual field, against which figures stand out.

■ **group**

two or more people who interact with and influence one another over a period of time, and who depend upon one another and share common goals and a collective identity.

■ **group cohesiveness**

the attractiveness that group members have for one another.

■ **group dynamics**

related to the study of how group processes change individual functioning.

■ **group polarisation**

the tendency of groups to arrive at decisions that are in the same direction but are more extreme than the mean of the pre-discussion decisions of the individuals in the group.

■ **group therapy**

a group discussion or other group activity with a therapeutic purpose participated in by more than one client or patient at a time.

■ group think

the tendency of members of a interconnected group to reach decisions without weighing all the facts, especially those cancelling out the majority opinion.

■ grouped frequency distribution

a table showing the number of occurrences for a grouping of scores. Used a lot in educational settings where a score of 90 to 100 may be grouped as an A, a score of 80 to 90 may be grouped as a B, etc.

■ groupthink

1. a deterioration of mental efficiency, reality testing, and moral judgment in a group that results from an excessive desire to reach consensus.
2. the tendency of members of some decision-making groups to suppress their own dissenting opinions in the interests of group consensus, thereby producing an inadequate decision-making process and poor decisions.

■ guided search

in visual perception, a parallel search of the environment for single, basic attributes that guides attention to likely locations of objects with more complex combinations of attributes.

■ guided visualisation

the use of mental imagery in therapy. Guided visualisation is used in hypnosis, to alter moods.

■ gustation

the sense of taste.

■ habit

a learned stimulus-response sequence.

■ habituation

the reduction in the strength of a response to a repeated stimulus. In general, almost any stimulus will produce habituation, for example, a pure tone sounded for a half-hour may decrease as much as 20 db in perceived loudness.

■ habituation method

a technique used to study perception in infants. It is based on the fact that while infants look directly at novel objects they soon tire of doing so (habituation). Hence one can determine the degree to which an infant perceives an object as novel by measuring the time spent looking at it.

■ haematoma

the collection of blood in tissues or a space following rupture of a blood vessel.

■ haemorrhage

abnormal internal or external discharge of blood. May be venous, arterial or capillary from blood vessels into tissues, into or from the body. Venous blood is dark red, flow is continuous. Arterial blood is bright red, flows in jets. Capillary blood is of a reddish colour, exudes from tissue.

■ hair cells

in audition, hairlike receptors in the cochlea that bend due to vibration of the basilar membrane and then send electrical impulses to the brain.

■ **hallucination**

a sense experience in the absence of appropriate external stimuli, a misinterpretation of imaginary experiences as actual perceptions.

■ **hallucinogens**

drugs whose main effect is to change perceptual experience and 'expand consciousness.' LSD and marijuana are examples (syn. psychedelic drugs).

■ **halo effect**

the tendency to bias our perception of another person in the direction of one particular characteristic that we like or dislike.

■ **halo traction**

the process of immobilising the upper body and cervical spine with a traction device. The device consists of a metal ring around the head, held in place with pins into the skull. A supporting frame is attached to the ring and to a body jacket or vest to provide immobilisation.

■ **handicapped**

a person who has a congenital or acquired mental or physical defect that interferes with normal functioning of the body, or the ability to be self sufficient in modern society.

■ **head injury**

refers to an injury of the head and/or brain, including lacerations and contusions of the head, scalp and/or forehead.

■ **health**

a general condition of soundness and vigour of body and mind but not simply the absence of illness or injury.

■ **health promotion**

the development and execution of general strategies and specific tactics to eliminate or reduce the risk that people will become ill.

■ **health psychology**

the field of psychology devoted to understanding the ways people stay healthy, the reasons they become ill and the ways they respond when they become ill.

■ **hedonic**

derived from ancient Greek, it means that which has a pleasurable quality.

■ **hedonic calculus**

a process of calculating happiness in actual units by measuring an action's intensity, duration, immediacy and the number of beings affected. The concept, associated with Jeremy Bentham and his utilitarianism, holds that happiness is measurable, such that 'the greatest good' can actually be ascertained.

■ **hedonism**

the ethical theory that claims that the pursuit of one's own pleasure should be the aim of all action.

■ **hedonistic paradox**

the notion that deliberate actions done in the pursuit of personal happiness are less likely to produce real happiness than the unintended

■ **holistic depth psychology**

a process through which the individual learns to work with progressively deepening layers of his or her psyche. Presumes that people have conscious and unconscious aspects of their being.

■ **holistic health**

in holistic health therapy, an individual is seen in the context of his or her life. This approach is based on the belief that the various parts of our lives - work, family, etc. - are related, and affect each other. Problems arising in one or more of these areas may be linked to problems in other areas.

■ **home sign**

a system of gestures used by deaf children that initially functions as a kind of simple pantomime but eventually takes on the properties of a language.

■ **homosexuality**

a primary or exclusive attraction to individuals of one's own sex.

■ **homunculus**

a little person residing within the brain, from where he/she governs human behaviour (based on ancient Egyptian beliefs).

■ **horizontal cells**

the cells that assimilate information across the retina. Rather than sending signals toward the brain, horizontal cells connect receptors to each other.

■ **hormone**

a chemical messenger produced by an organ in one part of the body and transported through the bloodstream to other parts of the body where it has a specific effect on cells that recognise its message.

■ **Horney, Karen (1885-1952)**

founded the American Institute of Psychoanalysis in 1941. Deviating from orthodox Freudian analysis, she emphasised environmental and cultural, rather than biological factors in neurosis.

■ **hozho**

a Navajo concept referring to harmony, peace of mind, goodness, ideal family relationships, beauty in arts and crafts and health of body and spirit.

■ **hue**

the dimension of colour from which major colour names are derived (red, yellow, green, and so on), corresponding to wavelength of light.

■ **human behaviour genetics**

the branch of study that assesses the genetic component of individual differences in behaviour and traits.

■ **humanism**

any view that stresses on the significance of human dignity, welfare and values, especially in contrast to theological or supernatural views.

■ **humanistic**

a mode of therapy which identifies interpersonal environments as the source of emotional problems. The role of the therapist is one of support and reinforcement of the person's sense of self.

■ humanistic perspective
a psychological model that emphasises an individual's phenomenal world and inherent capacity for making rational choices and developing to maximum potential.

■ humanistic psychology
a psychological approach that emphasises the uniqueness of human beings, it is concerned with subjective experience and human values. See also **phenomenology**.

■ humanistic therapies
a general term for approaches to psychotherapy that emphasise the individual's subjective experiences, free will, and ability to solve his or her own problems. Client-cantered therapy and Gestalt therapy are examples.

■ human-potential movement
the therapy movement that includes all those practices and methods that release the potential of the average human being for greater levels of performance and greater richness of experience.

■ hunger drive
a drive based on food deprivation.

■ hydrocephalus
excess cerebrospinal fluid in the brain, usually requiring a shunt to reduce pressure of enlarged ventricles.

■ hypercomplex cell
a cell in the visual cortex that responds to a particular orientation and length.

■ hyperflexia
increased action of the reflexes.

■ hyperphagia
pathological overeating.

■ hypertonicity
spacticity.

■ hypnosis
1. the responsive state achieved following a hypnotic induction or its equivalent. In this state, one person (the subject) responds to suggestions offered by another person (the hypnotist).
2. an artificially induced sleep-like state in which the individual is highly susceptible to suggestions. This technique is used for a variety of purposes in therapy, from pain relief to habit control and retrieval of repressed memories.

■ hypnotherapy
utilises relaxation to access the unconscious mind - the part of the mind in which memories are stored. Through the imagination, it is possible to tap into the mental programming which is normally beneath conscious awareness. With the understanding of this information comes the capability of altering the sometimes negative effects this programming can have on both mind and body.

■ hypnotic induction
the procedure used in establishing hypnosis in a responsive person. It usually involves relaxation and stimulated imagination.

■ hypnotic trance
the dreamlike state of heightened

suggestibility induced in a subject by a hypnotist.

■ **hypnotisability**

the degree to which an individual is receptive to standardised hypnotic suggestion.

■ **hypothalamus**

a small but very important structure located just above the brain stem and just below the thalamus. Considered a part of the central core of the brain, it includes centres that govern motivated behaviour such as eating, drinking, sex, and emotions, it also regulates endocrine activity and maintains body homeostatis.

■ **hypothermia**

a technique used to cool the spinal cord after injury. Hypothermia may reduce metabolic and oxygen requirements of the injured tissue and may reduce edema (swelling), which in turn may reduce secondary nerve fibre damage.

■ **hypotheses**

specific propositions or expectations about the nature of thins derived from a theory.

■ **hypothesis testing**

gathering information and testing alternative explanations of some phenomenon.

■ **hypothetical construct**

one form of inferred intermediate mechanism. The construct is conceived of as having properties of its own, other than those specifically required for the explanation, for example, drive that is inferred from the behaviour of a deprived organism and is used in the explanation of later behaviour.

■ **hypothetical imperative**

these are ethical obligations arising from a particular goal or desire, for example, 'If we want world peace, we should destroy all nuclear weapons.'

■ **hypoxia**

insufficient oxygen reaching the tissues of the body.

■ **iconic memory**

sensory memory in the visual domain, which permit large amounts of information to be stored for very brief durations.

■ **id**

in Freud's tripartite division of the personality, the most primitive part, consisting of the basic biological impulses (or drives). The source of psychic energy or libido. Operates on the pleasure principle, endeavouring to obtain pleasure and to avoid pain, regardless of external circumstances.

■ **ideal self**

humanistic term indicating the characteristics, behaviour, emotions and thoughts which a person desires.

■ **idealism**

a metaphysical view holding that reality is basically mental and that sensations are not produced by anything material. In less extreme forms, any view that contradicts that there is a reality independent of the mind and mental states.

identification
changing one's beliefs, attitudes, or behaviours in order to be like an admired reference group.

identification and recognition
these are the two ways of attaching meaning to precepts.

identification figures
adult models (especially parents) copied, partly unconsciously, by the child.

identity crisis
the critical point in an individual's life when he experiences intense emotional pain and confusion about his worth and his view of himself as a member of society.

identity of indiscernibles
also called Leibniz's Law, it states that if two things share all of the same properties, then they are the same. It is a way of specifying when two things are logically the same.

identity status
an individual's position on Erickson's identity-formation continuum, which includes identity achievement, foreclosure, moratorium, and identity diffusion (or confusion).

identity thesis
sometimes called 'physicalism', it is the view in the philosophy of the mind that mental events are similiar to the physical events in the brain.

ideology
a set of beliefs and values held by the members of a social group, which explains its culture both to itself and to other groups.

idiosyncracy credits
interpersonal influence that a leader earns by helping the group achieve task goals and by conforming to group norms.

illusion
in perception, a misinterpretation of the relationships among presented stimuli so that what is perceived does not correspond to physical reality, especially, but not exclusively, an optical or visual illusion.

illusory contours
as the name suggests these are contours perceived in a figure when no contours are physically present.

illusory correlation
the belief that two variables are associated with one another when in fact there is little or no actual association.

imagery
using the mind to generate a mental representation of a sensory experience.

imago
based on the belief that couples often unconsciously bring unfinished business from childhood into our romantic partnerships, placing the burden of meeting these child hood needs on their partners.

■ imitation

behaviour that is modelled on or copies that of another.

■ immanence

the state of being inherent in or coming from within something.

■ immune response

the body's defence function that produces antibodies to foreign antigens. It is important in organ and tissue transplantation since the body is likely to reject new tissues. Some theorise that injury to the nervous system exposes the immune system to previously unrecognised central nervous system autoantigens, which interfere with regeneration.

■ immune system

an intricate system of cellular and molecular components having the primary function of distinguishing self from not self and defence against foreign organisms or substances.

■ impaired social sensitivity

diminished ability to take the first step in beginning an action. Diminished capacity to feel, act or react with an appreciation of the expectations, standards and needs of others.

■ impairment

a deficiency that interferes with normal activity.

■ implication

a rational relationship between two statements where the truth of the first statement certifies the truth of a second. For example, given the statement, 'Jane is a woman', one can draw the implication that 'Jane is a human being'.

■ implicit personality theory

assumptions or naive belief systems people make about which personality traits go together.

■ implicit uses of memory

accessibility of information through memory processes without the use of any conscious effort to encode or recover information.

■ implosion therapy

it is a behavioural therapeutic technique that exposes a client to anxiety-provoking stimuli, through his or her own imagination, in an attempt to put out the anxiety associated with the stimuli.

■ impossible figures

a figure in which recognition is normal when attending to each part, but the parts do not fuse into a single coherent picture.

■ impression formation

the process by which one integrates various sources of information about another into an overall judgment.

■ imprinting

a type of early learning in which a newborn forms an attachment with some kind of model (normally, a parent).

■ impulse control

individual's ability to withhold inappropriate verbal or motor responses while completing a task.

Persons who act or speak without first considering the consequences are viewed as having poor impulse control.

■ **impulsive aggression**

impulsive or emotion-driven aggression formed in reaction to situations in the 'heat of the moment'.

■ **inappropriate affect**

the unusual way of expressing contradictory behaviour when describing or experiencing an emotion (e.g., smiling when discussing something sad, laughing when talking about the death of a dear one).

■ **incentive**

an external event or stimulus that is the target of a motivation, and that can serve as a reward. Incentive theories of motivation stress the role of external targets in eliciting and satisfying motivational states.

■ **incentive theory**

a theory of motivation that emphasises the importance of negative and positive incentives in determining behaviour, internal drives are not the sole instigators of activity.

■ **incommensurability**

the inability to arrive at a single measure by which two different things can be objectively assessed and compared.

■ **incompatibilism (incompatibilist)**

a view that claims that determinism and free will are incompatible and cannot exist together.

■ **incontinent**

inability to control bowel and bladder functions. Many people who are incontinent can become continent with training.

■ **independence**

not being subject to control by others.

■ **independent construals of self**

the abstraction of the self as an individual whose behaviour is organised primarily by reference to one's own thoughts, feelings and actions, rather than by reference to the thoughts, feelings and actions of people around him or her.

■ **independent living**

community-based to maximise a person's ability to be empowered and self-directed, allows an individual to live in one's own home with maximum personal control over how services are delivered, combined with the opportunity to work as appropriate.

■ **independent samples**

sample data that is independent or not related to each other.

■ **independent variable**

the variable under experimental control with which the changes studied in the experiment are correlated.

■ **indeterminism**

a view associated with Jean-Paul Sartre and existentialism, it holds the view that some things, including human choice, are not caused or determined.

indexical

they are a kind of expressions whose meanings are dependent on the context in which they are said and therefore may vary with context. Personal pronouns: 'I', 'you', 'he', 'she', and 'it' are examples of indexicals.

individual differences

relatively persistent dissimilarities in structure of behaviour among persons or members of the same species.

individualism

a philosophy of life stressing the priority of individual needs over group needs, a preference for loosely knit social relationships, and a desire to be relatively autonomous of others' influence.

indubitable

something which cannot be doubted. Descartes wanted to build his views on indubitable truths.

induced motion

the perception of motion caused when a larger object surrounding a smaller object moves, the smaller object may appear to be the one that is moving even if it is stationary.

induction

is the process of analysis that infers a general statement from a class of specific instances, contrasted with deduction.

induction, problem of

sometimes called Hume's problem, it questions whether it is justifiable to infer a general statement from some samples of a population because we never know whether the samples we've take are representative or skewed. More accurately, even if we have representative samples, there is an assumption that nature is basically and continuously uniform, such that standard samples will reveal the same kinds of things over time. Hume pointed out that we can never be certain that nature is uniform in this way.

inductive reasoning

reasoning about arguments in which it is improbable that the conclusion is false if the premises are true.

industrial psychologist

a psychologist who is concerned with such problems as selecting people most suitable for particular jobs, developing job training programs, and figuring out the determinants of consumer behaviour.

infancy

the period of helplessness and dependency in humans and other organisms, in humans, roughly the first 2 years.

infarct

tissue that dies as a result of blocked blood flow.

inference

the method of drawing conclusions from a set of existing facts.

inference to the best explanation

a line of reasoning that allows inferring the existence of unknown, unseen and immeasurable entities, if this inference is the best way of understanding known facts.

■ **inferential statistics**

mathematical analyses that move beyond mere description of research data to make inferences about the larger population from which the sample was drawn.

■ **infinite**

lacking limits or bounds, extending beyond measure or comprehension: without beginning or end, endless.

■ **infinite regress**

an objection to a solution because it posits a series of explanations, each dependent on a previous one, going back without end into time. This objection is commonly made, for example, by the atheist Bertrand Russell, to the first cause argument for God's existence.

■ **inflammation**

the body's defence reaction to injury or infection.

■ **inflexible**

inability or unwillingness to adjust to changes.

■ **information campaigns**

attempts to persuade people to alter their lifestyles in more healthful directions through the use of the mass media and other communication channels.

■ **information dependence**

dependence upon others for information about the world that reduces uncertainty.

■ **informational influence**

group effects that arise from individuals' desire to be correct and right and to understand how best to act in a given situation.

■ **informational social influence**

conformity, compliance, or obedience due to a desire to gain information (information dependence).

■ **informed consent**

1. a patient's right to know the risks and benefits of a medical procedure.
2. a procedure by which people freely choose to participate in a study only after they are told about the activities they will perform.

■ **ingratiation**

saying positive things about someone in order to get them to like you.

■ **ingroup**

a group to which a person belongs and that forms a part of his or her social identity.

■ **ingroup bias**

the tendency to give more favourable evaluations and greater rewards to ingroup members than to outgroup members.

■ **inhalant**

these are substances that produce an intoxicating effect when inhaled. Examples are spray paint, freon and glue.

■ **inhibitory inputs**

information entering a neuron signalling it not to fire.

■ inhibitory synapse

a synapse at which the neurotransmitter changes the membrane permeability of the receiving cell in the direction of the resting potential, in other words, keeps it from firing.

■ initiative

refers to the individual's ability to begin a series of behaviours directed toward a goal.

■ innate

something which is inborn.

■ innate idea

a thought that is believed to be inborn, present within the mind, at birth.

■ inner ear

the internal portion of the ear containing, in addition to the cochlea, the vestibular sacs and the semicircular canals.

■ insanity

the legal (not clinical) designation for the state of an individual judged to be legally irresponsible or incompetent.

■ insight

1. in problem-solving experiments the perception of relationships leading to solution. Such a solution can be repeated promptly when the problem is again confronted.
2. in psychotherapy, the discovery by the individuals of dynamic connections between earlier and later events so that they come to recognise the roots of their conflicts.

■ insight therapy

a technique by which the therapist guides a patient towards discovering insights between present symptoms and past origins.

■ insomnia

dissatisfaction with the amount or quality of one's sleep. The diagnosis is subjective because many people who complain of insomnia are found to have normal sleep when studied in the laboratory, whereas others who do not complain of insomnia are found to have detectable sleep disturbances.

■ instinct

an innately determined behaviour that is specific to a certain species and appears in the same form in all members of the species.

■ instinctual drift

tendency for learned behaviour to shift toward instinctual behaviour over time.

■ instrumental aggression

the intentional use of harmful behaviour so that one can achieve some other goal.

■ instrumental conditioning

a form of learning in which a behaviour becomes more or less probable, depending on its consequences. Rewards increase the probability that the behaviour will be repeated, whereas punishment or no reward reduces the probability.

■ instrumental value

worth that a thing has because it contributes to a further good, not because it has intrinsic value of its own.

■ **instrumentalism**

the view that scientific theories are not capable of being proven true or false, but are merely instrumental in furthering scientific knowledge. Also, the view that such theories should only be seen as instruments in the pursuit of truth, not the grander view that they themselves reveal truth.

■ **insulin**

the hormone secreted by the pancreas.

■ **intellectualisation**

a defence mechanism whereby a person tries to gain detachment from an emotionally threatening situation by dealing with it in abstract, intellectual terms.

■ **intelligence**

1. that which a properly standardized intelligence test measures.
2. the ability to learn from experience, think in abstract terms, and deal effectively with one's environment.

■ **Intelligence Quotient (IQ)**

a scale unit used in reporting intelligence test scores, based on the ratio between mental age and chronological age. The decimal point is omitted so that the average IQ for children of any one chronological age is set at 100.

■ **intension**

the meaning of a thing, rather than the class in which it falls.

■ **intentionality**

the feature of our consciousness that is directed to something outside itself, the 'aboutness' of our conscious states.

■ **interaction effects**

interaction effect is the effect of one variable on another which is contingent on a third variable.

■ **interactionism**

1. within personality-development theory, a framework in which personality is seen as resulting from the interaction between the child's genotype (inherited characteristics) and the environment in which he or she is raised.
2. in personality theory, a framework in which behaviour is seen as resulting from the interaction between consistent personality dispositions or traits and the situations in which people find themselves.

■ **interaural intensity difference**

the difference in intensity of sounds reaching the two ears, it aids in the localisation of sounds at high frequencies.

■ **interaural time difference**

the difference in time between the arrival of sound waves at the two ears, it aids in the localisation of sounds at low frequencies.

■ **interdependent construals of self**

theorisation of the self as part of an encompassing social relationship, recognising that one's behaviour is determined, contingent on an also to a large extent organised by what the actor observes to be the thoughts, feelings and actions of others.

■ **interdisciplinary approach**

a method of diagnosis, evaluation, and individual program planning in which two or more specialists, such as medical doctors, psychologists, recreational therapists, social workers, etc. participate as a team, contributing their skills, competencies, insights, and perspectives to focus on identifying the developmental needs of the person with a disability and on devising ways to meet those needs.

■ **interference**

a factor that can impair retrieval from long-term memory. It arises when different items are associated with the same retrieval cue, attempted retrieval of one of these items can be blocked by the inadvertent retrieval of the other item.

■ **interjudge reliability**

the consistency achieved by two or more observers when assessing or rating some behaviour (for example, in rating the aggressiveness of nursery-school children). Also called inferater agreement.

■ **internal attribution**

an attribution that locates the cause of an event to factors internal to the person, such as personality traits, moods, attitudes, abilities, or effort.

■ **internal consistency**

a form of test reliability. Specifically, the homogeneity of a set of items on a test, the degree to which they are all measuring the same variable.

■ **internal locus of control**

the belief that an individual has more control over life circumstances than the environment does.

■ **internal validity**

a measure of the trustworthiness of a sample of data. Internal validity looks at the subject, testing and environment in which the data collection took place.

■ **internalisation**

changing one's beliefs, attitudes, and behaviours because one genuinely believes in them. Incorporating them into one's own value system.

■ **internalism**

the view that one can directly experience the natural world in conscious states that can never be proven to relate to the external world in any objective way.

■ **interneurons**

neurons in the central nervous system that receive messages from sensory neurons and send them to other interneurons or to motor neurons.

■ **interpersonal attraction**

a person's desire to approach another individual.

interpretation

in psychoanalysis, the analyst's calling attention to the patient's resistances in order to facilitate the flow of associations, also the explanation of symbols, as in dream interpretation.

interquartile range

the difference between the scores (or estimated scores) at the 75th percentile and the 25th percentile. Used more than the range because it eliminates extreme scores.

interval estimation

the estimation of the population statistics based on a range around a sample statistics.

interval scale

refers to any scale of measurement possessing magnitude and equal intervals, but not an absolute zero.

interval schedules

in operant conditioning, reinforcement schedules in which reinforcement occurs only after a certain time interval has elapsed. On a fixed interval (FI) schedule, the organism is reinforced for its first response only after a certain amount of time has passed since its last response. On a variable interval (VI) schedule, reinforcement still depends on time since last response, but the interval's duration varies unpredictably.

intervening variable

a process inferred to occur between stimulus and response, thus accounting for one response rather than another to the same stimulus. The intervening variable may be inferred without further specification, or it may be given concrete properties and become an object of investigation.

interview

a conversation between an investigator (the interviewer) and a subject (the respondent) used for gathering pertinent data for the subject's benefit (as in the psychotherapeutic interview) or for information-gathering (as in a sample survey).

intimacy

sharing that which is inmost with others.

intimidation

arousing fear and gaining power by convincing others that one is dangerous.

intracellular fluid

water contained within the body's cells, one of the critical variables monitored in the control of thirst.

intracellular reservoir

water inside the body's cells.

intracranial haematoma

rupture of a blood vessel, producing a blood clot that exerts pressure on the brain.

Intracranial Pressure (ICP)

cerebrospinal fluid (CSF) pressure measured from a needle or bolt introduced into the CSF space surrounding the brain. It reflects the pressure inside of the skull.

intracranial pressure monitor

an ICP monitor. A monitoring device to determine the pressure within the brain. It consists of a small tube (catheter) attached to the person at the skull by either a ventriculostomy, subarachnoid bolt, or screw, and is then connected to a transducer, which registers the pressure.

intraspinal

within the vertebral column, which contains the spinal cord and cerebrospinal fluid.

Intravenous Pyelogram (IVP)

an x-ray of the kidney to determine function.

intrinsic motivation

the motivation or desire to do something based on the enjoyment of the behaviour itself rather than relying on or requiring external reinforcement.

intrinsic value

refers to the value of a thing that it has in and of itself, independent of its relationship to any further end.

introspection

the method of examining self-consciousness.

introversion

the tendency to focus energy internally which results in decreased social interaction.

introversion-extraversion

the personality dimension first identified by Carl Jung that refers to the degree to which a person's basic orientation is turned inward toward the self or outward toward the external world. At the introversion end are shy individuals who tend to withdraw into themselves, at the extraversion end are sociable individuals who prefer to be with others.

intuition

the direct consciousness of basic truths without aid of sensation or reasoning.

intuitionism

a view associated with G. E. Moore which states that knowledge of ultimate good and morality is apprehended directly by some special faculty in us of moral sense. The idea that certain fundamental and necessarily truths about reality are known directly, without inference or reasoning.

ion channel

a specialised protein molecule that permits specific ions to enter or leave cells. Some ion channels open or close in response to appropriate neurotransmitter molecules, others open or close in response to voltage changes across the cell membrane. This process regulates depolarisation and the firing of nerve impulses.

ion pump

a protein molecule that helps to maintain an uneven distribution of electrically charged ions across the cell membrane of a neuron by pumping them into or out of the cell. Ion pumps work with ion channels to regulate depolarisation and firing of nerve impulses.

■ **ipso facto**

a Latin term that means 'by the fact itself'; the very fact.

■ **irritability**

easy to excite to annoyance, impatience or anger, the action of nerve cells in generating and transmitting electrical impulses in response to stimuli.

■ **is/ought gap**

a view, attributed to Hume, which says that evaluative conclusions cannot be validly derived from purely factual premises. Hume held that people incorrectly move from 'is' statements to 'ought' statements.

■ **ischemia**

a reduction of blood flow that is thought to be a major cause of secondary injury to the brain or spinal cord after trauma.

■ **isomorphic**

term used to describe two or more objects which have the same shape or form.

■ **jamais vu**

familiar places, people and things seem foreign or alien.

■ **james-lange theory**

a classical theory of emotion, named for the two men who independently proposed it. The theory states that the stimulus first leads to bodily responses, and then the awareness of these responses constitutes the experience of emotion.

■ **jargon**

spoken language that has a normal rate and rhythm but is full of nonsense words.

■ **jealousy**

the negative emotional reaction experienced when a relationship that is important to a person's self-concept is threatened by a real or imagined rival.

■ **jigsaw classroom**

a cooperative group-learning technique designed to reduce prejudice and raise self-esteem.

■ **jin shin do**

a psychotherapy, which combines acupressure, Taoist yogic breathing and Reichian segmental theory (addresses how emotional tension affects the physical body) with the goal of releasing physical and emotional tension and armouring. The objective of this therapy is to promote a state in which the patient can address the emotional factors that underlie various physical conditions.

■ **job analysis**

involves the systematic study of an occupation in terms of what the worker does in relation to data, people, and things, the methods and techniques employed, the machines, tools, equipment, and work aids used, the materials, products, subject matter or services which result, and the traits required of the worker.

■ **job burnout**

the state of emotional exhaustion, depersonalisation and reduced personal accomplishment, often experienced by workers in high-stress jobs.

■ **judgment**

the ability to form a correct conclusion based on knowledge and experience.

■ **Jung, Carl (1875-1961)**

initially a follower of Sigmund Freud, Jung came to disagree with Freud and established the discipline of analytical psychology. He divided personality into introverts and extroverts and developed a theory of the unconscious mind that included both the personal and the collective. Along with Freud, Jung has perhaps had the most effect on modern psychology.

■ **Jungian**

a psychoanalytic orientation which stresses the role of spirituality and spiritual needs in dealing with emotional disorders. Based on the work of psychoanalyst Carl Jung.

■ **just noticeable difference (JND)**

a barely perceptible physical change in a stimulus, a measure of the difference threshold. The term is used also as a unit for scaling the steps of sensation corresponding to increases in the magnitude of stimulation. See also **difference threshold, Weber's law.**

■ **justice**

commonly divided into retributive and distributive, the former deals with punishments that correct the imbalance to society caused by a crime, the latter concerns the fair allocation of benefits and burdens in society.

■ **justification**

the reasons for doing, supporting, or believing something.

■ **just-world belief**

a belief that the world is a fair and equitable place, with people getting what they deserve in life.

■ **karma**

an idea related to Hinduism and Buddhism which holds that our inner self is affected by our actions in this life in future, reincarnated lives.

■ **key-word method**

a technique for learning vocabulary of a foreign language via an intermediate key word related to the sound of the foreign word and the meaning of the English equivalent.

■ **kin selection**

a theory that people will exhibit preferences for helping blood relatives because this will increase the odds that their genes will be transmitted to subsequent generations.

■ **kinesthesis**

the muscle, tendon and joint senses, yielding discrimination of position and movement of parts of the body.

■ kinesthetic sense

the sense which is concerned with the positions of the body and movement of the body parts relative to each other.

■ knowledge by acquaintance

knowledge we obtain through direct experience.

■ kub

an x-ray of the abdomen, showing the kidneys, urethra, and bladder.

■ kurtosis

the shape of a curve or distribution of scores (See **Leptokurtic, Mesokurtic** and **Platykurtic**).

■ laboratory experiment

an experiment conducted in a carefully controlled environment that simulates real-life settings.

■ laminectomy

state of having notable shifts in emotional state (e.g., uncontrolled laughing or crying).

■ language production

these are the tools people use to get their messages across. These include saying, signing and writing.

■ language-making capacity

the inherent guidelines or operating principles that children bring to the task of learning a language.

■ late selection

selective attention that occurs in the later stages of recognition, after the organism has determined the meaning of the input.

■ latency

a temporal measure of response, referring to the time delay between the occurrence of the stimulus and the onset of the response.

■ latency period

in Freud's psychoanalytic theory, a period in middle childhood, roughly the years 6-12, when both sexual and aggressive impulses are said to be in a quiescent state.

■ latency stage

Freud's fourth stage of psychosexual development where sexuality is repressed in the unconscious and children focus on identifying with their same sex parent and interact with same sex peers.

■ latent content

the underlying significance of a dream (such as the motives of wishes being expressed by it) as interpreted from the manifest content.

■ latent learning

it is the learning that takes place without apparent reinforcement but is not demonstrated until such time as reinforcement occurs.

■ lateral

side.

■ lateral anterior decompression

surgical procedure to reduce pressure on the spinal cord by removing bone fragments. Some patients report dramatic functional improvement. It must be noted that medical success depends on patient selection since not all people qualify and not all benefit from this kind of surgery.

■ **lateral fissure**

a deep fissure at the side of each cerebral hemisphere, below which lies the temporal lobe (syn. fissure of Sylvius).

■ **Lateral Hypothalamus (LH)**

an area of the hypothalamus important to the regulation of food intake. Electrical stimulation of this area will make an experimental animal start to eat, destruction of brain tissue here causes an animal to stop eating.

■ **law of common fate**

a law of grouping that states that elements moving in the same direction at the same rate are grouped together.

■ **law of effect**

the phenomenon that any behaviour that is followed by reinforcement is strengthened, from the infinite pool of possible responses, those that lead to reinforcement are repeated, whereas those that do not are extinguished.

■ **law of non-contradiction**

a basic principle of logic wherein a statement and its negation cannot both be true or false at the same time, for example, 'Our father has a car' and 'It is false that our father has a car'.

■ **law of proximity**

law of grouping that states that the nearest, or most proximal, elements are grouped together.

■ **law of similarity**

another law of grouping that states that the most similar elements are grouped together.

■ **leader**

the person who exerts the most influence on group behaviour and beliefs.

■ **leap of faith**

a phrase related to Soren Kierkegaard, originally referring to the absolute acceptance of God's will, even when doing so results in immoral behaviour. Now more generally used to refer to belief in God, or the incarnation of God-as-Jesus, despite reason and evidence to the contrary.

■ **learned helplessness**

a condition of apathy or helplessness created experimentally by subjecting an organism to unavoidable trauma (such as shock, heat, or cold). Being unable to avoid or escape an aversive situation produces a feeling of helplessness that generalises to subsequent situations.

■ **learning**

1. the process of acquiring knowledge or skill through study, practice or experience.
2. a relatively permanent change in behaviour that occurs as the result of practice. Behaviour changes due to maturation or temporary conditions of the organism (such as fatigue, the influence of drugs, adaptation) are not included.

■ **learning theory**

a theory based on the idea that changes in behaviour result more from experience and less from our personality or how we think or feel about a situation.

■ **learning-performance distinction**

the difference between what has been learned and what is expressed in overt behaviour.

■ **left hemisphere**

the left cerebral hemisphere. Controls the right side of the body and, for most people, speech and other logical, sequential activities (syn. major hemisphere).

■ **legal realism**

an idea that holds the view that the law is best understood by analysing what actually occurs in courts, law offices and legislatures rather than by studying theories, concepts, or principles about law.

■ **legitimate power**

power derived through one's position, such as a police officer or elected official.

■ **lens**

the part of the eye that helps focus light rays on a single point of the retina.

■ **lesions**

any bruise, injury or wound.

■ **levels-of-processing theory**

a theory which states that the deeper the level at which information was processed, the more likely it is to be retained in memory.

■ **liability**

state of having notable shifts in emotional state (e.g., uncontrolled laughing or crying).

■ **liar's paradox**

an ancient paradox where some grammatical sentences seem to assert both truth and falsity at the same time. An example is the statement, 'This statement is false', which can only be true if it is false, and only false if it is true.

■ **liberty**

the liberty to perform those acts that one wants to do. For example, the ability to say what one wants in public, without fear of reprisals.

■ **libido**

latin for lust. In Freud's psychoanalytic theory, the psychic energy of the id.

■ **life-change units (lcus)**

the measure of the stress levels of different types of change experienced during a certain period of time.

■ **lifelong living**

for persons discharged from rehabilitation who need ongoing lifetime supports, located in residential or skilled nursing environment, structured activities available on individual and group basis.

■ **light adaptation**

the decreased sensitivity of the eye to light when the subject has been continuously exposed to high levels of illumination.

■ **light box**

a set of bright, full-spectrum light bulbs inside a box with a reflective background and diffusing screen. Produces light that's 10 to 20 times stronger than ordinary indoor light. Used to treat winter depression, or SAD (seasonal affective disorder). Treatment typically involves spending 15 minutes to 3 hours in front of a light box every day in the fall, winter, and early spring. Research suggests that bright lights help regulate the body's internal clock, which controls hormone secretion and sleep patterns.

■ **lightness**

in sensory psychology, the degree to which a light appears white (which is different from brightness, in that a dimly lit object can still appear white).

■ **lightness constancy**

the propensity to perceive the whiteness, greyness, or blackness of objects as constant across changing levels of illumination.

■ **limbic system**

a set of structures in and around the midbrain, forming a functional unit regulating motivational and emotional types of behaviour, such as waking and sleeping, excitement and quiescence, feeding, and mating.

■ **linear perspective**

in perspective, a monocular cue for depth. When parallel lines appear to converge, they are perceived as vanishing in the distance.

■ **linguistic relativity hypothesis**

the proposition that one's thought processes, the way one perceives the world, are determined by one's language.

■ **lithium carbonate**

a compound based on lithium, an element related to sodium. Has been successful in treating bipolar disorders.

■ **lobe**

one of four areas within a cerebral hemisphere.

■ **localised functions**

behaviour controlled by known areas of the brain, for example, vision is localised in the occipital lobes.

■ **location constancy**

the tendency to perceive the place at which a resting object is located as remaining the same even though the relationship to the observer has changed.

■ **locked-in syndrome**

a condition in which a patient is awake and retains the ability to perceive, but is unable to communicate, except by limited eye movements. This is due to an interruption of motor pathways in the ventral pons, usually by infarction. This interruption disconnects the motor cells in the lower brain stem and spinal cord from the controlling signals issued by the brain.

■ **logical possibility**

an event or thing that, while it may

not be likely in this world, cannot be ruled out as prevented by the law of non-contradiction. For example, while cylindrical cubes are logically impossible, it is logically possible that elephants could one day fly (perhaps by genetic modifications).

■ **logically possible world**

a way of imagining alternative possibilities to our existence and reality, regardless of whether it is physically possible to bring it about, with the only criterion being that it doesn't violate the law of non-contradiction. The basic use of this concept is in modal logic, a branch of logic whose fundamental concepts are necessity and possibility.

■ **loneliness**

having a smaller or less satisfactory network of social and intimate relationships than one desires.

■ **longitudinal design**

a research design in which the same participants are observed repeatedly, which may sometimes continue over many years.

■ **longitudinal study**

a research method that studies an individual through time, taking measurements at periodic intervals.

■ **long-term memory (LTM)**

the relatively permanent component of the memory system, as opposed to short-term memory.

■ **long-term potentiation**

a phenomenon concerning the neural bases of learning. Once stimulated, neurons will show an increase in their rate of activity when subsequently stimulated (at least up to a period of months).

■ **loudness**

an intensity dimension of hearing correlated with the amplitude of the sound waves that constitute the stimulus. Greater amplitudes yield greater loudnesses.

■ **low-ball technique**

a two-step compliance strategy in which the influencer secures agreement with a request by understating its true cost.

■ **lower confidence limit**

the lower limit of a confidence interval. If prediction states that the true score falls between 90 and 100, then the lower confidence level is 90.

■ **lower motor neuron lesions**

any damage to the lower motor neuron or its axon (peripheral nerve) that separates the lower motor neuron from control of its muscle fibres. This type of lesion leads to flaccidity and muscle atrophy.

■ **lower motor neurons**

these nerve fibres originate in the spinal cord and travel out of the central nervous system to muscles in the body. An injury to these nerve cells can destroy reflexes and may also affect bowel, bladder and sexual function.

■ **lucid dream**

a dream in which events seem so normal (lacking the bizarre and illogical character of most dreams) that the dreamer believes he or she is awake and conscious.

■ **lumbar**

pertaining to that area immediately below the thoracic spine, the strongest part of the spine, the lower back.

■ **lumbar puncture**

a procedure used to measure pressure exerted by cerebrospinal fluid and to remove samples for analysis.

■ **lunch-line effect**

an example of peripheral attention. Even though you may be absorbed in conversation in a room full of people, the sound of your name in another conversation will usually attract your attention, this phenomenon suggests a nonconscious monitoring of that conversation.

■ **lysergic acid diethylamide**

a powerful psychoactive drug capable of producing extreme alterations in consciousness, hallucinations, distortions in perception, and unpredictable mood swings.

■ **Magnetic Resonance Imaging (MRI)**

a computer-based scanning procedure that uses strong magnetic fields and radio-frequency pulses to generate a picture of a cross section of the brain or body. Provides greater precision than the CT scanner.

■ **magnetic therapy**

this special therapy involves the use of magnets, magnetic devices or magnetic fields to treat various of physical and emotional conditions, including circulatory problems, certain forms of arthritis, chronic pain, sleep disorders, and stress.

■ **magnitude**

a scale of measurement where the individual units possess the qualities of greater than, equal to, or less than.

■ **main effect**

the effect of one variable on another without any other variable's or subgroup's participation.

■ **major depressive disorder**

a mood disorder characterised by intense feelings of depression for a long period time, without the manic high phase of bipolar depression.

■ **malingering**

to pretend inability so as to avoid duty or work.

■ **manic episode**

a component of bipolar disorder characterised by periods of extreme elation, unbounded euphoria without sufficient reason and grandiose thoughts or feelings about personal abilities.

■ **manifest content**

the remembered content of a dream, the characters, and their actions, as distinguished from the inferred latent content. A Freudian dream analysis

■ **mannitol**

a solution that reduces intracranial pressure by removing water from the brain through stimulating increased urinary excretion.

■ **marital therapy**

psychotherapy with both members of a couple aimed at resolving problems in their relationship (syn. couples therapy).

■ **masculinity**

possession of instrumental personality traits.

■ **Maslow, Abraham**

humanistic theorist most famous for the development of the Hierarchy of Needs.

■ **masochism**

a pathological desire to inflict pain on oneself or to suffer pain at the hands of others. See also **sadism**.

■ **master status**

a socially defined position occupied by a person in society that is very important in shaping his or her self-concept and life choices.

■ **matching hypothesis**

the proposition that people are attracted to others who are similar to them in particular characteristics, such as attitudes and physical attractiveness.

■ **materialism**

it is the metaphysical view that reality is composed only of causally determined physical matter and nothing else; the view in Marxism that the economic structure of society, for example, the inequality under capitalism and its resulting unequal economic classes of workers and owners, determine more than any other factors how social and political life work.

■ **maternal drive**

the drive, particularly in animals, induced in the female through bearing and nursing young, leading to nest building, retrieving, and other forms of care.

■ **matters of fact**

a phrase related to Hume, it refers to statements that are grounded in empirical observation or personal experience, providing knowledge of the world.

■ **maturation**

growth processes in the individual that result in orderly changes in behaviour, whose timing and patterning are relatively independent of exercise or experience though they may require a normal environment.

■ **mauvaise foi**

derived from French, it mean 'bad faith', it is a term attributed to Sartre and refers to one's unwillingness to take responsibility for the self one has created by one's decisions when faced with crucial choices in life. Instead, one blames uncontrollable circumstances such as genetics, bad luck, and one's family for what one is. A person who does this is called 'inauthentic'.

■ **maze**

a device use in the study of animal and human learning, consisting of a correct path and blind alleys.

■ **mean**

the arithmetical average, the sum of all scores divided by their number.

■ **means-ends analysis**

a problem-solving strategy in which one compares one's current state to the goal state in order to find the most important difference between them, eliminating this difference then becomes the main subgoal.

■ **measure of central tendency**

a value representative of a frequency distribution, around which other values are dispersed, for example, the mean, the median, or mode of a distribution of scores.

■ **measure of variation**

a measure of the dispersion or spread of scores in a frequency distribution, such as the range or the standard deviation.

■ **measurement**

assigning numbers to different levels, amounts, or sizes of a variable.

■ **measurement, scales of**

categories of data based on their numerical characteristics.

■ **measures of variability**

a statistic, such as a range or standard deviation, that indicates how tightly the scores in a set of observations cluster together.

■ **medial-temporal-lobe amnesia**

a form of amnesia or memory loss that results from damage to the middle of the temporal lobe of the brain.

■ **median**

the score of the middle case when cases are arranged in order of size of score.

■ **medication**

the use of drugs to alleviate psychological symptoms such as anxiety, depression, and thinking disorders.

■ **medicine, holistic**

a type of holistic medicine. It is a broadly descriptive term for a healing philosophy that views a patient as a whole person, not as just a disease or a collection of symptoms. In the course of treatment holistic medical practitioners may address emotional and spiritual dimensions as well as the nutritional, environmental and lifestyle factors that may contribute to an illness. Many holistic practitioners combine conventional forms of treatment with natural or alternative treatments.

■ **meditation**

an altered state of consciousness in which the individual is extremely relaxed and feels divorced from the outside world, the individual loses self-awareness and gains a sense of being involved in a wider consciousness. This meditative state is achieved by performing certain rituals, including regulating breathing, sharply restricting one's field of attention, and assuming yogic body positions.

medulla

the lowest section of the brainstem, a slight enlargement of the spinal cord as it enters the skull, the point at which the major nerve tracts cross over so that the right cerebral hemisphere controls the left side of the body, and the left cerebral hemisphere controls the right side.

medulla oblongata

part of the brainstem that controls vital life-sustaining functions such as heartbeat, breathing, blood pressure and digestion.

melatonin

a hormone produced by the pineal gland that enhance the immune system and helps people with jet lag or sleeplessness.

meliorism

derived from the Latin word melior, which mean 'better', it is the view that the world is capable of becoming increasingly better through human action, thus improving the human condition. In theology, it is the view that God wanted the world to be as good as possible for humanity, a view that may contradict the free will defence, which holds that an evil world may provide the best test for salvation.

memory

the mental capacity to encode, store and recover information.

memory decay

a major cause of forgetting in short-term memory in which information simply fades with time.

memory effect

error in research that results from subjects recollect previous testing and applying that knowledge to current testing.

memory span

the number of items (digits, letters, words) that can be reproduced in order after a single presentation, usually 762.

memory trace

the inferred change in the nervous system that persists between the time something is learned and the time it is recalled.

memory, episodic

memory for ongoing events in a person's life. More easily impaired than semantic memory, perhaps because rehearsal or repetition tends to be minimal.

memory, immediate

the ability to recall numbers, pictures, or words immediately following presentation. Patients with immediate memory problems have difficulty learning new tasks because they cannot remember instructions. Relies upon concentration and attention.

memory, long term

in neuropsychological testing, this refers to recall thirty minutes or longer after presentation. Requires storage and retrieval of information which exceeds the limit of short term memory.

■ memory, short term

primary or 'working' memory, its contents are in conscious awareness. A limited capacity system that holds up to seven chunks of information over periods of 30 seconds to several minutes, depending upon the person's attention to the task.

■ menarche

the first menstrual period, indicative of sexual maturation in a girl.

■ meninges

membrane that covers the brain and spinal cord.

■ meningitis

inflammation of the membranes that cover the brain and spinal cord.

■ mental age (MA)

a scale unit proposed by Binet for use in intelligence testing. If an intelligence test is properly standardised, a representative group of children of age 6 should earn an average mental age of 6, those of age 7, a mental age of 7, and so on. A child whose MA is above his or her chronological age (CA) is advanced, one whose MA lags behind is retarded. See also **chronological age, intelligence quotient**.

■ mental imagery

mental representations that are picture-like. Not the same as eidetic imagery.

■ mental inflexibility

a rigidity in thinking which impairs the individual's ability to be objective and process new information, inability to appreciate alternatives.

■ mental model

a concrete mental representation of a problem situation that may be useful in solving the problem.

■ mental practice

the imagined rehearsal of a perceptual-motor skill in the absence of gross body movements. For example, picturing yourself serving a tennis ball and making mental corrections when the movement seems faulty, without actually moving your arm.

■ mental retardation

subnormal intellectual functioning with impairment in social adjustment.

■ mental rotation

the notion that a mental image of an object can be rotated in the mind in fashion analogous to rotating the real object.

■ mental set

the inclination to respond to a new problem in the manner used to respond to a previous problem.

■ mental status

the degree of competency an individual displays when given standardised tests to determine intellectual, emotional, psychological and personality functions.

mental status examinations

standardised tests which evaluate verbal responses and behavioural reactions, a procedure used to determine the mental competency of an individual.

mere exposure effect

the tendency to develop more positive feelings toward objects and individuals the more we are exposed to them.

mesokurtic

a curve or distribution that has a stable amount of variance so that is similar to a normal curve.

mesolimbic dopamine system

a set of neurons in the upper brainstem that is crucial to incentive motivation for food and other rewards. The neurons begin in the midbrain and project their axons upward to limbic structures in the forebrain, where they release dopamine as a neurotransmitter.

meta

in philosophy, it is a term which refers to the analysis not on the ordinary level, but at a deeper level that views the adequacy or inadequacy of concepts at the ordinary level.

meta-analysis

a statistical technique to combine information from many empirical studies on a topic to objectively estimate the reliability and overall size of the effect.

metamemory

implicit or explicit knowledge about memory abilities and effective memory strategies, cognition about memory.

metaphilosophy

study of the nature of philosophy including its objectives, the appropriate questions for philosophical investigation and philosophy's relationship with other disciplines.

metaphysics (metaphysical)

the branch of philosophy that investigates questions concerning the nature of reality and that moves beyond scientific inquiry to exploring questions about self, God, free will and the origins of the universe. Named after a book by Aristotle for the study of questions left over after the study of this world, 'physica' or nature.

method of constant stimuli

a psychophysical method for determining sensory thresholds. Stimuli with magnitudes varying around the threshold are presented to a subject many times to see what percentage of the time the subject detects them.

method of loci

an aid to serial memory. Verbal material is transformed into mental images, which are then located at successive positions along a visualised route, such as an imaged walk through the house or down a familiar street.

methodological holism

view that, in analysis in the social sciences (politics, economics, sociology) some social groups or institutions are not reducible to individuals.

methodological individualism

the view that any theory in the social sciences about social groups or institutions must invariably be reduced to theories about individual human beings, so that the individual becomes the primary basis for investigation.

microexpressions

fleeting facial signals lasting only a few tenths of a second.

middle ear

part of the ear that transmits sound waves from the eardrum to the oval window of the inner ear by means of three tiny connecting bones (malleus, incus, and stapes).

mind

the seat of human consciousness.

mind/matter dualism

see **dualism**.

mind-body problem

a recurrent issue in philosophy: does the mind truly exist in nature as a separate entity from the body and, if so, as what kind of stuff or thing? Also, how do mind and body affect each other, if at all?

mindlessness

responding without thinking about the behaviour and its implications.

minnesota multiphasic personality inventory, 2nd. edition

an Objective test using 567 items which have been empirically derived to measure a variety of psychological concerns.

minor head injury

trauma to the head regardless of severity that does not necessarily result in the loss of consciousness. Frequently called Concussion, Traumatic Brain Injury, and Closed Head Injury.

misattribution of arousal

a situation in which the explanation of the physiological symptoms of arousal is switched from the real source to another one.

mnemonics

a system for improving memory often involving a set of symbols that can substitute for the material to be remembered, for example, in attempting to remember a number sequence, one may translate the sequence into letters of the alphabet that in turn approximate words that are easily remembered.

modal logic

an offshoot of logic whose fundamental concepts are necessity and possibility.

mode

the most frequent score in a distribution, or the class interval in which the greatest number or cases fall.

model

1. miniature systems are often constructed according to a logical, mathematical, or physical model. That is, the principles according to which data are organised and made understandable parallel those of the model, for instance, the piano keyboard is a model for understanding the basilar membrane, the thermostat is a model for the feedback principle of homeostasis.

2. in behaviour therapy, one who models or performs behaviours that the therapist wishes the patient to imitate.

modelling

in social learning theory, the process by which a person learns social and cognitive behaviours by observing and imitating others.

modesty

under-representing one's positive traits, contributions, or accomplishments.

monad

the primary, irreducible element of nature in Gottfried Leibniz's metaphysics.

money management

ability to distinguish the different denominations of money, count money, make change, budget.

monism

metaphysical view that all of nature is composed of only one substance. Idealists believe that the one substance is the mind, materialists believe it is matter.

Monoamine Oxidase (MAO)

one of the enzymes responsible for the breakdown of a group of neurotransmitters called biogenic amines (norepinephrine, dopamine, and serotonin are examples), believed to be important in the regulation of emotion. Drugs that inhibit the action of this enzyme (MAO inhibitors) are used in treating depression. See also **antidepressant, monamine oxidase inhibitor, neurotransmitter**.

Monoamine Oxidase Inhibitor (MAOI)

a class of drugs used to treat depression, the drug inhibits the action of an enzyme (monoamine oxidase) that breaks down certain neurotransmitters (such as dopamine, norepinephrine, and serotonin), thereby prolonging the action of these neurotransmitters.

monochromatism

total colour blindness, the visual system being achromatic. A rare disorder.

monotheism

the belief that there is only one God.

monozygotic (mz) twins

twins developed from a single egg. They are always of the same sex and commonly much alike in appearance, although some characteristics may be in mirror image, for example one right-handed, the other left-handed (syn. identical twins).

■ mood disorder

a mental disorder characterised by disturbances of mood. Depression, mania (exaggerated excitement), and bipolar disorders in which the individual experiences both extremes of mood are examples.

■ moon illusion

a perceptual illusion that makes the moon appear as much as 50 percent larger when it is near the horizon than when it is at its zenith, even though at both locations the moon produces the same retinal image.

■ moral pluralism

a common view about morality which holds that there are a variety of irreducible views about morality, none of which are entirely true and more importantly, it posits that humans will never agree about which theory of morality is true. As such, it encourages tolerance when discussing ethical issues instead of simplistic absolutism.

■ moral realism

in Piaget's theory of cognitive development, the preoperational child's treatment of social rules as absolute and unchangeable.

■ morality

a system of beliefs and values that ensures that individuals will keep their obligations to others in society and will behave in ways that do not interfere with the rights and interests of others.

■ morbidity

an illness or abnormal condition or quality.

■ morpheme

the smallest meaningful unit in the structure of a language, whether a word, base, or affix, such as man, strange, ing, pro.

■ mortality

subject dropouts in a research study. Mortality may pose a problem when a disproportionate drop out rate occurs between two or more groups (Example: 50% of males drop out of group one while only 5% of males drop out in group two, resulting in uneven groups).

■ motion after-effect

the illusion of movement in a static object that occurs after viewing motion for an extended period of time, the after-effect occurs in the opposite direction of the viewed motion.

■ motion parallax

a monocular cue to depth perception. When you are moving rapidly, nearby objects appear to move more quickly in the opposite direction than distant objects do. This difference in apparent speed provides a cue to the respective depths of the objects.

■ motivation

the need or desire together with environmental stimuli that causes an individual to act.

■ **motivation**

factors that energise behaviour and give it direction.

■ **motive**

any condition of the organism that affects its readiness to start on or continue in a sequence of behaviour.

■ **motor control**

regulation of the timing and amount of contraction of muscles of the body to produce smooth and coordinated movement. The regulation is carried out by operation of the nervous system.

■ **motor cortex**

the region of the cerebral cortex in the brain that controls the action of the body's voluntary muscles.

■ **motor neuron**

a nerve cell whose cell body is located in the brain and spinal cord and whose axons leave the central nervous system by way of cranial nerves or spinal roots. Motor neuron supply information to muscle. A motor unit is the combination of the motor neuron and the set of muscle fibres it innervates.

■ **motor planning**

action formulated in the mind before attempting to perform.

■ **multiple correlation**

a correlation technique used when there is one A and two or more B, e.g. the correlation between age and Maths and English ability.

■ **multivariate experiment**

a type of experiment that involves the simultaneous manipulation of several independent variables.

■ **muscle tone**

used in clinical practice to describe the resistance of a muscle to being stretched. When the peripheral nerve to a muscle is severed, the muscle becomes limp. When nerve fibres in the brain or spinal cord are damaged, the balance between facilitation and inhibition of muscle tone is disturbed. The tone of some muscles may become increased and they resist being stretched—a condition called spasticity.

■ **mutatis mutandis**

a Latin term which mean, 'the necessary changes having been made', in ordinary terms, making the necessary substitutions or changes.

■ **myelin**

a white, fatty insulating material for axons which produced in the peripheral nervous system by Schwann cells, and in the central nervous system by oligodendrocytes. Myelin is necessary for rapid signal transmission along nerve fibres, ten to one hundred times faster than in bare fibres lacking its insulation properties. Loss of myelin accompanies many central nervous system injuries and is the principal cause of multiple sclerosis. The process of remyelination is very important in spinal cord injury research. If this is possible in the body, as many researchers believe, it may be possible to return function to intact nerve fibres. Oligodendrocytes are apparently unable to provide myelin in the mature central nervous system.

■ **myelin sheath**

the fuzzy sheath surrounding certain nerve fibres known as myelinated fibres. Impulses travel faster and with less energy expenditure in myelinated fibres than in unmyelinated fibres.

■ **myelogram**

a diagnostic test in which an opaque liquid is injected into the spinal canal, producing an outline of it on X-rays or fluoroscope. Now somewhat outdated by modern imaging diagnostics. Some dyes are suspected of causing additional neurological problems.

■ **naive realism**

see **direct realism**.

■ **nanometer (nm)**

a billionth of a meter. Wavelength of light is measured in nanometers.

■ **narcissism**

self-love, in Freud's psychoanalytic theory, the normal expression of pregenital development.

■ **narcolepsy**

a sleep disturbance characterised by an uncontrollable tendency to fall asleep for brief periods at inopportune times.

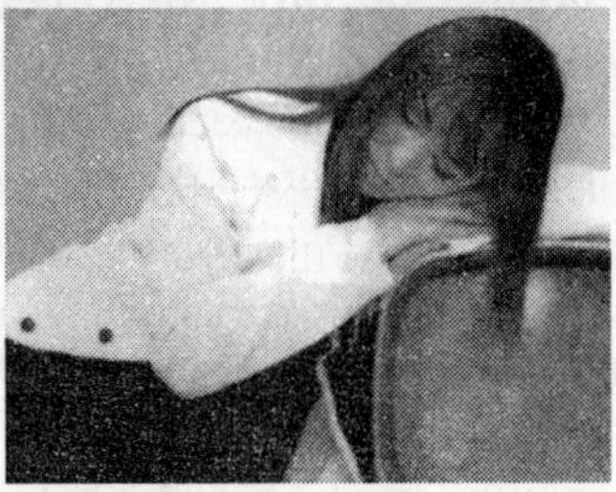

■ **nasogastric tube (ng tube)**

a tube that passes through the patient's nose and throat and ends in the patient's stomach. This tube allows for direct 'tube feeding' to maintain the nutritional status of the patient or removal of stomach acids.

■ **nativism**

the view that behaviour is innately determined.

■ **natural law**

objective doctrines for social, legal and moral behaviour that are derived from what is believed to be the rational, ordered character of the world.

■ **naturalistic fallacy**

a contentious claim, related to Moore, that says that evaluative concepts cannot be analysed in terms of factual (naturalistic) terms. Sometimes this claim is associated with jumping the is-ought gap.

■ **naturalistic observation**

a research method where the subject(s) is (are) observed without interruption under normal or natural circumstances.

■ nature–nurture controversy

the debate related to the relative importance of heredity (nature) and learning or experience (nurture) in determining development and behaviour.

■ nature-nurture issue

the problem of determining the relative importance of heredity (nature) and the result of upbringing in a particular environment (nurture) on mature ability.

■ nce score

a standard score that sets the mean to fifty and standard deviation to 21.06, allowing the 99th percentile to have a score of 99 and the first percentile a score of 1.

■ necessary truth

a statement that is correct by virtue of its definition. For example, 'an orphan is one whose parents have died'.

■ necessary/sufficient conditions

a necessary condition is a condition that must be satisfied before a thing can be included in a class or category, but it is not the only condition that must be satisfied before such inclusion. For example, being an athlete is a necessary condition for inclusion in the class of Olympic medallists. A sufficient condition is a condition that, when met, ensures an item's inclusion in that class. For example, being an unmarried male is a sufficient condition for inclusion in the class of bachelors.

■ necessity

the characteristic of a statement whereby it must be true and impossible to be false because it depends on no other factor for its truth. For example, the statement, 'for every number there is always a greater number,' possesses the property of necessity.

■ need

a physical state involving any lack or deficit within the organism.

■ need for achievement (n ach)

an assumed basic human need to strive for attainment of goals that inspires a wide range of behaviour and thinking.

■ need for cognition

an individual preference for and tendency to engage in effortful cognitive activities.

■ negative correlation

a correlation where two variables tend to move in contrasting directions (example: the number of pages printed and the amount of ink left in your printer are negatively correlated. The more pages printed, the less ink you have left.)

■ negative incentive

an object or circumstance away from which behaviour is directed when the object or circumstance is perceived or anticipated.

■ negative punishment

a form of behaviour, which is followed by the removal of an

appetitive stimulus, decreasing the probability of that behaviour.

■ negative reinforcement

reinforcing a response by the removal of an aversive stimulus.

■ negative reinforcer

any stimulus that, when removed following a response, increases the probability of the response. Loud noises, electric shock, and extreme heat or cold classify as negative reinforcers.

■ negative skew

a curve or distribution of scores that has extreme scores below the mean that are atypical of the majority of scores.

■ negative state relief model

a theory suggesting that for those in a bad mood, helping others may be a way to lift their own spirits if the perceived benefits for helping are high and the costs are low.

■ negative symptoms

in schizophrenia, behavioural deficits such as flattened affect, apathy, and poverty of speech. Presumed to result from abnormalities in brain structure.

■ negativity bias

the tendency for negative traits to be weighted more heavily than positive traits in impression formation.

■ neglect

paying little or no attention to a part of the body.

■ neologism

nonsense or made-up word used when speaking. The person often does not realise that the word makes no sense.

■ nerve

a bundle of elongated axons belonging to hundreds or thousands of neurons, possibly both afferent and efferent neurons. Connects portions of the nervous system to other portions and to receptors and effectors.

■ Nerve Growth Factor (NGF)

a 'vitamin' for nerve cells. NGF, a protein, supports survival of embryonic neurons, and regulates neurotransmitters. NGF is one of several growth factors that have been identified in the central nervous system. It is theorized that these factors, including the much rarer BDNF (brain derived neurotrophic factor) and CNTF (ciliary neurotrophic factor) have important roles in regeneration. Exact knowledge of the role of growth factors continues to be a major area of neuroscience, and may lead to drugs that enhance growth of nerve tissue.

■ neuralgia

sharp pain that runs along the course of a nerve.

■ neurogenic bladder

loss of bladder control due to an injury of the nervous system.

neurogenic bowel
loss of bowel function due to an injury of the nervous system.

neuroimaging
newly developed techniques that can create visual images of a brain in action, with an indication of which regions of the brain show the most neural activity during a particular task. One of the most widely used neuroimaging techniques is positron emission tomography (PET).

neurolinguistic programming
is based on the observation that all internal processing of experience is represented in neurological channels that correspond to the major sensory channels, i.e. kinesthetic, visual, and auditory. The therapist and client strive to find out which channel the client is best at communicating through and then build a therapeutic rapport focused on that communication.

neurologist
a physician who specialises in the nervous system and its disorders.

neurolysis
destruction of peripheral nerves by radio frequency, heat, cutting or by chemical injection. Used to treat spasticity.

neurolytic
a substance or procedure that destroys nerves.

neuromodulator
a substance that changes or modulates the activities of the post-synaptic neurons.

neuron
a nerve cell that can receive and send information by way of synaptic connections.

neuropathic pain
pain caused by abnormal functioning or over activity of nerves. It results from injury or disease of nerves.

neuropathy
disease of the nerves.

neuropsychologist
a psychologist who specialises in evaluating (by tests) brain/behaviour relationships, planning training programs to help the survivor of brain injury return to normal functioning and recommending alternative cognitive and behavioural strategies to minimise the effects of brain injury. Often works closely with schools and employers as well as with family members of the injured person.

neuroreceptor molecule
a protein molecule in a cell membrane that is sensitive to a particular chemical, such as a neurotransmitter. When the appropriate chemical activates a neuroreceptor molecule, changes occur in the cell membrane that either increase or decrease its permeability. Some neurotransmitters have an excitatory effect when locked to their

neuroreceptors, others have an inhibitory effect.

■ **neuroscience**

the science related to the study of the brain and of the links between brain activity and behaviour.

■ **neurosis (pl. neuroses)**

a mental disorder in which the individual is unable to cope with anxieties and conflicts and develops symptoms that he or she finds distressing, such as obsessions, compulsions, phobias, or anxiety attacks. In Freud's psychoanalytic theory, neurosis results from the use of defence mechanisms to ward off anxiety caused by unconscious conflicts. No longer a diagnostic category of DSM-IV.

■ **neurotic anxiety**

fear that is out of proportion to the actual danger posed (such as stage fright).

■ **neurotic disorders**

mental disorders in which a person does not have signs of brain abnormalities and does not display grossly irrational thinking or violate basic norms but does experience subjective distress, a category dropped from DSM-III.

■ **neuroticism**

the name of the emotional instability-stability dimension in Eysenck's factor-analytic theory of personality. Moody, anxious, and maladjusted individuals are at the neurotic or unstable end, calm, well-adjusted individuals are at the other.

■ **neurotransmitter**

a chemical involved in the transmission of nerve impulses across the synapse from one neuron to another. Usually released from small vesicles in the synaptic terminals of the axon in response to the action potential, diffuses across synapse to influence electrical activity in another neuron.

■ **nightmare**

a frightening dream occurring in REM (the periodic, rapid, jerky movement of the eyeballs under closed lids during stages of sleep associated with dreaming) sleep.

■ **nihil es in intellectu quod non prius fuerit in sensu**

a Latin phrase meaning, 'Nothing is in the intellect that was not previously in the senses', a central claim of empiricism claiming that all knowledge arises from the senses and experience and hence, that no knowledge is innate.

■ **n-methyl d-aspartate receptor (nmda receptor)**

a receptor molecule that requires two successive chemical signals to activate it, the first signal makes the receptor more responsive (a phenomenon known as long-term potentiation) so that when a second chemical signal occurs (the neurotransmitter glutanate), the receptor is activated. NMDA receptors are particularly dense in the hippocampus and may explain how memories are stored by linking neurons to form new neural circuits.

■ **nociceptive pain**

the pain induced by a noxious external stimulus. Specialised nerve endings in the skin send this pain message from the skin, through the spinal chord, into the brain.

■ **nociceptors**

nerve endings attached to peripheral nerves that sense tissue damage (or the threat of) by conveying heat, cold, or pressure.

■ **nominal scale**

any scale that contains no magnitude. Often nominal is thought of as name only, meaning that the variables of a nominal scale can be identified but not measured.

■ **nominalism**

the view that rejects universals and holds that only particular instances of things are real and that the only thing a class of items really has in common is its name. For example, humanity does not exist in general but only as individual instances of humans who only have a name, 'humanity', in common.

■ **non sequitur**

a Latin term which mean, 'does not follow', it is used for a conclusion that is not logically supported by its premises.

■ **non-ambulatory**

not able to walk.

■ **non-conscious**

information not generally available to consciousness or memory.

■ **non-conscious processes**

a considerable body of research indicates that we register and evaluate stimuli that we are not consciously aware of. The stimuli are said to influence us unconsciously or to operate at an unconscious (or subconscious) level of awareness.

■ **non-declarative memory**

a subsystem within long term memory which consists of skills one acquires through repetition and practice (e.g., singing, playing, and driving a car)

■ **nonparametric test**

any statistic that is designed for ordinal or nominal data or data that is not normally distributed

■ **non-rem (nrem) sleep**

the period during which a sleeper does not show rapid eye movement, characterised by less dream activity than REM sleep.

■ **nonverbal behaviour**

communicating feelings and intentions without words.

■ **norepinephrine**

one of the hormones secreted by the adrenal medulla, its action in emotional excitement is similar in some, but not all, respects to that of epinephrine. It is also a neurotransmitter of the central nervous system. Norepinephrine synapses can be either excitatory or inhibitory. Believed to play a role in depression and bipolar disorders (syn. noradrenaline).

■ **norm**

an expected standard of behaviour and belief established and enforced by a group.

norm crystallisation

the amalgamation of the expectations of a group of individuals into a common viewpoint as they talk and carry out activities together.

norm of social justice

a social norm stating that we should help only when we believe that others deserve our assistance.

norm of social responsibility

a social norm stating that we should help when others are in need and dependent on us.

normal curve

the plotted form of the normal distribution.

normal distribution

the standard symmetrical bell-shaped frequency distribution, whose properties are commonly used in making statistical inferences from measures derived from samples.

normal distribution

the scores of a sample or population that, when graphed, fall on or close to a normal curve. A normal distribution is often ideal in research because the data can then be said to have all of the characteristics of a normal curve.

normative ethics

the area of ethics that seeks answers to questions about which acts should be advocated and which prohibited. The phrase contrasts with metaethics.

normative influence

group effects that arise from individuals' desire to be liked, accepted and approved of by others.

normative investigations

research efforts designed to describe what is characteristic of a specific age or developmental stage.

normative social influence

conformity, compliance, or obedience due to a desire to gain rewards or avoid punishments (outcome dependence).

norms

standards based on measurements of a large group of people. Used for comparing the scores of an individual with those of others within a well-defined group.

note

in philosophy, students should be careful to differentiate the mention of a word from the use of scare quotation marks to stress on an odd or different meaning of a word. For example, "Money is 'God' for them", is not an example of mentioning a word, but of using quotation marks to mean something other than actually quoting some person.

noumenal world

term attributed to Kant, which refers to the world as it really is, beyond human experience, rather than the world one can experience and obtain knowledge about.

noumenon
a part of reality that is not revealed by direct sensory experience, the underlying stuff beneath or beyond phenomena and hence, a term used in dualistic metaphysics.

nous
Greek term for 'mind'.

nuclei (sing. nucleus)
a collection of nerve cell bodies grouped in the brain or spinal cord.

null hypothesis
a statistical hypothesis that any difference observed among treatment conditions occurs by chance and does not reflect a true difference. Rejection of the null hypothesis means that we believe the treatment conditions are actually having an effect.

numinous experience
a phrase associated with theologian Rudolf Otto— sacredness, accompanied by a feeling of holiness and transcendence.

nystagmus
involuntary horizontal, vertical, or rotary movement of the eyeballs.

obedience
the performance of an action in response to a direct order.

object
refers to anything, abstract or concrete, also, any actual physical thing.

object permanence
Piaget's term for the child's realisation that an object continues to exist even though it is hidden from view.

object relations theory
an outgrowth of psychoanalytic theory that deals with the person's attachments to others over the course of development. Emphasises ego functioning more than did classical psychoanalytic theory.

object size
the size of an object as determined from measurement at its surface. When size constancy holds, the observer perceives a distant object as being near its object size.

objective
the kind of viewpoint that is unbiased by individual prejudices, sensory and perceptual distortions, or misinterpretations.

objective anxiety
fear that is proportionate to the danger posed.

objective techniques
a generic term for the psychological procedures used to measure personality which rely on measurable or objective techniques such as the MMPI-2 and WAIS-III.

objectivism
it belief that moral values can be objectively true independent of individual, or subjective feelings. Capitalised, the word is used by Ayn Rand in a very different sense to defend ethical egoism.

obligation
a binding contract, a moral responsibility.

observational learning

learning by watching the actions of others and noting that subsequent rewards they receive.

observational method

studying events as they occur in nature, without experimental control of variables, for instance, studying the nest-building of birds, or observing children's behaviour in a play situation.

observer bias

the misrepresentation of evidence because of the personal motives and expectations of the viewer.

obsession

a persistent, unwelcome, intrusive thought, often suggesting an aggressive or sexual act.

obsessive-compulsive disorder

an anxiety disorder taking one of three forms: (a) recurrent thoughts, often disturbing and unwelcome (obsessions), (b) irresistible urges to repeat stereotyped or ritualistic acts (compulsions), (c) both of these in combination.

occasionalism

the dualistic belief that although mind and body are diverse entities that appear to interact, they do not; God alone causes effects. Events in the natural world merely serve as 'occasions' for God to work and bring about synchrony between mind and body.

occipital lobe

region in the back of the brain which processes visual information. Damage to this lobe can cause visual deficits.

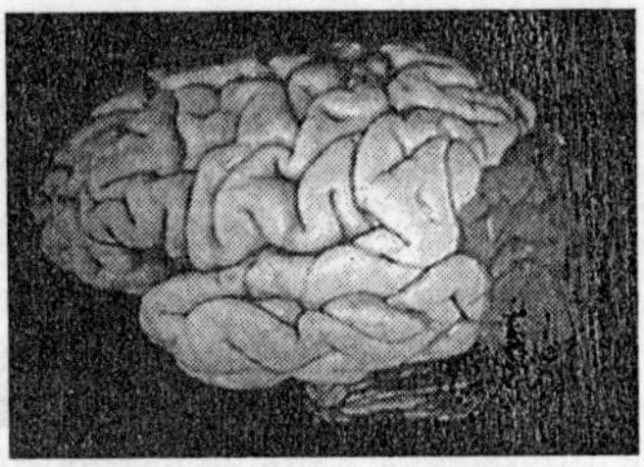

occupational therapy

therapeutic use of self-care, work and play activities to increase independent function, enhance development and prevent disability, may include the adaptation of a task or the environment to achieve maximum independence and to enhance the quality of life. The term occupation, as used in occupational therapy, refers to any activity engaged in for evaluating, specifying and treating problems interfering with functional performance.

Ockham's razor

sometimes called the principle of parsimony, it holds that explanations should be as simple and economical as possible and that no more assumptions should be applied to an explanation than those that are completely necessary.

odd-even reliability

the correlation coefficient determined by comparing odd items of the measurement to the even items. One method to determine the internal consistency of a test or measuring device.

■ **oedema**

increase water content in the brain, causing brain swelling.

■ **oedipal conflict**

in Freud's psychoanalytic theory, the conflict that arises during the phallic stage of psychosexual development in which the individual is sexually attracted to the parent of the opposite sex and perceives the same-sex parent as a rival.

■ **oestrogen**

a group of female sex hormones produced principally by the ovaries. They are responsible for the development of female body characteristics and hair distribution, and for preparing the reproductive system for pregnancy.

■ **oestrous cycle**

recurring episodes of sexual receptivity that precede ovulation in most female mammals. They are characterised by rising and falling levels of estrogens and progesterone in the bloodstream.

■ **old-fashioned racism**

blatantly negative stereotypes based upon white racial superiority, coupled with open opposition to racial equality.

■ **olfaction**

the sense of smell.

■ **olfactory bulb**

a region of the brain involved in olfaction (smell), it is a way station between the receptors in the nasal passage and the olfactory cortex.

■ **olfactory epithelium**

the specialised skin within the nasal cavity that contains the receptors for the sense of smell.

■ **oligodendrocyte**

a central nervous system glial cell, oligodendrocytes are the site of myelin manufacture for central nervous system neurons (the job of Schwann cells in the peripheral nervous system). A myelin protein from oligodendrocytes is known to be a potent inhibitor of nerve growth.

■ **omentum**

well-vascularised tissue of the gut believed to reduce swelling and increase blood flow to the spinal cord when transposed to the injured site.

■ **omnipotence**

power that is limitless, normally attributed to God.

■ **omniscience**

knowledge that is limitless, usually attributed to God.

■ **one-way ANOVA**

an analysis of variance used when there is only one main effect.

■ **ontology**

ancient Greek, 'ontos', being- the branch of metaphysics which studies, questions, analyses and criticises assumptions and theories about the nature of being and existence.

■ open head injury

trauma to the brain due to the penetration of a foreign object that tears soft tissue and blood vessels in its path.

■ open question argument

originated by G. E. Moore who argued that good cannot be synonymous with any other property, for then the question would always be relevant as to whether the thing that satisfies the definition was really good? For example, if one equates good with pleasure and one presents a pleasureful thing as good, the question remains, is that thing really good? Therefore, good has still not been defined.

■ operant

behaviour shown by an organism that can be characterised in terms of the observable effects it has on the environment.

■ operant behaviour

behaviour defined by the stimulus to which it leads rather than by the stimulus that elicits it, such as behaviour leading to reward (syn. instrumental behaviour).

■ operant conditioning

the strengthening of an operant response by presenting a reinforcing stimulus if, and only if, the response occurs (syn. instrumental conditioning, reward learning).

■ operant extinction

when a behaviour no longer produces predictable consequences, it returns to the level of occurrence it had before operant conditioning.

■ operational definition

a definition of a variable or condition in terms of the specific operation or procedure used to determine its presence.

■ opiates

opium or one of its chemical derivatives: codeine, morphine, or heroin. Central nervous system depressants that relieve pain and produce euphoria, all highly addictive (syn. narcotics). See also **heroin**.

■ opinion molecule

a cognitive unit comprising a belief, an attitude, and a perception of social support for the individual's view on the matter. For example, 'I believe that Democrats are compassionate toward the poor' (belief), 'I prefer having Democrats in office' (attitude), 'And I think the American people agree with me' (perception of social support).

■ opioid receptors

neuroreceptor molecules in specific areas of the brain and spinal cord to which a group of neurotransmitters, called endorphins, bind. These molecules also have an affinity for opiates. There are several distinct types of opioid receptors, each has a different affinity for binding with various opiates.

opponent-colour theory

a theory of colour perception that postulates two types of colour-sensitive units that respond in opposite ways to the two colours of an opponent pair. One type of unit responds to red or green, the other to blue or yellow. Since a unit cannot respond in two ways at once, reddish-greens and yellowish-blues cannot occur.

opponent-process theory

the theory that all colour experiences arise from three systems, each of which includes two 'opponent' elements (red versus green, blue versus yellow, and black versus white).

optic chiasma

a cross-over junction of the optic nerves, located near the base of the brain, where nerve fibres from the inner half of each retina (nearest the nose) cross to the opposite side of the brain. The resulting left optic tract carries data about objects seen in the right-hand side of the field of vision, and the right optic tract carries signals from objects seen on the left.

optic nerve

in vision, a nerve formed out of axons of the ganglion cells, which leads to the brain.

optimal level of arousal

theory arguing that humans are driven to increase or decrease arousal to produce a comfortable level that is not over nor under stimulating.

optimistic explanatory style

a habitual tendency to attribute negative events to external, unstable, and specific causes, and positive events to internal, stable, and global causes.

optometrist

a key member of the rehab team uniquely qualified to diagnose and treat visual disorders resulting from brain injury or defect.

oral aggressive personality

stemming from the Oral stage, a child who becomes fixated due to over stimulation transfers his or her unresolved oral issues into aggression and hostility.

oral receptive personality

stemming from the Oral stage, a child who becomes fixated due to under stimulation transfers his or her unmet oral needs into smoking, drinking, talking, biting fingernails, or sucking one's own thumb, for example.

oral stage

in Freud's psychoanalytic theory, the first stage of psychosexual development, pleasure derives from the lips and mouth, as in sucking at the mother's breast.

order effects

the effects of administering treatments in a particular order.

ordered array

a table consisting of data in order of highest to lowest or lowest to highest where each data is given a numbered rank depicting its difference from the highest or lowest score.

■ **ordinal scale**

any scale that reflects only magnitude but does not contain equal intervals or an absolute zero.

■ **ordinary language philosophy**

a form of philosophy that analyses concepts by looking at the their usage in ordinary language, in contrast to their built-up, acquired usage in the history of philosophy.

■ **organisational psychologists**

psychologists who study various aspects of the human work environment, such as communication among employees, socialisation or enculturation of workers, leadership, job satisfaction, stress and burnout, and overall quality of life.

■ **organismic variables**

the inner determinants of an organism's behaviour.

■ **orientation**

awareness of one's environment and/or situation, along with the ability to use this information appropriately in a functional setting.

■ **orientation constancy**

the ability to perceive the actual orientation of objects in the real world despite their varying orientation in the retinal image.

■ **orienting reflex**

1. a non-specific response to change in stimulation involving depression of cortical alpha rhythm, galvanic skin response, pupillary dilation, and complex vasomotor responses (a term introduced by Russian psychologists).
2. head or body movements that orient the organism's receptors to those parts of the environment in which stimulus changes are occurring.

■ **original position**

see **veil of ignorance**.

■ **orthopaedics**

the branch of medicine devoted to the study and treatment of the skeletal system, its joints, muscles and associated structures.

■ **orthosis**

splint or brace designed to improve function or provide stability.

■ **osmoreceptors**

hypothesised cells in the hypothalamus that respond to dehydration by stimulating the release of ADH by the pituitary gland, which, in turn, signals the kidneys to reabsorb water into the bloodstream.

■ **osteoporosis**

loss of bone density, common in immobile bones.

■ **otoliths**

'Ear stones.'

■ **outcome dependence**

dependence upon others for positive outcomes or rewards (also know as normative dependence).

■ **outer ear**

the external ear and auditory canal, whose purpose is to funnel sound waves towards the inner ear.

■ out group

any group with which a person does not share membership.

■ out group homogeneity effect

perception of out group members as being more similar to one another than are members of one's ingroup.

■ outpatient

the patient residing outside the hospital but returning on a regular basis for one or more therapeutic services.

■ oval window

a membrane on the cochlea of the inner ear that receives vibrations from the ear drum via three connecting bones (malleus, incus, and stapes). Vibrations at the oval window set up similar vibrations in the internal fluid of the cochlea, ultimately activating the hair cells that serve as auditory receptors.

■ over learning

a technique used to improve memory where information is learned to the point that it can be repeated without mistake more than one time.

■ over-regularisation

a grammatical error, usually appearing during early language development, in which rules of the language are applied too widely, resulting in incorrect linguistic forms.

■ overtone

a higher frequency tone, a multiple of the fundamental frequency that occurs when a tone is sounded by a musical instrument.

■ pag

a region of the midbrain called the perioqueductal gray, or PAG for short, that is involved in sensing pain. When PAG neurons are active, a neural gate is closed and consequently the sensation of pain is diminished.

■ pain

the body's response to noxious stimuli that are intense enough to cause, or threaten to cause, tissue damage.

■ palsy

paralysis.

■ pancreas

a bodily organ situated near the stomach. As a duct gland, it secretes pancreatic juice into the intestines, but some specialised cells function as an endocrine gland, secreting the hormone insulin into the bloodstream.

■ panic attack

period of extreme anxiety and physical symptoms such as heart palpitations, shakiness, dizziness, and racing thoughts. Initial attacks are often reported to feel like a heart attack due to the heart palpitations. A medical exam should be conducted to rule out any such condition.

■ **panic disorder**

an anxiety disorder in which the individual has sudden and inexplicable episodes of terror and feelings of impending doom accompanied by physiological symptoms of fear (such as heart palpitations, shortness of breath, muscle tremors, faintness).

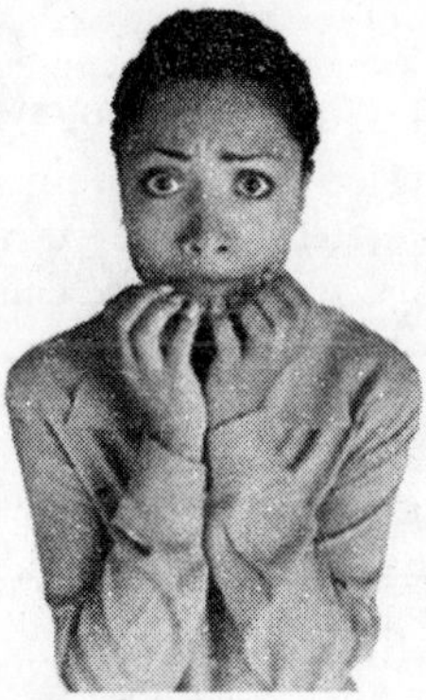

■ **panpsychism**

the belief that the whole of the natural world is composed of certain ultimate units that are conscious and sentient.

■ **paradigm**

a standard, framework, model, or pattern for a concept, around which subsequent investigation is structured.

■ **paradox**

the problem that arises when an argument with seemingly incontrovertible premises leads to contradictory conclusions. A famous example is one of Zeno's paradoxes: if a runner must run from A to B, first he must reach the midpoint, M. Before he can reach M, he must reach the midpoint between A to M, which is N, and before N, the midpoint between A and N, ad infinitum. Therefore the runner can never start or complete the journey. Paradoxes are usually generated by an ambiguous term or terms and are dissolved by carefully specifying the key meanings.

■ **parallel form reliability**

the correlation coefficient determined by comparing the scores of the two similar measuring devices (or forms of the same test) administered to the same people at one time.

■ **parallel forms**

different versions of a test used to assess test reliability. The change of forms reduces effects of direct practice, memory, or the desire of an individual to appear consistent on the same items.

■ **parallel processes**

two or more mental processes that are carried out simultaneously.

■ **parallel processing**

a theoretical interpretation of information processing in which several sources of information are all processed simultaneously.

■ **parallelism**

see **occasionalism**.

■ paralytic ileus

loss of movement in the small intestine, resulting in gas and fluid build-up. It usually lasts a few days after injury.

■ parameter

a summary value of a specific population characteristic (e.g., mean age, standard deviation of IQ's, median income).

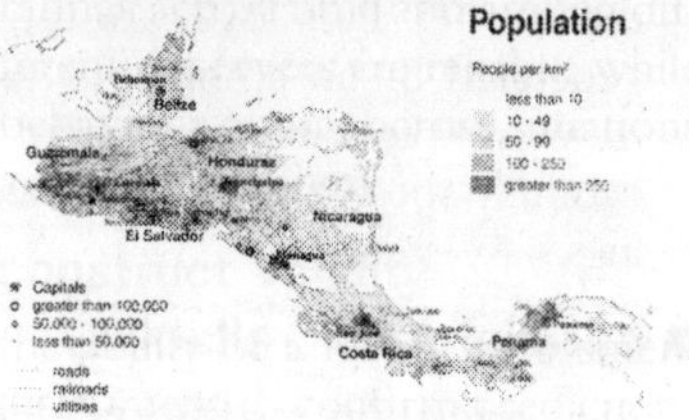

■ paranoid schizophrenia

a schizophrenic reaction in which the patient has delusions of persecution.

■ paraphilias

same as sexual perversions. Sexual attraction to unusual objects as well as sexual activities that are unusual in nature. Examples are fetishism (sexual attractions to an inanimate object or some specific non-genital part of a person), exhibitionism (obtaining sexual gratification by exposing one's genitals to an unwilling observer), and paedophilia (a preference for obtaining sexual gratification through contact with youngsters who are legally underage).

■ paraplegia

paralysis of the legs (from the waist down).

■ parapsychology ('beside psychology')

a sub field of psychology that studies psi phenomena (extrasensory perception and psychokinesis). See also **clairvoyance, extrasensory perception, precognition, psi, psychokinesis, telepathy**.

■ parasympathetic division

the subdivision of the autonomic nervous system that monitors the routine operation of the body's internal functions and conserves and restores body energy.

■ parasympathetic system

a division of the automatic nervous system, the nerve fibres of which originate in the cranial and sacral portions of the spinal cord. Active in relaxed or quiescent states of the body and to some extent antagonistic to the sympathetic division, or system.

■ parathyroid glands

endocrine glands adjacent to the thyroid gland in the neck, whose hormones regulate calcium metabolism, thus maintaining the normal excitability of the nervous system. Parathyroid inadequacy leads to tetany.

■ parental investment

the time and energy parents must spend raising their offspring.

■ parenting practices

specific parenting behaviour that arises in response to particular parental goals.

■ **parenting styles**

the manner in which parents rear their children. An authoritative parenting style, which balances demands and responsiveness, is seen as the most effective.

■ **parietal lobe**

one of the two parietal lobes of the brain located behind the frontal lobe at the top of the brain.

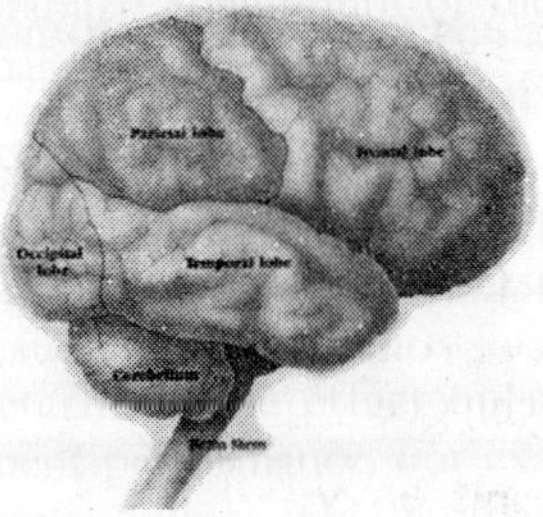

■ **parietal lobe, left**

damage to this area may disrupt a person's ability to understand spoken and/or written language.

■ **parietal lobe, right**

damage of this area can cause visuo-spatial deficits (e.g., the person may have difficulty finding their way around new or familiar places).

■ **parsimony**

see **Ockham's razor.**

■ **partial reinforcement effect**

the behavioural principle that states that responses acquired under intermittent reinforcement are more difficult to extinguish than those acquired with continuous reinforcement.

■ **participant modelling**

a therapeutic technique in which a therapist demonstrates the desired behaviour and a client is aided, through supportive encouragement, to imitate the modelled behaviour.

■ **particulars**

individual things, as opposed to aggregates, or universals.

■ **Pascal's wager**

associated with Blaise Pascal who argued that even if all arguments for God's existence fail, it is still the more prudential bet to believe in God, because if God does exist we have eternity to gain, and if God does not, we have lost little by believing.

■ **passionate love**

an intensely emotional state in which tender and sexual feelings, elation and pain, anxiety and relief, altruism and jealousy coexist in a confusion of feelings. Combines physiological arousal with perception that the arousal is evoked by the beloved.

■ **pastoral counsellor**

a member of a religious order who specialises in the treatment

of psychological disorders, often combining spirituality with practical problem solving.

■ **paternalism**

from Latin, pater, 'father', the belief that restrictions on freedoms of the individual are justified when the agency, individual, or institution acts as a benign parent. In medical ethics, it was a view that came under attack after the patients' rights movements attacked the paternalism of physicians, especially of male physicians towards female patients.

■ **path analysis**

a correlational procedure that divides an overall correlation between two variables into separate components or paths. For example, path analysis can help to determine whether a link between childhood temper tantrums and later occupational problems is direct or is due to some intervening link like dropping out of school.

■ **patient**

the term used by those who take a biomedical approach to the treatment of psychological problems to describe the person being treated.

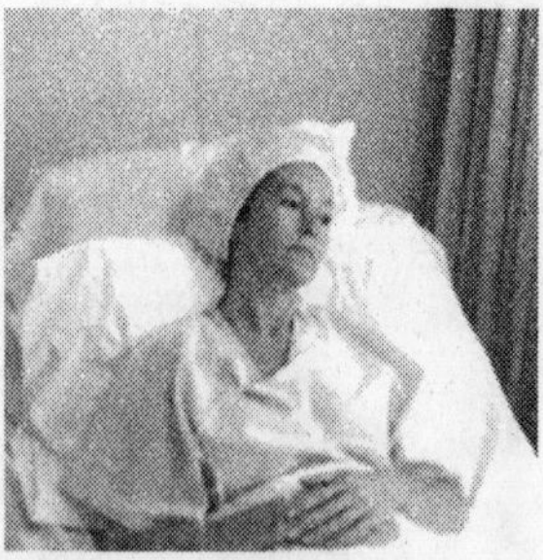

■ **pattern recognition**

the perceptual process of determining what an object is.

■ **peace psychology**

an interdisciplinary approach to the prevention of nuclear war and the maintenance of peace.

■ **peak experience**

a life experience considered paramount due to the feeling of unity with the world.

■ **Pearson product-moment correlation**

a correlation statistic used primarily for two sets of data that are of the ratio or interval scale. The most commonly used correlation technique.

■ **penis envy**

in Psychoanalytic thought, the desire of girls to posses a penis and therefore have the power that being male represents.

■ **per se**

Latin, 'in and of itself', intrinsically.

■ **perceived control**

the belief that one has the ability to make a difference in the course or the consequences of some event or experience, often helpful in dealing with stressors.

■ **percentile rank**

percentage of scores falling at or below a specific score. A percentile rank of 95 means that 95% of all of the scores fall at or below this point. In other words, the score is as good as or better than 95% of the scores.

■ **percept**

the result of the perceptual process, that which the individual perceives.

■ **perception**

a general term to describe the whole process of how we come to know what is going on around us, the entire sequence of events from the presentation of a physical stimulus to the phenomenological experiencing of it. Perception is viewed as a set of sub processes that occur in a multilevel, interactive system. The lower levels in this system, the parts closely associated with the sense organs, are called sensory processes.

■ **perceptual constancy**

the tendency to see objects as relatively unchanged under widely altered conditions of illumination, distance, and position.

■ **perceptual defence**

the supposed prevention of an individual's conscious perceptual system from recognizing an anxiety-producing situation perceived by the individual's unconscious perceptual system.

■ **perceptual organisation**

the processes that put sensory information together to give the perception of a coherent scene over the whole visual field.

■ **perceptual patterning**

the tendency to perceive stimuli according to principles such as proximity, similarity, continuity, and closure. Emphasized by Gestalt psychologists.

■ **perfect correlation**

a correlation of either +1.0 or -1.0. A perfect correlation is extremely rare and when it occurs means that predicting one score based on another score is perfect or without error.

■ **perfectionism**

the ethical theory that the ideal of ethics is to make oneself as perfect as possible, to make society similarly perfect, and finally, to perfect humanity.

■ **performance**

overt behaviour, as distinguished from knowledge or information not translated into action. The distinction is important in theories of learning.

■ **Peripheral Nervous System (PNS)**

nerves that extend from the spinal cord to other parts of the body, transmitting messages to and from these parts and sending sensory signals back to the spinal cord and brain. The PNS is not part of the CNS (central nervous system). Peripheral nerves have the ability to regenerate if they are damaged.

■ **peripheral route to persuasion**

persuasion that occurs when people do not think carefully about a communication and instead are influenced by cues that are irrelevant to the content or quality of the communication.

■ **permissive [parents]**

parenting style consisting of very few rules and allowing children to make most decisions and control their own behaviour.

■ **perseveration**

the inappropriate persistence of a response in a current task which may have been appropriate for a former task. Perseverations may be verbal or motoric.

■ **Persistent Vegetative State (PVS)**

a long-standing condition in which the patient utters no words and does not follow commands or make any response that is meaningful.

■ **person**

a major area of inquiry in metaphysics and ethics, it is usually defined as a being who is sentient, self-consciousness, has the ability to communicate with others, and is a self-moving agent. In this minimal sense, dolphins and chimpanzees may be persons, but some humans may not be if they are in permanent comas and lack sentience.

■ **person centred therapy**

the therapeutic technique based on humanistic theory which is non-directive and empathic.

■ **personal construct**

in George Kelly's theory of personality, a dimension used by an individual to interpret or 'construe' his or her environment. Considered by Kelly to be the basic unit of personality organisation.

■ **personal distress**

an unpleasant state of arousal in which people are preoccupied with their own emotions of anxiety, fear, or helplessness upon viewing a victim's plight.

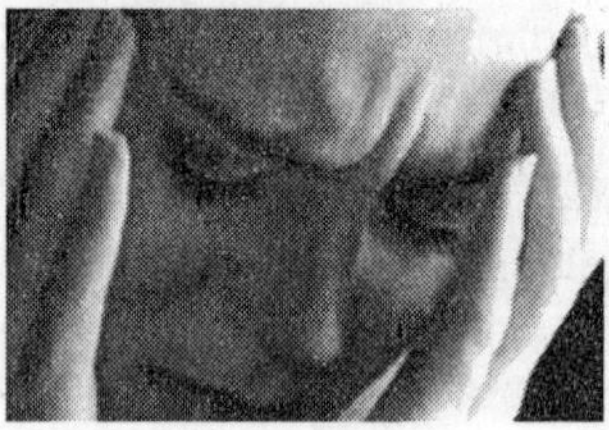

■ **personal identity**

that property which causes a single individual to have consciousness of his or her own identity over and through time. It enables one to differentiate herself

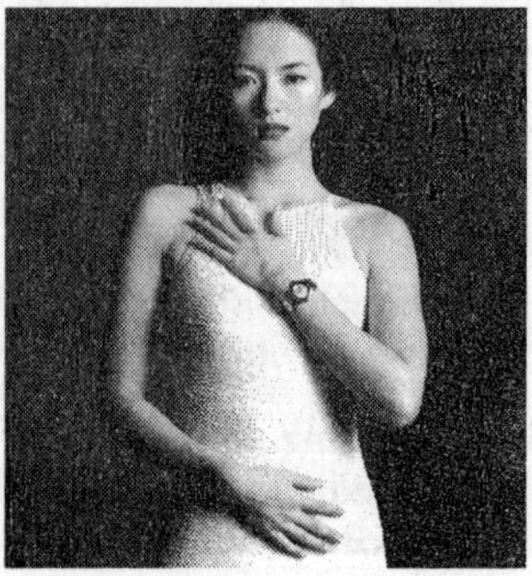

from all others. The major candidates for grounding this kind of identity are memory and the continuity of a human body over time.

■ **personality**

the distinctive and characteristic patterns of thought, emotion, and behaviour that define an individual's personal style of interacting with the physical and social environment.

■ **personality assessment**

the measurement or appraisal of personality.

■ **personality disorder**

a chronic, inflexible, maladaptive pattern of perceiving, thinking, and behaving that seriously impairs an individual's ability to function in social or other settings.

■ **personality inventory**

an inventory for self-appraisal, consisting of many statements or questions about personal characteristics and behaviour that the person judges to apply or not to apply to him or her.

■ **personality psychologist**

a psychologist whose area of interest focuses on classifying individuals and studying the differences between them. This specialty overlaps both developmental and social psychologists to some extent.

■ **personality types**

distinct patterns of personality characteristics used to assign people to categories- qualitative differences, rather than differences in degree, used to discriminate among people.

■ **person-cantered therapy**

see client-cantered therapy.

■ **persuasion**

the process of consciously attempting to change attitudes through the transmission of some message.

■ **pet scans**

brain images produced by a device that obtains detailed pictures of activity in the living brain by recording the radioactivity emitted by cells during different cognitive or behavioural activities.

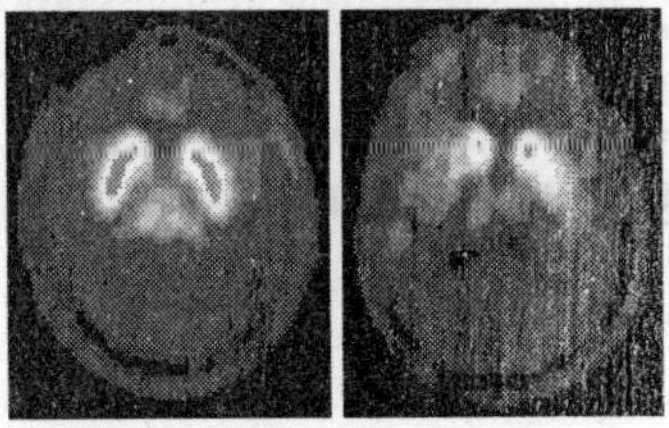

■ **pet therapy**

a therapeutic approach based on the idea that expressing affection for a pet helps people feel happier, maintain a positive outlook, and therefore improve their health. According to several studies, having a pet can reduce stress, lower blood pressure, and ward off loneliness and depression. Many nursing homes and some prisons have developed pet therapy programmes, with excellent results.

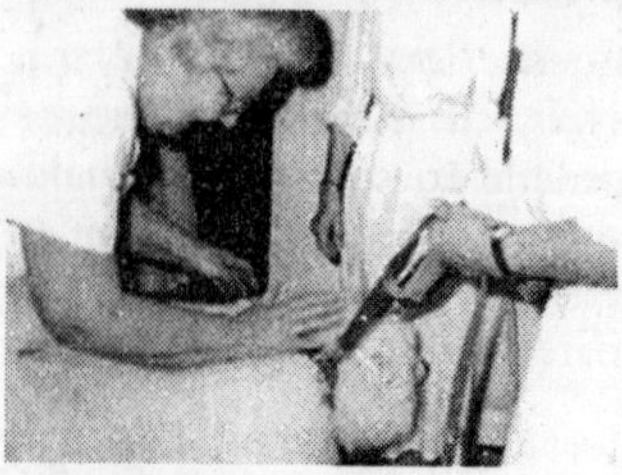

■ **petit mal**

a term used to describe a mild form of seizure characterised by a blank stare and temporary pause in activity.

■ **petitio principii**

Latin, 'begging the question', see **begging the question.**

■ **phallic personality**

stemming from the Phallic stage, a child who becomes fixated may develop a personality characterised by selfishness, impulsivity, and a lack of or reduced ability to feel empathy.

■ **phallic stage**

in Freud's psychoanalytic theory, the third stage of psychosexual development in which gratification is associated with stimulation of the sex organs and sexual attachment is to the parent of the opposite sex.

■ **phantom limb phenomenon**

as experienced by amputees, extreme or chronic pain in a limb that is no longer there.

■ **phantom pain**

sensation of a limb that has been amputated from the body.

■ **phasic pain**

the kind of sharp pain experienced immediately upon suffering an injury, usually brief with a rapid increase in intensity followed by a decrease.

■ **phencyclidine (PCP)**

originally developed as an anaesthetic but discontinued because of the bizarre reactions it produced, this drug causes an insensitivity to pain and makes the users feel dissociated from themselves and from their environments. Overdoses result in prolonged periods of stupor or coma.

■ **phenomenalism**

the view that the reality of physical objects does not exist apart from its perception by a perceiver and therefore, the material world does not exist apart from the actual or potential perceptions of the mind.

■ **phenomenological perspective**

an approach to psychology that focuses on subjective experience and tries to describe it from each individual's unique perspective.

■ **phenomenology**

the study of an individual's subjective experience or unique perception of the world. Emphasis is on understanding events from the subject's point of view rather than focusing on behaviour.

phenomenon

(plural, phenomena) ancient Greek, 'appearance', it is that which is manifested or shown through sensory experience, contrasted with noumenon.

phenothiazines

a group of antipsychotic drugs that relieve the symptoms of schizophrenia by blocking the access of the neurotransmitter dopamine to its receptors. Chlorpromazine (Thorazine) and fluphenazine (Prolixin) are examples.

phenotype

in genetics, the characteristics that are displayed by the individual organism such as eye colour or intelligence as distinct from those traits that one may carry genetically but not display.

pheromones

special chemicals secreted by many animals that float through the air to attract other members of the same species. They represent a primitive form of communication.

phi correlation

a correlation technique used when both variables are binary (Example true/false, yes/no, or on/off).

phi phenomenon

stroboscopic motion is its simpler form. Commonly produced by successively turning on and off two separated stationary light sources, as the first is turned off and the second turned on, the subject perceives a spot of light moving from the position of the first to that of the second.

philosophy

Greek, 'love of wisdom', it is the study of the most abstract and general questions about the world, and how we think, experience and should behave.

phobia

excessive fear in the absence of real danger.

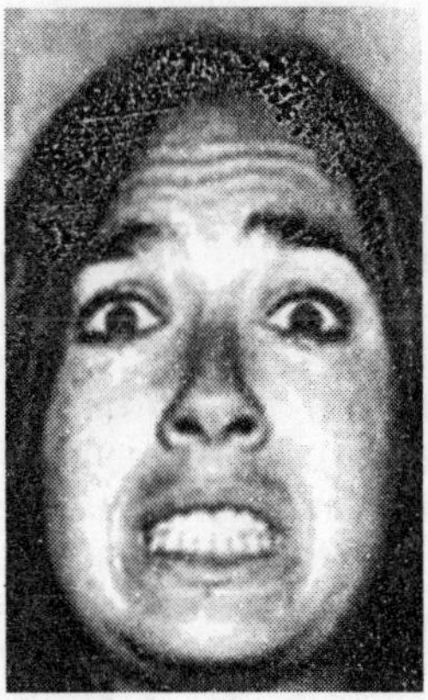

phobic disorder

an anxiety disorder in which phobias are severe or pervasive enough to interfere seriously with the individual's daily life.

phonation

the production of sound by means of vocal cord vibration.

phoneme

the smallest unit in the sound system of a language, it serves to distinguish utterances from one another.

■ **photopigments**

chemicals contained in the rods and cones (the receptor cells in the eye). These chemicals absorb light, which starts a process that results in a neural impulse.

■ **photoreceptors**

receptor cells in the retina which are sensitive to light.

■ **physiatrist**

a physician who specialises in physical medicine and rehabilitation. Some physiatrists are experts in neurological rehabilitation, trained to diagnose and treat disabling conditions. The physiatrist examines the patient to assure that medical issues are addressed, provides appropriate medical information to the patient, family members and members of the treatment team. The physiatrist follows the patient closely throughout treatment and oversees the patient's rehabilitation program.

■ **physical attractiveness stereotype**

the belief that physically attractive individuals possess socially desirable personality traits and lead happier lives than less attractive persons.

■ **physical development**

the bodily changes, maturation, and growth that occur in an organism starting with conception and continuing across the life span.

■ **physical therapist**

the physical therapist evaluates components of movement, including: muscle strength, muscle tone, posture, coordination, endurance, and general mobility. The physical therapist also evaluates the potential for functional movement, such as ability to move in the bed, transfers and walking and then proceeds to establish an individualised treatment program to help the patient achieve functional independence.

■ **physicalism**

the form of metaphysical monism that maintains that all existence is physical and can be governed by laws of physics. See also **identity thesis**.

■ **physiological dependence**

the process by which the body becomes adjusted to and dependent on a drug.

■ physiological motive

a motive based on an evident bodily need, such as the need for food or water.

■ pia

one of three membranes holding the brain together.

■ pitch

a qualitative dimension of hearing correlated with the frequency of the sound waves that constitute the stimulus. Higher frequencies yield higher pitches.

■ pituitary gland

an endocrine gland joined to the brain just below the hypothalamus. It consists of two parts, the anterior pituitary and the posterior pituitary. The anterior pituitary is the more important part because of its regulation of growth and of other endocrine glands (syn. hypophysis).

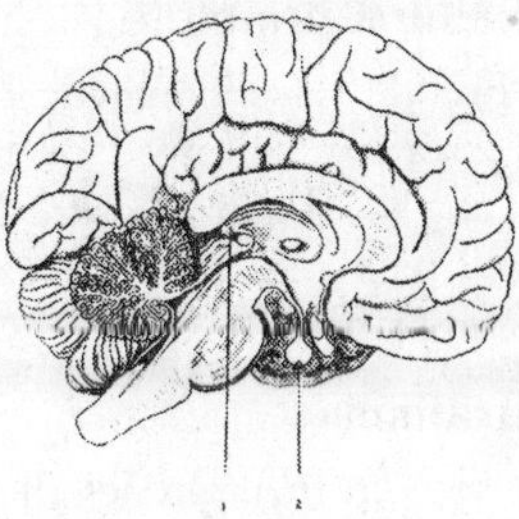

■ pituitary gland

located in the brain, the gland that secretes growth hormone and influences the secretion of hormones by other endocrine glands.

■ place theory

the theory that different frequency tones produce maximum activation at different locations along the basilar membrane, with the result that pitch can be coded by the place at which activation occurs.

■ place theory of pitch

a theory of hearing that associates pitch with the place on the basilar membrane where activation occurs.

■ placebo

an inert substance used in place of an active drug, given to the control group in an experimental test.

■ placebo control

an experimental condition in which treatment is not administered. It is used in cases where a placebo effect might occur.

■ placebo effect

a situation where people experience some change or improvement from an empty, fake, or ineffectual treatment.

■ placebo effect

a situation where people experience some change or improvement from an empty, fake, or ineffectual treatment.

■ placebo therapy

a therapy independent of any specific clinical procedures that results in improvement.

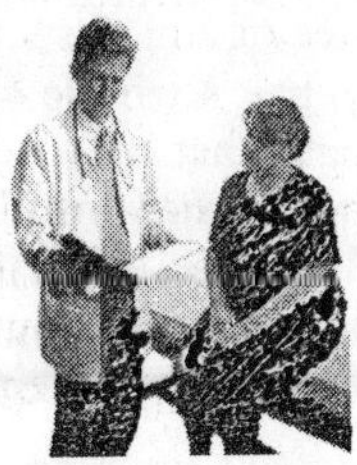

■ **plasticity**

the ability of cellular or tissue structures and their resultant function to be influenced by an ongoing activity.

■ **plateau**

a temporary or permanent levelling off in the recovery process.

■ **Plato (427-347 B.C.)**

a pupil and friend of Socrates. Plato founded (c.387 B.C.) The Academy near Athens, where he taught until his death. His most famous pupil was Aristotle.

Plato's dialogues show the relationship between the soul, the state and the cosmos, in the study of law, mathematics, philosophic problems, and natural science. He regarded the rational soul as immortal, and he believed in a world soul and a creator of the physical world. He argued for the independent reality of ideas as the only guarantee of ethical standards and of objective scientific knowledge. He taught that only he who understands the harmony of all parts of the universe is capable of ruling the just state. He touched upon virtually every problem that has occupied subsequent philosophers and his teachings have been among the most influential in Western civilisation.

■ **platonism**

term referring to Plato's view that abstract concepts and numbers have an independent existence as (what is variously translated as) Forms, Ideas, or Essences, while physical objects are mere imperfect copies or shadows of these Forms.

■ **platykurtic**

a curve or distribution of scores that has a lot of variance.

■ **play therapy**

a psychodynamic technique which encourages children to explore their conflicts through symbolic play rather than through verbal expression.

■ **pleasure principle**

in Freud's psychoanalytic theory, the strategy followed by the id, seeking to obtain pleasure and to avoid pain regardless of external circumstances.

■ **pluralism**

the view in metaphysics that reality is irreducible to one or even two things, and that there are several essential substances. Contrasts with monism and dualism. See also **moral pluralism**.

■ **pluralistic ignorance**

the tendency for persons in a group to mislead each other about a situation, for example, to define an emergency as a nonemergency because others are remaining calm and are not taking action.

■ point biserial correlation

a correlation technique used when one variable is numeric and the other is binary (Example age and sex or income and true/false)

■ point estimation

estimating the population statistics based on a single sample statistic.

■ polygenic traits

characteristics, intelligence, height, emotional stability, determined by many sets of genes.

■ polygraph

a device that measures simultaneously several physiological responses that accompany emotion, for instance, heart and respiration rate, blood pressure, and GSR. Commonly known as a 'lie detector' because of its use in determining the guilt of a subject through responses while he or she answers questions.

■ pons

1. the region of the brain stem that connects the spinal cord with the brain and links parts of the brain to one-another.
2. part of the brain that plays a role in the regulation of states of arousal, including sleep and dreaming.

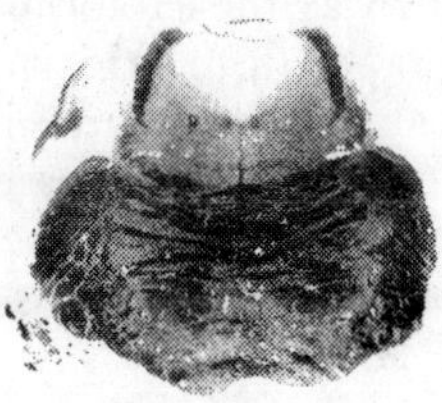

■ pornography

the combination of sexual material with abuse or degradation in a manner that appears to endorse, condone, or encourage such behaviour.

■ positive correlation

a correlation where as one variable increases, the other also increases, or as one decreases so does the other. Both variables move in the same direction.

■ positive incentive

an object or circumstance toward which behaviour is directed when the object or circumstance is perceived or anticipated.

■ positive punishment

a behaviour is followed by the presentation of an aversive stimulus, decreasing the probability of that behaviour.

■ positive reinforcement

reinforcing a response by the presentation of a positive stimulus.

■ positive reinforcer

any stimulus that, when applied following a response, increases the probability of the response (syn. reward).

■ positive skew

a curve or distribution of scores that has extreme scores above the mean that are atypical of the majority of scores.

■ positive symptoms

in schizophrenia, behavioural excesses such as hallucinations and bizarre behaviour. Contrasted with negative symptoms and presumed to be caused by irregularities in neural transmission.

positivism

a very general term describing various beliefs holding that the scientific method is the best means of obtaining knowledge.

positivity bias

the tendency for people to evaluate individual human beings more positively than groups or impersonal objects.

Positron Emission Tomography (PET)

a computer-based scanning procedure that measures regional changes in blood flow to map the neural activities of the living brain.

possible selves

the ideal selves that a person would like to become, the selves a person could become, and the selves a person is afraid of becoming, components of the cognitive sense of self.

post concussion syndrome

a particular group of impairments that characterise the effects of injury on the brain and behaviour. PCS include impairments in the ability to think, to do, and to know. PCS is characterised by diminished, self-awareness and diminished ability to benefit from experience. Other difficulties includes unreliable memory, rapid mood swings, poor concentration, headache, dizziness, hypersensitivity, depression and anxiety.

post hoc, ergo propter hoc

Latin, 'after this, therefore because of this', it is a fallacy that argues that because B happened after A, therefore A caused B. An example of this fallacy is the statement, "The midtown bus stopped at Fourth Street where Mary got on and John got off; therefore Mary caused John to leave the bus."

Post Traumatic Amnesia (PTA)

a period of hours, weeks, days or months after the injury when the patient exhibits a loss of day-to-day memory. The patient is unable to store new information and therefore has a decreased ability to learn. Memory of the PTA period is never stored, therefore things that happened during that period cannot be recalled. May also be called Anterograde Amnesia.

post traumatic stress disorder

not long ago, post traumatic stress disorder, PTSD, used to be known as 'shell shock' or 'battle fatigue.' The old terms were popularised during World War II, and continued to be so until just recently. Back then, PTSD was thought to affect only combat veterans. Now, scientist know that, in fact, survivors of atrocities such as the Holocaust, torture, rape, domestic violence, child abuse, war, natural disasters, catastrophic illnesses, and horrific accidents, are susceptible to post traumatic stress disorder, PTSD.

■ **post-acute rehabilitation**

programs designed to provide intensive, 24-hour rehabilitation to improve cognitive, physical, emotional, and psychosocial abilities, to facilitate better independent living skills. Facilities typically provide a full spectrum of clinical therapies, as well as life-skills training in a residential setting.

■ **posterior attentional system**

neural structures in the back of the brain that mediate our ability to selectively attend to a particular location.

■ **posthypnotic amnesia**

a particular form of posthypnotic suggestion in which the hypnotised person forgets what has happened during the hypnosis until signalled to remember.

■ **posthypnotic suggestion**

a suggestion made to a hypnotised person that he or she will perform in a prescribed way (commonly to a prearranged signal) when no longer hypnotised. The activity, the posthypnotic response, is usually carried out without the subject's awareness of its origin.

■ **postmodernism**

a modern movement in philosophy and the humanities that rejects the optimistic view that science and reason will improve humanity.

■ **Post-Traumatic Stress Disorder (PTSD)**

an anxiety disorder characterised by the persistent re-experience of traumatic events through distressing recollections, dreams, hallucinations, or dissociative flashbacks. Develops in response to rapes, life-threatening events, severe injuries, and natural disasters.

■ **postural drainage**

using gravity to help the clear lungs of mucus by positioning the head lower than chest.

■ **postural hypotension**

the reduction of blood pressure resulting in light-headedness. Due to changes in the autonomic nervous system of persons with spinal cord injury, blood vessels do not decrease in size in response to lowered blood pressure. The result is that blood pools up in legs or pelvic region.

■ **posture**

attitude of the body. Posture is maintained by low-grade, continuous contraction of muscles which counteract the pull of gravity on body parts. Injury to the nervous system can impair the ability to maintain normal posture, for example, holding up the head.

■ **power**

the strength or the data to find a difference when there truly is a difference. Power is abbreviated with the capital Greek letter beta (?).

■ **pqrst method**

a technique for reading and studying information presented in textbook form. The method takes its name from the first letter of the five steps one follows in reading a textbook chapter: Preview, Question, Read, Self-recitation, Test.

■ **pragmatic rules**

rules used in deductive reasoning that are less abstract than logical rules, but still applicable to many different domains of life. An example is the permission rule.

■ **pragmatism**

a form of American philosophy associated with William James and Charles Pierce that holds that the truth of an idea should be measured by its practical applications in the ordinary world.

■ **prana**

the yogic concept of a cosmic energy or life force, similar to the Chinese idea of chi, that enters the body with the breath. Prana is thought to flow through the body, bringing health and vitality. It is considered the vital link between the spiritual self and the material self.

■ **pre-attentive processing**

processing of sensory information that precedes attention to specific objects.

■ **precognition**

perception of a future event that could not be anticipated through any known inferential process (for example, predicting that a particular number will come up on the next throw of dice).

■ **preconscious**

in Freud's topograhic model, the part of the mind containing thoughts and memories that are not part of conscious awareness at the moment, but which can be brought to awareness when needed.

■ **predestination**

the doctrine that all individuals have been predestined from birth for salvation or damnation regardless of their deeds in life.

■ **predicate**

a condition; a property or attribute that qualifies another thing.

■ **predictive validity**

see criterion validity.

■ **predictive validity**

a measurements ability to predict scores on another measurement that is related or purports to measure the same or similar construct

■ **preferential looking method**

a method of examining infants' perceptual preferences by presenting them two stimuli simultaneously and noting the amount of time the infants gaze at each object.

■ prefrontal lobotomy

an operation that severs the nerve fibres connecting the frontal lobes of the brain with the diencephalon, especially those fibres of the thalamic and hypothalamic areas-best-known form of psychosurgery.

■ prejudice

negative feelings toward a group. Derived from 'pre-judgment,' usually implies negative feelings not based on adequate or valid data about the group.

■ premise

a proposition or statement, a number of which make up an argument, from which a conclusion is finally drawn.

■ pre-morbid condition

characteristics of an individual present before the disease or injury occurred.

■ preoperational stage

piaget's second stage of cognitive development (ages 2-7 years). The child can think in terms of symbols but does not yet comprehend certain rules or operations, such as the principle of conservation.

■ pre-operational stage

Piaget's second stage of cognitive development in which a child develops objects permanency and language.

■ prepared conditioning

the proposal that humans are biologically predisposed, or prepared, by evolutionary selection to associate fear with objects or situations that were dangerous in earlier times. Explains why people develop phobias (conditioned fears) of snakes and heights but not of lambs or guns.

■ pressure release

regular procedure to relieve pressure from sitting on the ischial turberosities. Necessary to avoid pressure sores.

■ pressure sore

also known as skin sore or decubitus ulcer, is an avoidable and potentially dangerous skin erosion due to pressure. They usually occur over bony prominences and are subject to infection and tissue death.

■ pretest-posttest method

a method of determining the amount of change that occurred in a set of data by measuring the data prior to treatment and then after treatment and comparing the two measurement outcomes.

■ prima facie

Latin, 'at first inspection', on the surface, at the first look, something assumed until something better comes along or until a strong enough reason arises to overturn it.

■ primacy effect

1. in memory experiments, the tendency for initial words in a list to be recalled more readily than later words.

2. in studies of impression formation, the tendency for initial information to carry more weight than information received later.

■ **primary abilities**

the abilities, discovered by factor analysis, that underlie intelligence test performance.

■ **primary auditory area**

a brain region located at the top of the temporal lobe of each cerebral hemisphere where auditory signals carried by the acoustic nerve are analysed. Because nerve fibres from each side of the head cross over at the brain stem before reaching the auditory area, signals from each ear reach both temporal lobes. Thus, damage to one lobe does not produce deafness in one ear.

■ **primary motor area**

a projection area in the brain lying in front of the central fissure. Electrical stimulation commonly results in movement, or motor, responses.

■ **primary reinforcer**

a reinforcer that meets our basic needs such as food, water, sleep, or love.

■ **primary sex characteristics**

the structural or physiological characteristics that make possible sexual union and reproduction.

■ **primary somatosensory area**

area in the parietal lobe of the brain that registers sensory experiences, such as heat, cold, touch, and pain (syn. body-sense area).

■ **primary visual area**

a projection area lying in the occipital lobe. In humans, damage to this area produces blindness in portions of the visual field corresponding to the amount and location of the damage.

■ **primary/secondary qualities**

primary qualities assumed to be inherent in an object as opposed to the qualities the mind perceives an object to have through sensory experience. They are very fundamental, abstract ones, such as 'taking up space' or 'being conscious'. Secondary qualities are what we normally call sensations: redness, heaviness, roughness, and so on, and can be due to the interaction of primary qualities with our sensory organs.

■ **prime matter**

the ultimate potential from which all things take form.

■ **prime move**

in Aristotle's worldview, the cause of all development in the universe. For Aristotle, the prime mover is merely a logical postulate, an X as the first cause, and completely non-anthropomorphic. It also 'moves' the world by 'attracting' development towards it, not by initiating development at creation.

■ **priming**

the increased accessibility or retrievability of information stored in memory produced by the prior presentation of relevant cues.

principle of sufficient reason

see sufficient reason, principle of.

Prisoner's dilemma

an ethical dilemma where two paired individuals must choose between two options: one which will benefit only one and harm the other, and the other choice, which will benefit both to a lesser degree, but only if both individuals choose it. Hence a dilemma of prudential choice in an extreme situation.

private language

a term associated with Wittgenstein, it is a language that can be known only to one person because its terms are defined by the individual's subjective experience.

private self-awareness

a psychological state in which one is aware of one's hidden private self-aspects.

private self-consciousness

the tendency to be aware of the covert, private aspects of the self.

privileged access

the unique, exclusive, and unerring access we have to the processes of our mind by means of introspection.

proactive interaction

the interaction between individuals and their environments that arises because different individuals choose to enter different situations and to shape those situations differently after entering them.

proactive interference

the interference of earlier learning with the learning and recall of new material.

probability of error

the likelihood that error caused the results of data analysis. If the probability of error is greater than the predetermined acceptable level of error then the results are said to be 'not significant.'

probability sample

also called representative samples, a probability sample consists of characteristics that are close to the population that they represent.

probe

in studies of memory, an item from a list to be remembered that is presented as a cue to the subject, for example, the subject could be asked to give the next item in the list.

problem of evil

see **evil, problem of.**

problem of induction

see induction, problem of.

problem solving

thinking that is directed toward solving specific problems and that moves from an initial state to a goal state by means of a set of mental operations.

problem space

the elements that make up a problem: the initial state, the incomplete information or unsatisfactory conditions the person starts with, the goal state, the set of information or state the person wishes to achieve, and the set of operations, the steps the person takes to move from the initial state to the goal state.

problem-focused coping

reducing anxiety or stress by dealing in some way with the anxiety-producing situation. Escaping the situation or finding a way to alter it are examples.

problem-solving skill

ability to consider the probable factors that can influence the outcome of each of various solutions to a problem, and to select the most advantageous solution. Individuals with deficits in this skill may become 'immobilized' when faced with a problem. By being unable to think of possible solutions, they may respond by doing nothing.

problem-solving strategies

the various strategies that can be employed in solving a problem. Of special interest are a class of strategies that involve breaking the solution to a problem into a series of subgoals. The subgoals are to be accomplished as intermediate steps toward ultimately reaching the final goal.

procedural memory

memory for how things get done-the way perceptual, cognitive, and motor skills are acquired, retained, and used.

progesterone

a female hormone secreted by the ruptured follicle.

prognosis

the prospect as to recovery from a disease or injury as indicated by the nature and symptoms of the case.

program

1. a plan for the solution of a problem, often used interchangeably with 'routine' to specify the precise sequence of instructions enabling a computer to solve a problem.
2. in teaching, a set of materials arranged so as to maximise the learning process.

projection

a defence mechanism by which people protect themselves from awareness of their own undesirable traits by attributing those traits excessively to others.

projective techniques

a generic term for the psychological procedures used to measure personality which rely on ambiguous stimuli.

projective test

a personality test in which subjects reveal ('project') themselves through imaginative productions. The projective test gives much freer possibilities of response than the fixed-alternative personality inventory. Examples of projective tests are the Rorschach Test (ink blots to be interpreted) and the Thematic Apperception Test (pictures that elicit stories).

■ prolactin

pituitary hormone prompting the secretion of milk.

■ proletariat

in Marxism, it is the oppressed working class, as opposed to the class of property owners, the bourgeoisie.

■ prone

lying on one's stomach.

■ proof

an argument with such irrefutable premises that it establishes a justified conclusion.

■ property

that which is true of a thing; an attribute or characteristic.

■ proposition

a sentence or component of a sentence that asserts something, the predicate, about somebody (or something), the subject. All sentences can be broken into propositions.

■ proprioception

the sensory awareness of the position of body parts with or without movement. Combination of kinaesthesia and position sense.

■ prosocial behaviour

voluntary behaviour that is carried out to benefit another person.

■ prosody

the inflections or intonations of speech.

■ prosopagnosia

a loss in the ability to recognise faces that results from brain damage.

■ prosthesis

replacement device for a body part, for example an artificial limb.

■ prototype

the part of a concept that contains the properties that describe the best examples of the concept.

■ proximal

next to, or nearest, the point of attachment.

■ proximal stimulus

the optical image on the retina. Contrasted with the distal stimulus, the physical object in the world.

■ proximity

the location of people relative to one another.

■ psi

processes of information and/or energy exchange not currently explicable in terms of known physical mechanisms.

■ psychiatric morbidity

mental illness.

■ psychiatric nurse

a nurse specially trained to deal with patients suffering from mental disorders.

■ **psychiatric social worker**

a social worker trained to work with patients and their families on problems of mental health and illness, usually in close relationship with psychiatrists and clinical psychologists.

■ **psychiatrist**

a medical doctor specialising in the treatment and prevention of mental disorders both mild and severe.

■ **psychiatry**

a branch of medicine concerned with mental health and mental illness.

■ **psychic determinism**

the assumption that mental and behavioural reactions are determined by previous experiences.

■ **psychic trauma**

an emotional shock or distressful situation that produces a lasting impression on the inner essence of an individual.

■ **psychoactive drugs**

drugs that affect one's behaviour and thought processes.

■ **psychoanalysis**

1. the method developed by Freud and extended by his followers for treating mental disorders.

2. the theory of personality which grew out of experiences with the psychoanalytic method of treatment. The theory emphasises the role of unconscious processes in personality development and in motivation.

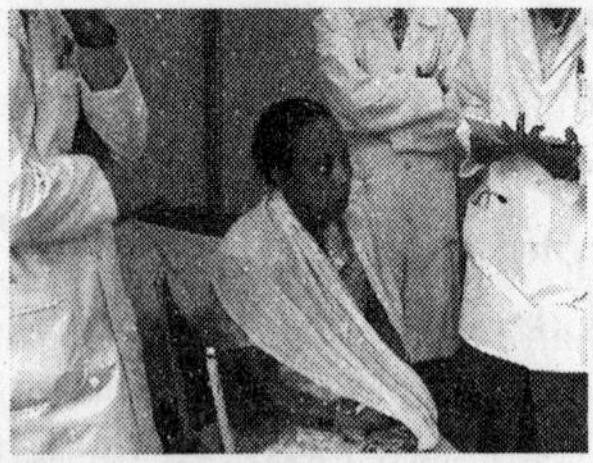

■ **psychoanalyst**

a psychotherapist, usually trained as a psychiatrist, who uses methods related to those originally proposed by Freud for treating neuroses and other mental disorders.

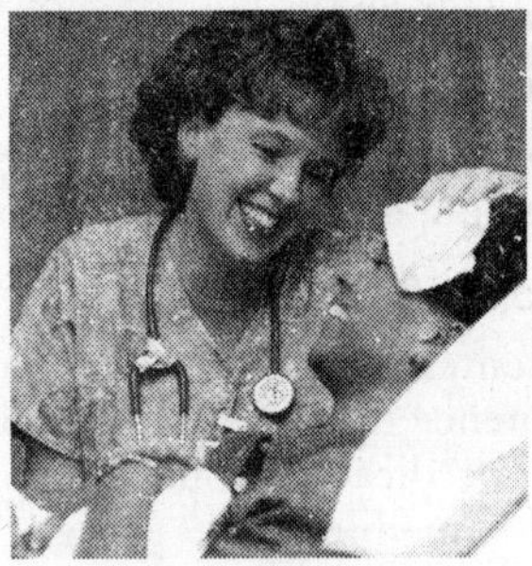

■ **psychoanalytic**

this approach attempts to help a person understand his or her thoughts, feelings, and behaviours in terms of unconscious inner drives. Sigmund Freud was the originator of psychoanalytic thought but other analytic theories have since been developed, including Jungian, Adlerian, and others.

■ **psychoanalytic perspective**

an approach to psychology that tries to explain certain kinds of behaviours in terms of unconscious beliefs, fears, and desires.

psychoanalytic psychotherapy

a method of treating mental disorders based on the theories of Freud but briefer and less intense than psychoanalysis. Less emphasis on exploration of childhood experiences and more attention to the client's current interpersonal problems.

psychobiography

the use of psychological (especially personality) theory to describe and explain an individual's course through life.

psychodrama

patients play different roles in a brief drama. For example, a person having difficulty finding a job might imagine a job interview and alternately play the roles of employer and prospective employee. By playing both roles the client develops skills in dealing with job interviews.

psychodynamic

a variation on the Freudian approach like classical psychoanalytic therapy, psychodynamic theory views, thoughts, feelings, and behaviours as manifestations of inner drives. However, psychodynamic therapy involves more direct interaction between the therapist and the client, and in general assigns a more active role to the client than in psychoanalysis.

psychodynamic personality theories

theories of personality that share the assumption that personality is shaped by and behaviour is motivated by powerful inner forces.

psychodynamic perspective

a psychological model in which behaviour is explained in terms of past experiences and motivational forces. Actions are viewed as stemming from inherited instincts, biological drives, and attempts to resolve conflicts between personal needs and social requirements.

psychodynamic therapy

a modern adaptation of psychoanalytic therapy which has made sometimes minor and sometimes major changes to Freud's original theories.

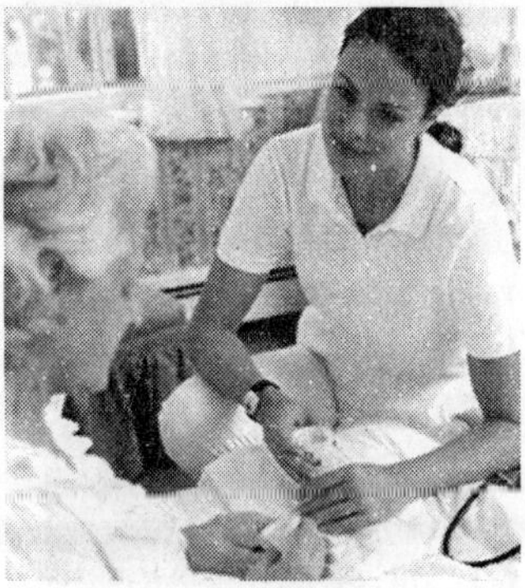

psychogenic

a physical symptom, disease or emotional state that is of mental in origin.

psychoimmunology

an area of research in behavioural medicine that studies how the body's immune system is affected by psychological variables. See also **behavioural medicine**.

■ **Psychokinesis (PK)**

mental influence over physical events without the intervention of any known physical force (for example, willing that a particular number will come up on the throw of dice).

■ **psycholinguistics**

the study of the psychological aspects of language and its acquisition.

■ **psychological assessment**

the use of specified procedures to evaluate the abilities, behaviour, and personal qualities of people.

■ **psychological dependence**

habitual use of a drug to relieve anxiety even though no physical dependence (addiction) has developed.

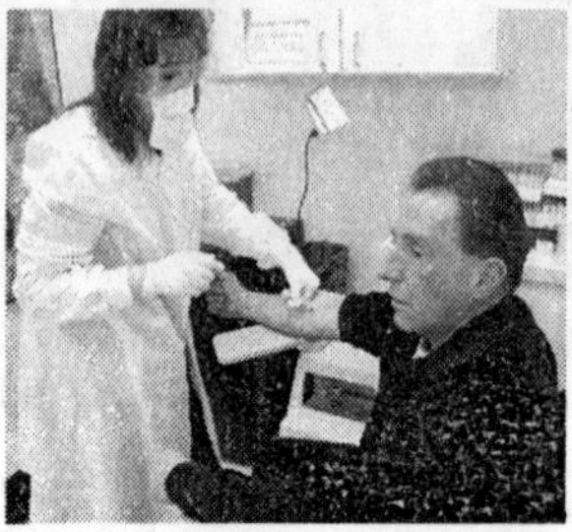

■ **psychological determinism**

the doctrine that all thoughts, emotions, and actions have causes.

■ **psychological diagnosis**

the label given to psychological abnormality by classifying and categorising the observed behaviour pattern into an approved diagnostic system.

■ **psychological egoism**

see **egoism, psychological**.

■ **psychological examination**

a group of standardised tests designed to measure an individual's intellectual capacity, motivation, perception, role behaviour, values, level of anxiety, coping mechanisms, depression and general personality integration.

■ **psychological motive**

a motive that is primarily learned rather than based on biological needs.

■ **psychological testing**

an assessment technique in which a person is presented with a series of stimuli to which he or she is asked to respond. This is part of an evaluation of an individual's functioning aimed at establishing a psychological diagnosis.

■ **psychologist**

a professional specialising in counselling, including adjustment to disability. Psychologists use tests to identify personality and cognitive functioning. This information is shared with team members to assure consistency in approaches. The psychologist may provide individual or group psychotherapy for the purpose of cognitive retraining, management of behaviour and the development of coping skills by the patient/client and members of the family.

■ **psychology**

the science that studies behaviour and mental processes.

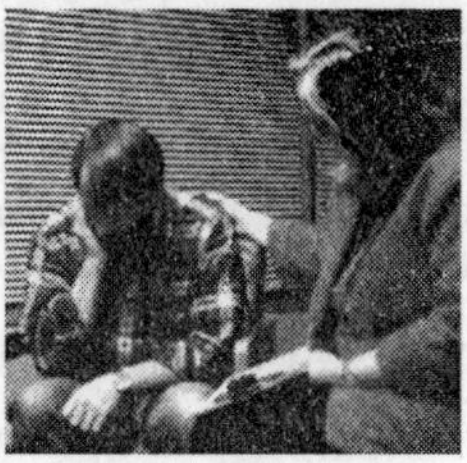

■ **psychometric function**

a curve plotting the percentage of times the subject reports detecting a stimulus against a measure of the physical energy of the stimulus.

■ **psychometrics**

the field of psychology that specialises in mental testing.

■ **psychoneuroimmunology**

the research area that investigates interactions between psychological processes, such as responses to stress, and the functions of the immune system.

■ **psychopathological functioning**

disruptions in emotional, behavioural, or thought processes that lead to personal distress or block one's ability to achieve important goals.

■ **psychopharmacology**

the study of the effects of drugs on behaviour.

■ **psychophysical methods**

procedures used to determine thresholds of sensory modalities.

■ **psychophysics**

a name used by Fechner for the science of the relationship between mental processes and the physical world. Now usually restricted to the study of the sensory consequences of controlled physical stimulation.

■ **psychosexual development**

in Freud's psychoanalytic theory, the idea that development takes place through stages (oral, anal, phallic, latent, genital), each stage characterised by a zone of pleasurable stimulation and appropriate objects of sexual attachment, culminating in adult sexuality.

■ **psychosis**

(pl. psychoses). A severe mental disorder in which thinking and emotion are so impaired that the individual is seriously out of contact with reality. No longer a major diagnostic category in DSM-IV.

■ **psychosocial stages**

a modification by Erikson of the psychoanalytic theory of psychosexual development, giving more attention to the social and environmental problems associated with the various stages of development and adding some adult stages beyond genital maturing.

■ **psychosomatic disorder**

physical illness that has psychological causes (syn. psychophysiological disorder).

■ **psychosurgery**

a surgical procedure performed on brain tissue to alleviate a psychological disorder.

■ **psychotherapy**

treatment of personality maladjustment or mental disorders by

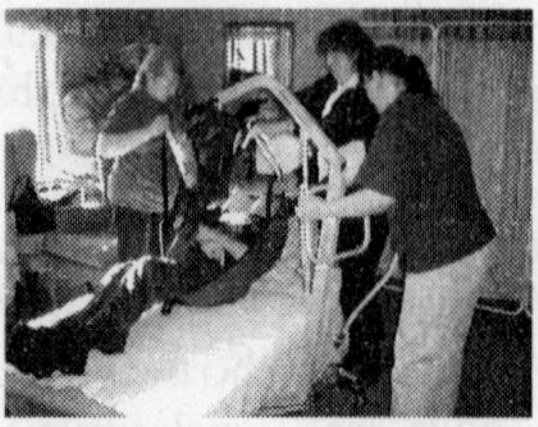

psychological means, usually, but not exclusively, through personal consultation.

psychotic behaviour

behaviour indicating gross impairment in reality contact as evidenced by delusions and/or hallucinations. May result from damage to the brain or from a mental disorder such as schizophrenia or a bipolar disorder.

psychotic disorders

severe mental disorders in which a person experiences impairments in reality testing manifested through thought, emotional, or perceptual difficulties. No longer used as a diagnostic category after DSM-III.

psychotropic medication

prescription medication used primarily to treat mental illness.

ptosis

drooping of a body part, such as the upper eyelid, from paralysis, or the displacement of visceral organs from weakness of abdominal muscles.

puberty

the period during which the reproductive organs become functionally mature. The development of the secondary sex characteristics (particularly the growth and pigmentation of underarm and pubic hair) marks the onset of puberty and the capacity for reproduction, the culmination.

public self-awareness

a psychological state in which one is aware of one's public self-aspects.

public self-consciousness

the tendency to be aware of the publicly displayed aspects of the self.

punisher

any stimulus that, when made contingent upon a response, decreases the probability of that response.

punishment

a procedure used to decrease the strength of a response by presenting an aversive stimulus whenever the response occurs. Note that such a stimulus when applied would be a punisher, when removed, it would act as a negative reinforcer, reinforcing whatever led to its removal.

pupil

in the eye, a circular opening in the iris (the coloured part of the eye) that expands and contracts, varying according to the intensity of light present.

pure alexia

a loss of the ability to recognise words that results from brain damage (in the left occipital lobe).

q sort

an assessment technique by which a rater provides a systematic description of an individual's personality by sorting a set of personality statements (for example, 'Has a wide range of interests') into groups, ranging from those that are least descriptive to those that are most descriptive of the individual.

■ **q. e. d.**

Latin abbreviation of quod erat demonstratum, 'that which was to be proved'. It signals the conclusion of an argument.

■ **qua**

Latin, 'as'.

■ **quadraparesis**

partial loss of function all four extremities of the body.

■ **quadriplegia**

complete paralysis of all four limbs.

■ **qualia**

the qualities of a thing that can be experienced by the direct sensory perception of that thing, for example, the sweetness of a peach, the softness and fuzziness of its skin, are all qualia.

■ **qualities**

see **primary/secondary qualities.**

■ **quasi-experimental research**

any research study that uses specific experimental methods but does not randomise subjects.

■ **quietism**

the theological concept that rejects active involvement in the world in favour of quiet contemplation and passivity.

■ **r**

symbol used for the Pearson-product moment correlation (correlation coefficient)

■ **racism**

discrimination against people based on their skin colour or ethnic heritage.

■ **rage attacks**

violent anger in the form of physical and verbal abuse.

■ **random assignment**

placement of research participants into experimental conditions in a manner which guarantees that all have an equal chance of being exposed to each level of the independent variable.

■ **random sample**

a group of subjects representing the population who are selected through chance.

■ **range**

the difference between the highest and the lowest scores in a set of observations- the simplest measure of variability.

■ **range of motion (rom)**

refers to movement of a joint (important to prevent contractures).

■ **Rank, Otto (1884-1937)**

one of Sigmund Freud's first and most valued pupils. Rank analysed the underlying significance of myths. He later diverged from Freud and emphasised the birth trauma as the central cause of neurosis.

■ **rank-ordered array**

a table consisting of data in order of highest to lowest or lowest to highest where each data is given a numbered rank depicting its difference from the highest or lowest score.

■ **rape myth**

the false belief that deep down, women enjoy forcible sex and find it sexually exciting.

■ **Rapid Eye Movements (REMS)**

eye movements that usually occur during dreaming and that can be measured by attaching small electrodes laterally to and above the subject's eye. These register changes in electrical activity associated with movements of the eyeball in its socket.

■ **rapport**

1. a comfortable relationship between the subject and the tester, ensuring cooperation in replying to test questions.
2. a similar relationship between therapist and patient.
3. a special relationship of hypnotic subject to hypnotist.

■ **rating scale**

a device by which raters can record their judgments of others (or of themselves) on the traits defined by the scale.

■ **ratio scale**

any scale of measurement possessing magnitude, equal intervals, and an absolute zero.

■ **ratio schedules**

in operant conditioning, reinforcement schedules where reinforcement depends on the number of responses the organism makes. On a fixed ratio (FR) schedule, the number of responses required is fixed at a particular value (for example, five responses for a reinforcement). On a variable ratio (VR) schedule, reinforcement occurs only after a certain number of responses, but that number varies unpredictably (for example, sometimes one response, other times ten, but with an average of five).

■ **rational-emotive therapy**

generally briefer than psychoanalysis. Based on the belief that disturbances are caused by 'shoulds' about oneself, others, and the surrounding world, RET is an action-oriented approach that focuses on examining such unconscious assumptions and working to change them. By challenging faulty beliefs with rational thoughts, clients are led to re-order their self-perceptions and decision-making processes.

■ **rationalisation**

a defence mechanism in which self-esteem is maintained by assigning plausible and acceptable reasons for conduct entered on impulsively or for less acceptable reasons.

■ **raw data**

the initial data gathered that has not yet been graphed, organised, or analysed.

■ **reaction formation**

a defence mechanism in which a person denies a disapproved motive through giving strong expressions to its opposite.

■ **reaction time**

the time between the presentation of a stimulus and the occurrence of a response.

■ **reactive interaction**

the interaction between individuals and their environments that arises because different individuals interpret, experience, and react to situations in different ways.

■ **realism**

the opposite of idealism, it is the belief that objects in the physical world have an existence independent of the mind.

■ **realistic conflict theory**

the theory that intergroup conflict develops from competition for limited resources.

■ **reality principle**

in Freud's psychoanalytic theory, the strategy followed by the ego, holding back the impulses of the id until they can be satisfied in socially approved ways.

■ **reality therapy**

emphasises personal responsibility for one's actions, the therapist acts as a coach, helping the client learn how to get desired results in life by changing his or her actions. Reality therapy stresses understanding and accepting the consequences of one's actions as cause and effect.

■ **reason**

the faculty of the mind that has to do with logic, analysis and rationality.

■ **reasoning**

the process of thinking in which conclusions are drawn from a set of facts. Thinking directed toward a given goal or objective.

■ **reasoning, abstract**

mode of thinking in which the individual recognises a phrase that has multiple meanings and selects the meaning most appropriate to a given situation. The term 'abstract' typically refers to concepts not readily apparent from the physical attributes of an object or situation.

■ **reasoning, concrete**

the ability to understand the literal meaning of a phrase.

■ **reasoning, problem-solving**

the ability to analyse information related to a given situation and generate appropriate response options. Problem-solving is a sequential process that typically proceeds as follows: identification of problem, generation of response options, evaluation of response option appropriateness, selection and testing of first option, analysis as to whether solution has been reached. A patient/client may discontinue making a cup of coffee because the sugar bowl is empty, even though sugar is readily available in a nearby cabinet. A patient/client may easily navigate his way into a room crowded with furniture, but request staff assistance to navigate his way out.

■ **reasoning, sequencing**

the ability to organise information or objects according to specified rules, or the ability to arrange information or objects in a logical, progressive manner. Nearly every activity, including work and leisure tasks, requires sequencing. For example, in cooking certain foods, it is important that ingredients be added and mixed in a specified order, in dressing, undergarments must be put on prior to outer garments.

■ **rebirthing**

also known as conscious-connected breathing or vivation. A technique in which the therapist guides clients through breathing exercises to help them re-experience past memories - including birth - and let go of emotional tensions stored in the body.

■ **recall**

a method of retrieval in which an individual is required to reproduce the information previously presented.

■ **receiver-operating-characteristic curve (roc curve)**

the function relating the probability of hits and false alarms for a fixed signal level in a detection task. Factors influencing response bias may cause hits and false alarms to vary, but their variation is constrained to the ROC curve.

■ **recency effect**

in memory experiments, the tendency for the last words in a list to be recalled more readily than other list words.

■ **receptive field**

in vision, a region of the retina that is associated with a specific cortical neuron, when a stimulus appears anywhere in the field, the associated neuron fires.

■ **receptor**

a specialised cell sensitive to particular kinds of stimuli and connected to nerves composed of afferent neurons (such as the retina of the eye). Used more loosely, the organ containing these sensitive portions (such as the eye or the ear).

■ **recessive gene**

a member of a gene pair that determines the characteristic trait or appearance of the individual only in the other member of the pair is recessive. If the other member of the pair is dominant, the effect of the recessive gene is masked.

■ **reciprocal altruism**

the idea that people behave altruistically because they expect that others will perform altruistic behaviour for them in turn.

■ **reciprocal determinism**

a concept of Albert Bandura's sociallearning theory that refers to the notion that a complex reciprocal interaction exists among the individual, his or her behaviour, and environmental stimuli and that each of these components affects the others.

■ **reciprocal helping**

a sociobiological principle stating that people expect that anyone helping another will have that favour returned at some future time. Also know as **reciprocal altruism**.

■ **Reciprocating Gait Orthosis (RGO)**

a type of long leg brace used for ambulation by paralysed people. Uses cables across the back to transfer energy from leg to leg, thereby simulating a more natural gait.

■ **reciprocity norm**

the expectation that one should return a favour or good deed.

■ **recoding**

a process for improving short-term memory by grouping items into a familiar unit or chunk.

■ **recognition**

to recognise something is to associate it correctly with a category, such as 'chair', or with a specific name, such as 'John Jones'. It is a high-level process that requires learning and remembering.

■ **reconstruction**

tendency to fill in the gaps in our memory and often believe these represent true memories.

■ **reconstructive memory**

the process of putting information together based on general types of stored knowledge in the absence of a specific memory representation.

■ **recreation therapist**

individual within the facility responsible for developing a program to assist persons with disabilities plan and manage their leisure activities, may also schedule specific activities and coordinate the program with existing community resources.

■ **red-green colour blindness**

the commonest form of colour blindness, a variety of dichromatism.

■ **reduced stimulation study**

an experimental situation in which sensory stimulation is markedly reduced (syn. sensory deprivation study).

■ **reducible/irreducible**

capable of being broken down into smaller parts and especially in philosophy, by analysis. Irreducible implies that no further breaking down or analysis is possible.

reductio ad absurdum

Latin, 'reduction to absurdity', it is a strategy used to refute an argument by demonstrating that something absurd results from it, so that the premises or inference must be rejected.

reductionism

in psychology, a kind of explanation that tries to explain (or reduce) psychological notions to biological ones.

reference group

any group to which an individual refers for comparing, judging, and deciding on his or her opinions and behaviours. We are said to 'identify' with such groups.

referent power

power given to an individual due to respect and/or desire to be similar to that individual.

reflected appraisal

perception of how others perceive us and evaluate us.

reflection

a therapeutic technique in humanistic therapy where the feelings and thoughts of the client are reflected or reworded back to the client to assist in understanding them.

reflective equilibrium

in John Rawls' theory of justice, equilibrium or balance is obtained when our rock-bottom moral beliefs are weighted against the fundamental principles of justice (assuming some give-and-take must take place in real-world applications), resulting in this state.

reflex

an involuntary response to a stimulus involving nerves not under control of the brain. In some types of paralysis, reflexes cannot be inhibited by the brain and they become exaggerated, thereby causing spasms.

reflux

a return or backflow.

refractory

a nerve or muscle that resists stimulation, or a condition that resists treatment.

refractory period

the period of rest during which a new nerve impulse cannot be activated in a segment of an axon.

refractory phase

the period of temporary inactivity in a neuron after it has fired once.

regeneration

in brain or spinal cord injury, regeneration is the regrowth of nerve fibre tissue by way of some as yet unknown biologic process. In the peripheral system, nerves do regenerate after damage, and reform functional connections. Regeneration researchers are confident central nerves can be induced to grow, provided the proper environment is created. The challenge remains to restore functional connections to effectively restore function.

■ registration

a term to describe receptive processing in which information is processed but not perceived.

■ regression

a return to more primitive or infantile modes of response.

■ regression analysis

used with a correlation to determine a regression equation that predicts or estimates a person's score on one variable if the other is known.

■ rehabilitation

comprehensive program to reduce/overcome deficits following injury or illness, and to assist the individual to attain the optimal level of mental and physical ability.

■ rehabilitation counsellor

also called Vocational Counsellor. A specialist in social and vocational issues who helps the patient develop the skills and aptitudes necessary for return to productive activity and the community.

■ rehabilitation facility

agency of multiple, coordinated services designed to minimise for the individual the disabling effects of one's physical, mental, social, and/or vocational difficulties and to help realise individual potential.

■ rehabilitation nurse

a nurse specialising in rehabilitation techniques as well as basic nursing care. Nurses assist the patient and family in acquiring new information, developing skills, achieving competence and exhibiting behaviours that contribute to the attainment of a healthy state.

■ rehearsal

the conscious repetition of information in short-term memory, usually involving speech. The process facilitates the short-term recall of information and its transfer to long-term memory.

■ reification

the act by which an abstract idea or concept is assumed to be a concrete reality, merely because it has verbal form. Generally, this word is negative and connotes a mistake, as in, "He thought numbers were things he could catch."

■ reincarnation

the belief in rebirth, in other words, that a person has lived before.

■ reinforcement

1. in classical conditioning, the experimental procedure of following the conditioned stimulus by the unconditioned stimulus.
2. in operant conditioning, the analogous procedure of following the occurrence of the operant response by the reinforcing stimulus.

3. the process that increases the strength of conditioning as a result of these arrangements.

■ reinforcement

stimuli offered following a given behaviour that increases the probability that the behaviour will be repeated.

■ reinforcement contingency

a consistent relationship between a response and the changes in the environment that it produces.

■ reinforcement schedule

a well-defined procedure for reinforcing a given response only some proportion of the time it occurs.

■ reinforcer

any stimulus that, when made contingent upon a response, increases the probability of that response.

■ reinforcing stimulus

1. in classical conditioning, the unconditioned stimulus.
2. in operant conditioning, the stimulus that reinforces the operant (typically, a reward) (syn. reinforcer).

■ relative motion parallax

a source of information about depth in which the relative distances of objects from a viewer determine the amount and direction of their relative motion in the retinal image.

■ relative size

in perception, a monocular cue for depth. If an image contains an array of objects of similar shape, the smaller objects are perceived as being farther away.

■ relativism

see both **cultural relativism** and **ethical relativism.**

■ relaxation response

a condition in which muscle tension, cortical activity, heart rate, and blood pressure decrease and breathing slows.

■ relaxation training

training in various techniques for relaxing muscle tension. The procedure is based on Jacobson's progressive relaxation method, in which the person learns how to relax muscle groups one at a time, the assumption being that muscular relaxation is effective in bringing about emotional relaxation.

■ releaser

a term used by ethologists for a stimulus that sets off a cycle of instinctive behaviour.

■ reliability

the self-consistency of a test as a measuring instrument. Reliability is measured by a coefficient of correlation between scores on two halves of a test, alternate forms of the test, or retests with the same test, a high correlation signifies high consistency of scores for the population tested.

■ reliability coefficient

the correlation coefficient is called the reliability coefficient when a correlation is used to determine or estimate reliability.

■ replication

the strength of a research study is only as good as its ability to be replicated. In other words, if a study has significant results but can not be done again, it is difficult to assess whether it was a good study or a result of error.

■ representative ideas (perceptions), theory of

the view that knowledge of the external world through direct sensory experience only represents or copies the real features of objects in the external world. One problem with this view is that the redness of a fire truck may be more in the interaction of the matter of the truck with our eyes than 'in' the truck itself.

■ representative sample

a subset of a population that closely matches the overall characteristics of the population with respect to the distribution of males and females, racial and ethnic groups, and so on.

■ representativeness heuristic

the tendency to judge the category membership of people based on how closely they match the 'typical' or 'average' member of that category.

■ repression

1. a defence mechanism in which an impulse or memory that is distressing or might provoke feelings of guilt is excluded from conscious awareness. See also **defence mechanisms**, **suppression**.
2. a theory of forgetting.

■ res cogitans

Latin, 'a thinking thing', according to Descartes, one of two substances, (the other is res extensa) that are irreducible to anything else and entirely different from each other.

■ res extensa

Latin, 'that which is extended' according to Descartes, the physical world, matter, including the matter of people, their bodies, that which takes up space and is in space. For Descartes, quantifiable stuff subject to the laws of physics and mathematics.

rescorla-wagner model

a model of classical conditioning. It assumes that the amount of conditioning between a conditioned stimulus and an unconditioned stimulus on any trial depends on the predictability of the unconditioned stimulus, the less predictable the unconditioned stimulus, the greater the amount of conditioning.

residential services

assumes a 24-hour residential environment outside the home and includes 24-hour provision of or access to support personnel capable of meeting the client's needs.

residual stress pattern

a chronic syndrome in which the emotional responses of post-traumatic stress persist over time.

resistance

in psychoanalysis, a blocking of free association, a psychological barrier against bringing unconscious impulses to the level of awareness. Resistance is part of the process of maintaining repression.

respite care

a means for taking over the care of a person temporarily (for a few hours to a few days) to provide a period of relief for the primary caregiver.

respondent behaviour

a type of behaviour corresponding to reflex action, in that it is largely under the control of and predictable from the stimulus (syn. elicited behaviour).

response

1. the behavioural result of stimulation in the form of a movement or glandular secretion.
2. sometimes, any activity of the organism, including central responses (such as an image or fantasy) regardless of whether the stimulus is identified and whether identifiable movements occur.
3. products of the organism's activity, such as words typed per minute.

response bias

the systematic tendency as a result of nonsensory factors for an observer to favour responding in a particular way.

response prevention

a therapeutic technique where stimuli is presented to the client but the client is not permitted to exercise his or her typical response. Used for the treatment of phobias, obsessive compulsive disorder and other anxiety disorders.

resting potential

the electrical potential across the nerve cell membrane when it is in its resting state (in other words, not responding to other neurons), the inside of the cell membrane is slightly more negative than the outside.

reticular formation

a system of ill-defined nerve paths and connections within the brain stem, lying outside the well-defined nerve pathways, and important as an arousal mechanism.

■ **retina**

the portion of the eye sensitive to light, containing the rods and the cones.

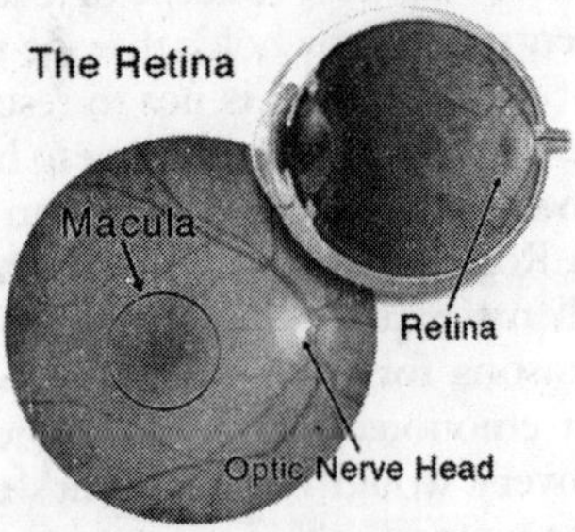

■ **retinal disparity**

1. the displacement between the horizontal positions of corresponding images in the two eyes. 2. the binocular cue to distance referring to the distance between the two images sent to the brain by our eyes. The farther apart these images, the closer the object.

■ **retinal image**

the image projected onto the retina by an object in the visual field.

■ **retinal size**

the size of the retinal image of an object, retinal size decreases in direct proportion to the object's distance.

■ **retribution**

punishment for a misdeed.

■ **retributive justice**

that part of the theory of justice which considers punishment on the basis of just desserts rather than on the basis of deterrence or rehabilitation, based on the idea of compensating for an injury; based on the idea of 'an eye for an eye, a life for a life'.

■ **retrieval**

locating information in memory.

■ **retrieval**

the recovery of stored information from memory.

■ **retrieval cue**

anything that can help you retrieve information from memory.

■ **retroactive interference**

the interference in recall of something earlier learned by something subsequently learned.

■ **retrograde amnesia**

inability to recall events that occurred prior to the accident, may be a specific span of time or type of information.

■ **reuptake**

the process by which a neurotransmitter is 'taken up' again (reabsorbed) by the synaptic terminals from which it had been released.

■ **reversal design**

any single subject design that includes the removal of treatment to determine if the subject reverts to baseline (ex. ABA, ABAB)

■ **reversal theory**

theory that explains human motivation in terms of reversals from one to the other opposing metamotivational states.

reversibility
a child's ability to reverse operations and therefore recognise that the qualities of an object remain the same despite changes in appearance. Occurs in Piaget's Concrete Operational Stage of Cognitive Development (e.g., 1+2=3 to 3-2=1).

reward
a synonym for positive reinforcement.

reward power
power derived through an ability to offer rewards.

right hemisphere
the right cerebral hemisphere. Controls the left side of the body and, for most people, spatial and patterned activities (syn. minor hemisphere).

rights
that which is one's due. There are legal rights, natural rights, human rights, and moral rights in a particular society. Rights are often short-hand for moral rules about how people should get along, for example, the right to a smoke-free workplace is becoming an ethical and legal right in contemporary American society.

ritual healing
ceremonies that infuse special emotional intensity and meaning into the healing process.

rod
in the eye, an element of the retina mediating achromatic sensation only, particularly important in peripheral vision and night vision.

Rogers, Carl
in Rogers' view, people have a basic need to realise their abilities and attain psychological health and well-being. His concept of client-centred therapy holds that the role of the counsellor is not to resolve client's conflicts, but rather to help them become the best they can be. A Rogerian counsellor might help clients explore and discover the reasons for occupational choices or emotional problems. The discovery would be the client's not the counsellor's.

role construct repertory test
a measuring instrument devised by George Kelly for eliciting a person's constructs. Also called the **Rep Test**.

role-playing
a method for teaching attitudes and behaviours important to interpersonal relations by having the subject assume a part in a sponta-

neous play, whether in psychotherapy or in leadership training.

■ **rorschach inkblot test**

a projective technique utilising ambiguous inkblots as stimuli. rubenfeld synergy method gentle touch, movement, verbal exchange, and imagination used to access memories and emotions locked in the body. Integrates elements of the Alexander Technique, Feldenkrais Method, Gestalt and Hypnotherapy. Combines bodywork and psychotherapy. May be used for physical or emotional problems or for personal growth.

■ **rules**

behavioural guidelines for acting in certain ways in certain situations.

■ **rule-utilitarianism**

see **utilitarianism, rule**.

■ **saccade**

the quick movement of the eyes between eye fixations.

■ **sadism**

a pathological motive that leads to inflicting pain on another person.

■ **safety signal hypothesis**

the suggestion that the reason organisms prefer predictable to unpredictable aversive events is because predictability provides a safe period.

■ **sample**

a selection of scores from a total set of scores known as the 'population'. If selection is random, an unbiased sample results, if selection is nonrandom, the sample is biased and unrepresentative.

■ **satiety sensors**

detectors located in different parts of the digestive or thirst systems that signal that the needed nutrients or fluids are on their way and that feeding or drinking can stop.

■ **saturation**

the dimension of colour that describes its purity, if highly saturated, it appears to be pure hue and free of grey, but if of low saturation, it appears to have a great deal of grey mixed with it.

■ **scaling**

converting raw data into types of scores more readily interpreted, such as ranks, centiles, standard scores.

■ **scapegoat**

a form of displaced aggression in which an innocent but helpless victim is blamed or punished as the source of the scapegoater's frustration.

■ **scapegoat theory of prejudice**

the theory that some hostility toward minority groups arises because prejudiced individuals repress their own unacceptable impulses and then express hostile attitudes toward others who are perceived to possess those same impulses. The hostility often takes the form of blaming the group for both personal and societal problems.

■ **scepticism**

schedules of reinforcement in operant conditioning, the patterns of delivering and withholding reinforcement.

■ **schacter-singer theory**

a theory of emotions stating that environmental stimuli lead to general physiological arousal, the individual's cognitive appraisal of the arousal then leads to the subjective experience of a specific emotion.

■ **schedule of reinforcement**

the frequency and/or timing with which reinforcement occurs.

■ **schema**

(pl. schemas). The term refers to cognitive structures stored in memory that are abstract representations of events, objects, and relationships in the real world. It is a key ingredient of cognitive theories of psychological phenomena.

■ **schemas**

organised systems of beliefs about some stimulus object, which are built up from experience and which selectively guide the processing of new information.

■ **schematic processing**

the cognitive process of searching for the schema in memory that is most consistent with the incoming information.

■ **schemes**

Piaget's term for cognitive structures that develop as infants and young children learn to interpret the world and adapt to their environment.

■ **schizoid**

having some characteristics that resemble schizophrenia but are less severe. Occurs with higher frequency in families of schizophrenics and thus tends to support a genetic basis for schizophrenia.

■ **schizophrenia**

a group of mental disorders characterised by major disturbances in thought, perception, emotion, and behaviour. Thinking is illogical and usually includes delusional beliefs, distorted perceptions may take the form of hallucinations, emotions are flat or inappropriate, bizarre behaviour includes unusual postures, stereotyped movements, and 'crazy talk'. The individual withdraws from other people and from reality. Inherited brain or biochemical abnormalities are implicated.

■ **schizophrenic disorder**

severe form of psychopathology characterised by the breakdown of integrated personality functioning, withdrawal from reality, emotional distortions, and disturbed thought processes.

■ **scholasticism**

theological philosophy, based on Aristotle's teachings and the work of Church scholars, taught primarily in medieval times (11th to 16th centuries) in religious training institutions.

■ **school psychologist**

a professional psychologist employed by a school or school system, with responsibility for testing, guidance, research, and so on.

■ **scientific method**

the set of procedures used for gathering and interpreting objective information in a way that

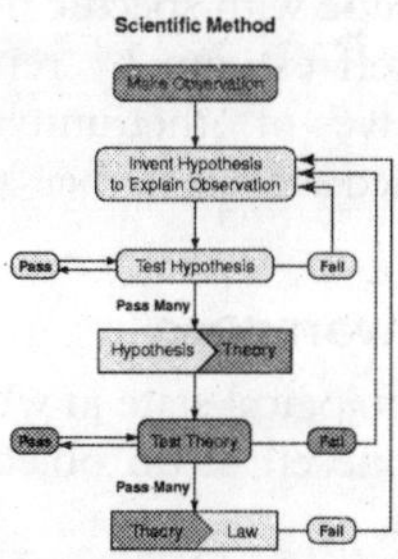

minimises error and yields dependable generalisations.

■ **second order conditioning**

conditioning in which the UCS is not biologically significant (such as food, water, or shock) but gains power as a UCS by being consistently paired with a biologically significant UCS.

■ **secondary qualities**

see **primary/secondary qualities.**

■ **secondary sex characteristics**

the physical features distinguishing the mature male from the mature female, apart from the reproductive organs. In humans, the deeper voice of the male and the growth of the beard are illustrative. See also **primary sex characteristics**.

■ **secure attachment style**

an expectation about social relationships characterised by trust, a lack of concern with being abandoned, and a feeling of being valued and well liked.

■ **seizure**

an uncontrolled discharge of nerve cells which may spread to other cells nearby or throughout the entire brain. It usually lasts only a few minutes. It may be associated with loss of consciousness, loss of bowel and bladder control and tremors. May also cause aggression or other behavioural change.

■ **selective adaptation**

in perception, a loss of sensitivity to motion that occurs when we view motion. The adaptation is selective because we lose sensitivity to the motion viewed, and to similar motions, but not to motion that differs significantly in direction or speed. Presumably the result of fatigued neurons in the cerebral cortex.

■ **selective attention**

the perceptual processes by which we select certain input, but not others, for recognition.

■ **selective breeding**

a method of studying genetic influences by mating animals that display certain traits and selecting for breeding from among their offspring those that express the trait. If the trait is primarily determined by heredity, continued selection for a number of generations will produce a strain that breeds true for that trait.

■ **selective optimisation with compensation**

a strategy for successful ageing in which one makes the most of gains while minimising the impact of losses that accompany normal ageing.

■ **selective social interaction theory**

the view that suggests that, as people age, they become more selective in choosing social partners who satisfy their emotional needs.

■ **self**

a symbol-using individual who can reflect upon his/her own behaviour.

■ **self awareness**

the ability to know and understand one's self.

■ **self concept**

the composite of ideas, feelings and attitudes that a person has about his own identity, worth, capabilities and limitations.

■ **self monitoring**

the ability to regulate, control and keep track of one's self.

■ **self psychology**

an analytic psychotherapy, utilising empathy and interpretation, to promote greater self-cohesion and self-esteem. The approach addresses experiences in the past and present which have been emotionally injurious or enhancing to self-esteem.

■ **self-actualisation**

a person's fundamental tendency toward maximal realisation of his or her potentials, a basic concept in humanistic theories of personality such as those developed by Maslow and Rogers.

■ **self-affirmation theory**

a theory predicting that people will often cope with specific threats to their self-esteem by reminding themselves of other unrelated but cherished aspects of their self-concept.

■ **self-awareness**

a psychological state in which one takes oneself as an object of attention.

■ **self-concept**

the composite of ideas, feelings, and attitudes people have about themselves. For some theorists, self-concept is synonymous with the self.

■ **self-consciousness**

a state of heightened self-awareness, the disposition to be self-attentive.

■ **self-disclosure**

the revealing of personal information about oneself to other people.

■ self-discrepancy theory

a theory that people experience specific negative emotions when they perceive a discrepancy between their self-concept and various self-guides.

■ self-efficacy

the set of beliefs that one can perform adequately in a particular situation.

■ self-efficacy theory

a theory that motivation is determined both by the belief that one is capable of successfully performing some behaviour, and by the belief that performing the behaviour will lead to certain outcomes.

■ self-enhancement

the process of seeking out and interpreting situations so as to attain a positive view of oneself.

■ self-esteem

a person's evaluation of his or her self-concept.

■ self-evaluation maintenance model

a theory predicting under what conditions people are likely to react to the success of others with either pride or jealousy.

■ self-fulfilling prophecy

the process by which someone's expectations about a person or group leads to the fulfillment of those expectations.

■ self-handicapping

actions that people take to sabotage their performance and enhance their opportunity to excuse anticipated failure.

■ self-monitoring

the tendency to use cues from other people's self-presentations in controlling one's own self-presentations.

■ self-perception

the individual's awareness of himself or herself, differs from self-consciousness because it may take the form of objective self-appraisal.

■ self-perception theory

the theory that we often infer our internal states, such as our attitudes, by observing our behaviour.

■ self-perception theory

the theory that attitudes and beliefs are influenced by observations of one's own behaviour, sometimes we judge how we feel by observing how we act.

■ self-promotion

conveying positive information about the self either through one's behaviour or by telling others about one's positive assets and accomplishments.

■ self-regulation

in behaviour therapy, monitoring one's own behaviour and using techniques such as self-reinforcement or controlling stimulus conditions to modify maladaptive behaviour.

■ self-report measures

the self-behaviour that is identified through a participant's own observations and reports.

■ **self-schema**

(pl. self-schemas). A generalisation or theory about oneself derived from past experience. Self-schemata are assumed to influence the way we selectively attend to, process, and recall personally relevant information (syn. self-concept).

■ **self-schemas**

the many beliefs people have about themselves that constitute the 'ingredients' of the self-concept.

■ **self-serving bias**

the tendency to assign an internal locus of causality for our positive outcomes and an external locus for our negative outcomes.

■ **self-verification**

the process of seeking out and interpreting situations so as to confirm one's self-concept

■ **semantic memory**

a type of memory that stores general knowledge, such as the meanings of words. Knowledge is encoded in relation to other knowledge rather than in relation to the memoriser.

■ **semantics**

a branch of semiotics, it studies the meaning of words and the relationship between the symbols of language and the actual world, whereas syntax studies grammar and the relation between kinds of words.

■ **semicircular canals**

three curved tubular canals, in three planes, which form part of the labyrinth of the inner ear and are concerned with equilibrium and motion. See also **equilibratory senses**.

■ **semiotics**

the general study of signs and symbols, including the study of language.

■ **sensation**

the conscious experience associated with a very simple stimulus like the onset of a tone or light. At one time, the distinction between sensation and perception had great theoretical importance with perception viewed as a combination of sensations. Today, the dividing line between sensation and perception is much less clear, and it seems best to view such experiences as lying along a continuum.

■ **sensation**

the process by which stimulation of a sensory receptor gives rise to neural impulses that result in an experience, or awareness of, conditions inside or outside the body.

■ **sense data**

the information provided to us by our senses.

■ **sensitisation**

a simple form of learning in which an organism learns to strengthen its reaction to a weak stimulus if a threatening or painful stimulus follows.

■ **sensorimotor**

refers to all aspects of movement and sensation and the interaction of the two.

■ **sensorimotor stage**

piaget's first stage of cognitive development (birth-2 years) during which the infant discovers relationships between sensations and motor behaviour.

■ **sensory adaptation**

the reduction in sensitivity that occurs with prolonged stimulation and the increase in sensitivity that occurs with lack of stimulation, most noted in vision, smell, taste, and temperature sensitivity.

■ **sensory integration**

interaction of two or more sensory processes in a manner that enhances the adaptiveness of the brain.

■ **sensory memory**

the initial memory processes involved in the momentary preservation of fleeting impressions of sensory stimuli.

■ **sensory modalities**

the individual senses.

■ **sensory neuron**

a neuron, or nerve cell, that conveys messages to the brain or spinal cord from the sense receptors informing the organism about events in the environment or within the body (syn. afferent neuron).

■ **sensory physiology**

the study of the way in which biological mechanisms convert physical events into neural events.

■ **sensory processes**

the subprocesses of the perceptual system that are closely associated with the sense organs. Sensory processes provide selectively filtered information about the stimuli that impinge on us, higher-level processes use this information to form a mental representation of the scene.

■ **sensory receptors**

specialised cells that convert physical signals into cellular signals that are processed by the nervous system.

■ **sensory-neural loss**

a hearing deficit in which threshold elevation (loss of sensitivity) is greater at high rather than low frequencies.

■ **sentience**

the ability to feel pleasure and pain.

■ **septal area**

a portion of the brain deep in the central part, between the lateral ventricles, that appears to yield a state akin to pleasure when stimulated electrically (in a rat, at least).

■ **sequelae**

residual symptoms frequently observed following recovery from a physical condition, treatment or injury.

■ **sequencing**

reading, listening, expressing thoughts, describing events or contracting muscles in an orderly and meaningful manner.

■ **serial memory search**

comparing a test stimulus in sequence to each item in short-term memory. See also **short-term memory**.

■ **serial position effect**

a characteristic of memory retrieval in which the recall of beginning and end items on a list is often better than recall of items appearing in the middle.

■ **serial processes**

two or more mental processes that are carried out in order, one after the other.

■ **serial processing**

a theoretical interpretation of information processing in which several sources of information are processed in a serial order, only one source being attended to at a time.

■ **serotonin**

a neurotransmitter in both the peripheral and central nervous systems. It is an inhibitory transmitter whose actions have been implicated in various processes including sleep, the perception of pain, and mood disorders (depression and manic-depression).

■ **serotonin reuptake inhibitors**

a class of antidepressant drugs that work by increasing levels of the neurotransmitter serotonin in the synapse.

■ **set**

a temporary readiness to perceive or react to a stimulus in a particular way.

■ **set point**

the weight at which an individual's body functions best.

■ **sex**

the biological status of being male or female.

■ **sex chromosomes**

chromosomes that contain the genes that code for the development of male or female characteristics.

■ **sex differences**

biologically based differences between males and females.

■ **sex role**

the full complement of attitudes and behaviours that a society considers appropriate for the individual because of his or her sex.

■ **sex therapy**

a therapeutic approach which focuses on sexual dysfunction, explores sexual history and attitudes, and teaches people new ways to think about and express sexual feelings.

■ **sex typing**

the acquisition of attitudes and behaviours that a society considers appropriate for the individual because of his or her sex. Distinguished from gender identity, which is the degree to which one regards oneself as male or female.

■ **sexism**

any attitude, action or institutional structure that subordinates a person because of his or her sex.

■ **sex-linked trait**

a trait determined by a gene transmitted on the same chromosomes that determine sex, such as red-green colour blindness. See also **X, Y chromosome**.

■ **sexual arousal**

the motivational state of excitement and tension brought about by physiological and cognitive reactions to erotic stimuli.

■ **sexual harassment**

unwelcome physical or verbal sexual overtures that create an intimidating, hostile, or offensive social environment.

■ **sexual orientation**

one's sexual attraction toward members of either one's own sex of the other sex.

■ **sexual orientation**

one's sexual attraction toward members of either one's own sex of the other sex.

■ **shamanism**

a spiritual tradition that involves both healing and gaining contact with the spirit world.

■ **shape constancy**

the tendency to see a familiar object as of the same shape regardless of the viewing angle.

■ **shaping by successive approximations**

a behavioural method that reinforces responses that successively approximate and ultimately match the desired response.

■ **shaping of behaviour**

modifying operant behaviour by reinforcing only those variations in response that deviate in the direction desired by the experimenter.

■ **shearing**

microscopic lesions in the brain caused when the movement of the brain within the skull puts strain on delicate nerve fibres and blood vessels causing them to stretch to the point of breaking.

■ **sheltered workshop**

a work setting certified as such by the Wage & Hour Division. It provides transitional and/or long-term employment in a controlled and protected working environment for those who are unable either to compete or to function in the open job market due to their disabilities. May provide vocational evaluation and work adjustment services.

■ **shock therapy**

extreme procedure used primarily as a last resort when no other methods seem to work. The brain can be likened to an extraordinarily complex electrical circuit board. The shock presumably helps to break up the unhealthy brain circuits that cause mental distress.

■ **short-term memory (STM)**

the component of the memory system has limited capacity and maintains information for only a brief time.

■ **shunt**

a procedure to remove excessive fluid in the brain by surgically-placing a tube that the ventricles into the abdominal cavity, heart or large veins of the neck.

■ **shyness**

an individual's discomfort and/or inhibition in interpersonal situations that interferes with pursuing interpersonal or professional goals.

■ **sibling**

a brother or sister.

■ **signal detection task**

a procedure whereby the subject must judge on each trial whether a weak signal was embedded in a noise background. Saying 'yes' when the signal was presented is called a hit and saying 'yes' when the signal was not presented is called a false alarm.

■ **signal detection theory**

a theory of the sensory and decision processes involved in psychophysical judgments, with special reference to the problem of detecting weak signals in noise.

■ **significant difference**

a difference between experimental groups or conditions that would have occurred by chance less than an accepted criterion. In psychology, the criterion most often used is a probability of less than 5 times out of 100, or $p < .05$.

■ **simple cell**

a cell in the visual cortex that responds to a bar of light or straight edge of a particular orientation and location in the visual field.

■ **simple phobia**

excessive fear of a specific object, animal, or situation in the absence of real danger.

■ **sine wave**

a cyclical wave that when plotted corresponds to the plot of the trigonometric sine function. The sound waves of pure tones yield this function when plotted.

■ **single positron emission computerized tomography (SPECT)**

an imaging technique used to measure blood flow in the brain.

■ **situational anxiety**

a feeling of apprehension, discomfort and dread which is precipitated by a new experience, or a change of situation or events.

■ **situational attribution**

attributing a person's actions to factors in the situation or environment, as opposed to internal attitudes and motives. See also **dispositional attribution**.

■ **situational depression**

an episode of emotional and psychological depression that occurs in response to a specific set of circumstances.

■ **situational variables**

external influences on behaviour.

■ **size constancy**

the tendency to see a familiar object as of its actual size regardless of its distance.

■ **size-distance invariance principle**

the proposal that the perceived size of an object is equal to the product of the retinal size of the object and the perceived distance of the object.

■ **skepticism**

from the Greek skepsis, 'questioning', in its most general use, it refers to a disbelieving and questioning state of mind. As a philosophical principle, it rejects the notion that real knowledge or truth are possible, perhaps because the mind is incapable of finding truth.

■ **Skinner, B.F.**

strong supporter of behaviourism. Advocated the use of controlled, scientific methods in studying human behaviour through a person's response to the environment. His work has influenced modern guidance and counselling. In Skinner's view, all behaviour is controlled by reinforcements - if one is offered a positive stimulus, he will respond in a positive way. From this standpoint, emotional problems are determined by the pattern of reinforcements a young person experiences while growing up. A counsellor working in this tradition

would explore with the client the reinforcements provided by the client's problematic ways of confronting issues in life.

■ **skull**

the bony structure of the head and face.

■ **slave/master morality**

slave morality is a derisive term used by Frederich Nietzsche to illustrate the kind of morality originating in the slave class, and according to Nietzsche, it values submissiveness, benevolence, humility, and patience. Nietzsche considered these qualities weak and likened Christian virtue to slave morality. Nietzsche contrasted this type of morality with master morality seen in the aristocratic, ruling classes, which exemplified pride, moral decisiveness, assertiveness, and affirmation of life.

■ **sleep apnea**

a sleep disorder of the upper respiratory system that causes the person to stop breathing while asleep.

■ **sleeper effect**

the delayed effectiveness of a persuasive message from a noncredible source.

■ **slippery slope argument**

also referred to as the 'camel's nose under the 'tent' and 'wedge' arguments, one of the most famous ideas in ethics and politics, it is often used to oppose any change in society involving medicine or restriction of rights. It envisions a continuous slope, where there is a good reason for taking the first step, but where at the bottom of the slope there is a morally repugnant result. Because it will be very difficult to say why, if we take the first step, the same kind of reasons won't also justify going from the first to second steps, it claims that we shouldn't take the first step. If we do, it says, we will soon end up where we didn't want to be at the start. For example, "If euthanasia is permitted for competent, consenting adults in cases of terminal illness and hopeless pain, before long, doctors will kill patients for lesser illnesses or for those who have not consented."

■ **smooth muscle**

the type of muscle found in the digestive organs, blood vessels, and other internal organs. Controlled via the autonomic nervous system.

■ **social anxiety**

the unpleasant emotion people experience due to their concern with interpersonal evaluation.

■ **social categorisation**

the classification of people into groups based on their common attributes.

■ **social comparison theory**

the theory that proposes that we evaluate our thoughts and actions by comparing them to those of others.

■ **social constructionism**

a perspective in the social sciences that states that individuals creatively shape reality through social interaction.

■ **social contract**

a concept associated with a number of philosophers such as Locke, Hobbes, Hume, Rousseau, and John Rawls, which proposes that humanity's emergence from the savage state of nature to organised, civilised society was accomplished by virtue of a tacit contract among its members and included legal and moral obligations that would ensure the continuation of civilisation.

■ **social dependency**

reliance on someone else for help and support with regard to basic human needs.

■ **social development**

the ways in which individuals' social interactions and expectations change across the life span.

■ **social dilemma**

any situation in which the most rewarding short-term choice for an individual will ultimately cause negative consequences for the group as a whole.

■ **social exchange theory**

the theory that proposes that we seek out and maintain those relationships in which the rewards exceed the costs.

■ **social facilitation**

the phenomenon in which an organism performs responses more rapidly when other members of its species are present.

■ **social identities**

aspects of a person's self-concept based upon his or her group memberships.

■ **social impact theory**

the theory that the amount of social influence others have depends on their number, strength, and immediacy to those they are trying to influence.

■ **social influence**

the exercise of social power by a person or group to change the attitudes or behaviour of others in a particular direction.

■ **social intelligence**

a theory of personality that refers to the expertise people bring to their experience of life tasks.

■ **social isolation**

a feeling of aloneness experienced by the individual as a threatening state imposed by others, a sense of aloneness caused by the absence of family and friends, the absence of a supportive or significant personal relationship caused by the patient's unacceptable social behaviour or social values, the inability to engage in social situations, immature interests, inappropriate attitudes for the developmental age of the individual, alterations in physical appearance, or mental status or illness.

■ **social learning theory**

a theory that proposes that social behaviour is primarily learned by observing and imitating the actions of others, and secondarily by being directly rewarded and punished for our own actions.

■ **social loafing**

group-induced reduction in individual output when performer's efforts are pooled, and thus, cannot be individually judged.

■ **social norms**

a group or community's unwritten rules that govern its members' behaviour, attitudes, and beliefs.

■ **social penetration theory**

a theory that describes the development of close relationships in terms of increasing self-disclosure.

■ **social perception**

the way we seek to know and understand other persons and events.

■ **social phobia**

extreme insecurity in social situations accompanied by an exaggerated fear of embarrassing oneself. See also **phobia, phobic disorder**.

■ **social physique anxiety**

anxiety about others observing and evaluating one's physique.

■ **social power**
the force available to the influencer to motivate attitude or behaviour change.

■ **social psychologist**
a psychologist who studies social interaction and the ways in which individuals influence one another.

■ **social psychology**
the scientific discipline that attempts to understand and explain how the thought, feeling, and behaviour of individuals are influenced by the actual, imagined, or implied presence of others.

■ **social role theory**
the theory that virtually all of the documented behavioural differences between males and females can be accounted for in terms of cultural stereotypes about gender and the resulting social roles that are taught to the young.

■ **social roles**
a cluster of socially defined expectations that individuals in a give situation are expected to fulfil.

■ **social roles**
a cluster of socially defined expectations that individuals in a give situation are expected to fulfil.

■ **social sensitivity**
adaptability to the expectations and standards of a group or society.

■ **social skills training**
a behavioural training program designed to improve interpersonal skills through observation, modelling, role-playing, and behavioural rehearsal.

■ **social support**
resources, including material aid, socio-emotional support, and informational aid, provided by others to help a person cope with stress.

■ **socialisation**
the shaping of individual characteristics and behaviour through the training that the social environment provides.

■ **socialism**
political system that avoids the totalitarian aspects of communism, but which advocates community rather than private ownership of a society's means of production, and the equitable distribution of benefits regardless of wealth or position.

■ **social-learning theory**
the application of learning theory to the problems of personal and social behaviour (syn. social behaviour theory).

■ **social-learning therapy**

a form of treatment in which clients observe models' desirable behaviour being reinforced.

■ **sociobiology**

a scientific discipline concerned with identifying biological and genetic bases for social behaviour in humans and other animals.

■ **Socrates (469-399 B.C.)**

Socrates left no writings, and most of our knowledge of him and his teachings comes from the dialogues of his most famous pupil. He spent his time discussing virtue, justice, and piety, seeking wisdom about right conduct so that he might guide the moral and intellectual improvement of Athens. Using a method now known as the Socratic dialogue, or dialectic, he drew forth knowledge from his students by asking questions and examining the implications of their answers. He equated virtue with knowledge of one's true self, holding that no one knowingly does wrong. He looked upon the soul as the seat of both waking consciousness and moral character, and held the universe to be purposively mind-ordered.

■ **soft determinism**

see determinism.

■ **solipsism**

the view that because there is no adequate bridge from the subjective mind to the external world, the only thing that exists is one's own consciousness and its contents. Generally, a position adopted as a way of forcing people to think about how much they can really prove about the fundamental assumptions they make each day, for example, that other people have minds like their own and that the world really exists when they go to sleep.

■ **soma**

the cell body of a neuron, containing the nucleus and cytoplasm.

■ **somatic nervous system**

a division of the peripheral nervous system consisting of nerves that connect the brain and spinal cord with the sense receptors, muscles, and body surface.

■ **somatosensory**

sensory activity having its origin elsewhere than in the special sense organs (such as eyes and ears) and conveying information to the brain about the state of the body proper and its immediate environment.

■ **somatosensory cortex**

area of the brain that processes incoming signals from the skin, muscles, and bones.

■ **sophism (sophistry)**

the use of arguments which appear to be strong and persuasive, but which are really fallacious in some way. The word comes from the Sophists of ancient Athens, who taught young aristocrats how to speak well to influence the newly-created democracy there. Socrates hated the Sophists, and hence, it is a term of derision.

■ **sophists**

group of transient Greek scholars in the 5th century B. C. who taught argument for the sake of winning to students and who themselves charged money to such students for doing so. Socrates and Plato regarded them as charlatans for their policy of charging a fee for their teachings and because they taught manipulation and persuasion rather than the pursuit of the truth.

■ **sorties**

also known as 'paradox of the heap', for example, one drop of water does not make an ocean, adding another drop also won't make an ocean. By this line of reasoning, we can never get an ocean or (if grains of sand) a heap.

■ **soul**

the living but immaterial thing that animates one's consciousness, maintains (some think even before birth) an identity throughout life, and (some think) survives beyond death.

■ **sound argument**

a valid deductive argument whose conclusion follows logically from its premises, and whose premises are all true.

■ **space boots**

plastic boots worn on the feet to prevent flaccidity.

■ **spasticity**

an involuntary increase in muscle tone (tension) that occurs following injury to the brain or spinal cord, causing the muscles to resist being moved. Characteristics may include increase in deep tendon reflexes, resistance to passive stretch, clasp knife phenomenon, and clonus.

■ **spatial ability**

ability to perceive the construction of an object in both two and three dimensions. Spatial ability has four components: the ability to perceive a static figure in different positions, the ability to interpret and duplicate the movements between various parts of a figure, the ability to perceive the relationship between an object and a person's own body sphere, and the ability to interpret the person's body as an object in space.

■ **spatial frequency**

in perception, the distance between successive dark bars in a grating consisting of alternating dark and light bars. Spatial frequency is a determinant of visual resolution.

■ **spatial localisation**

the perceptual process of determining where in the visual field an object is.

spatial resolution

the ability to see spatial patterns. Visual actuity and the contrast threshold are measures of spatial resolution.

speaker's intention

the speaker's goal in uttering a particular sentence, which is distinct from the actual content of the sentence.

specific hunger

hunger for a specific food incentive, such as a craving for sweets.

specific phobias

phobias that occur in response to specific types of objects or situations.

speech-language pathology services

a continuum of services including prevention, identification, diagnosis, consultation, and treatment of patients regarding speech, language, oral and pharyngeal sensorimotor function.

sphincteronomy

the cutting of the bladder sphincter muscle to eliminate spasticity and related voiding problems. A non-surgical sphincterotomy uses a chemical block to inactivate transmitter-release between sphincter nerve and muscle, gradually stopping contractions, it is also reversible.

spinal shock

similar to a concussion in the brain, spinal shock causes the system to shut down. In spinal cord injury, shock causes immediate flaccid paralysis, which lasts about three or four weeks. Improvement then occurs to a great extent, due to several possibilities: restoration of blood flow, synaptic reconnection, restoration of myelin integrity and axonal connection.

spindle

an EEG characteristic of Stage 2 sleep, consisting of short bursts of rhythmical responses of 13-16 Hz, slightly higher than alpha.

spiritual

presupposes that human beings have an inner spirit, which through various practices may be aligned with a higher power, however that is defined.

split-brain subject

a person who has had an operation that severed the corpus callosum, thus separating the functions of the two cerebral hemispheres.

spontaneous recovery

the recovery which occurs as damage to body tissues heals. This type of recovery occurs with or without rehabilitation and it is very difficult to know how much improvement is spontaneous and how much is due to rehabilitative interventions. However, when the recovery is guided by an experienced rehabilitation team, complications can be anticipated and minimised, the return of function can be channelled in useful directions and in progressive steps so that the eventual outcome is the best that is possible.

spontaneous-remission effect
the improvement of some mental patients and clients in psychotherapy without any professional intervention, a baseline criterion against which the effectiveness of therapies must be assessed.

sports psychology
the study of human behaviour in sport. The goal of much of the work is to help athletes develop psychological skills that maximise performance and enhance the sport experience. For example, hypnosis and biofeedback have been used to control an athlete's anxiety level during competition and mental imagery has been employed to help perfect the synchrony and flow of certain body movements.

spreading activation
a proposed model of retrieval from long-term memory in which activation subdivides among paths emanating from an activated mental representation.

spurious association
a plausible but nonexistent relation between two stimuli. Human learners frequently report such relations when trying to learn less-than-perfect relations.

stabilised retinal image
the image of an object on the retina when special techniques are used to counteract the minute movements of the eyeball that occur in normal vision. When an image is thus stabilised it quickly disappears, suggesting that the changes in stimulation of retinal cells provided by the eye movements are necessary for vision.

stages of development
developmental periods, usually following a progressive sequence, that appear to represent qualitative changes in either the structure or the function of the organism (such as Freud's psychosexual stages, Piaget's cognitive stages).

standard deviation
the square root of the mean of the squares of the amount by which each case departs from the mean of all the cases (syn. root mean square deviation).

standardisation
a set of uniform procedures for treating each participant in a test, interview, or experiment or for recording data.

state of nature
the human condition outside of organised society or civilisation. Philosophers have disagreed on the description of such a state. Some like Hobbes view it as "solitary, poor, nasty, brutish, and short" where each person is in a "war against all", others like Rousseau see nobility in such a state, positing "noble savages" uncorrupted by private property, schooling, and the artifices of civilised society.

state-dependent learning
learning that occurs during a particular biological state such as when drugged so that it can best

be demonstrated or is most effective when the person is put in the same state again.

■ statistical significance

the trustworthiness of an obtained statistical measure as a statement about reality, for example, the probability that the population mean falls within the limits determined from a sample. The expression refers to the reliability of the statistical finding and not to its importance.

■ statistics

the discipline that deals with sampling data from a population of individuals, and then drawing inferences about the population from the sample.

■ stereoscopic vision

1. the binocular perception of depth and distance of an object owing to the overlapping fields of the two eyes.
2. the equivalent effect when slightly unlike pictures are presented individually to each eye in a stereoscope.

■ stereotype

a schema of the personality traits or physical attributes of a class or group of people. The schema is usually an overgeneralisation, leading us to assume that every member of the group possesses the particular characteristic, for instance the false stereotype that all homosexual males are effeminate.

■ stereotype threat

the threat associated with being at risk for confirming a negative stereotype of one's group.

■ stereotype vulnerability

a disturbing awareness among members of a negatively stereotyped group that anything one does, or anything about oneself that fits the stereotype, may confirm it as a self-characterisation.

■ stereotypes

generalisations about a group of people in which the same characteristics are assigned to all members of a group.

■ steroids

complex chemical substances, some of which are prominent in the secretions of the adrenal cortex and may be related to some forms of mental illness.

■ stigma

an attribute that serves to discredit a person in the eyes of others.

■ stimulants

psychoactive drugs that increase arousal. Amphetamines, cocaine, and caffeine are examples.

■ stimulation-produced analgesia

an analgesic effect produced by the stimulation of a region of the midbrain.

■ stimulus

an internal or external event which generates nervous system activity or response.

■ stimulus discrimination

a conditioning process in which an organism learns to respond differently to stimuli that differ from the conditioned stimulus on some dimension.

■ **stimulus generalisation**

the automatic extension of conditioned responding to similar stimuli that have never been paired with the unconditioned stimulus.

■ **stimulus-driven capture**

a determinant of why people select some parts of sensory input for further processing. It occurs when features of stimuli—objects in the environment—automatically capture attention, independent of the local goals of a perceiver.

■ **stimulus-response (s-r) psychology**

a psychological view that all behaviour is in response to stimuli and that the appropriate tasks of psychological science are those identifying stimuli, the responses correlated with them, and the processes intervening between stimulus and response.

■ **stoicism, stoic**

school of philosophy founded by Zeno around 300 BC in ancient Greece, it views the world as a divinely organised whole in which all things eventually happen for the best. Therefore, the wise and ethical man should be resigned and accept the inevitability of the universe.

■ **storage**

the retention of encoded material over time.

■ **strabismus**

in vision, a lack of binocular depth perception caused by a person's eyes not pointing in the same direction early in life.

■ **strategic self-presentation**

conscious and deliberate efforts to shape other people's impressions in order to gain power, influence, sympathy or approval.

■ **straw-man argument**

an argument that unfairly interprets the opposing position as so weak and untenable that the power of the opposing position is lost and difficult to support; attacking a position easy to refute rather than the real, complex position of an opponent.

■ **stress**

a state that occurs when people encounter events that they perceive as endangering their physical or psychological well-being.

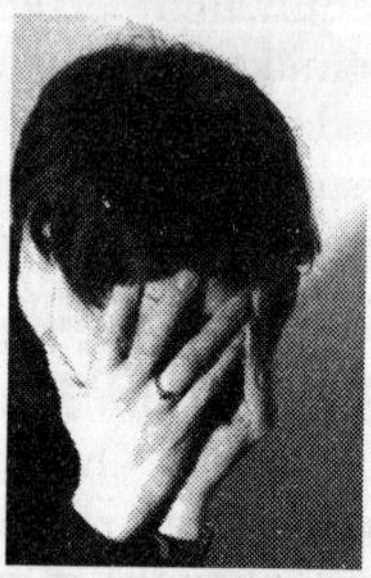

■ **stress management**

a cognitive behavioural approach that teaches people to handle stressful situations by understanding their own stressors and coping skills to find appropriate responses.

■ stress moderator variables
variables that change the impact of a stressor on a given type of stress reaction.

■ stress responses
reactions to events an individual perceives as endangering his or her well-being. These may include bodily changes that prepare for emergency (the fight-or-flight response) as well as such psychological reactions as anxiety, anger and aggression, apathy and depression, and cognitive impairment.

■ stressors
events that an individual perceives as endangering his or her physical or psychological well-being.

■ striate muscle
striped muscle, the characteristic muscles controlling the skeleton, as in the arms and legs. Activated by the somatic, as opposed to the autonomic, nervous system.

■ stroboscopic motion
an illusion of motion resulting from the successive presentation of discrete stimulus patterns arranged in a progression corresponding to movement, such as motion pictures.

■ structuralism
the study of the structure of mind and behaviour. The view that all human mental experience can be understood as a combination of simple elements or events.

■ sub specie aeternitatis
Latin, loosely 'from the viewpoint of the Eternal', closely associated with Spinoza.

■ subacute care
may follow a period of acute rehabilitation, not necessarily hospital based, typical length of rehabilitation stay 6-24 months (short to intermediate term), stay based on demonstrated improvement, identifiable team and program with specialised unit.

■ subcortical
the region beneath the cerbral cortex.

■ subculture
a social group exhibiting a lifestyle sufficiently different to distinguish itself from others within the larger culture.

■ subdural
beneath the dura, a tough membrane that covers the brain and spinal cord.

■ subjective
a personal point of view, and hence, a possibly odd position, contrasts with objective.

■ subjective idealism
see **idealism**.

■ subjectivism
the belief that the answer to what is right and wrong is held by each individual's personal beliefs, and that moral decisions are made by consulting one's own conscience.

■ subliminal perception
the processing of information which is below one's threshold of conscious awareness.

■ **subluxation**

complete or partial dislocation of a joint.

■ **substance**

that which can exist independently of all else, something that is not a quality or predicate but more fundamental, something that has an unchangeable essence, contains properties, and exists independently in reality.

■ **substance p**

a protein that stimulates nerve endings at the site of an injury, enhancing the awareness of pain.

■ **subtractive mixture**

colour mixture in which the results differ from additive mixture obtained by mixing projected lights. Subtractive mixture occurs when transparent coloured filters are placed one in front of the other and when pigments are mixed.

■ **sufficient condition**

see **necessary/sufficient condition.**

■ **sufficient reason, principle of**

a term associated with Gottfried Leibniz, it is the belief that nothing exists without a reason.

■ **sui generis**

Latin, 'of its own kind', unique.

■ **Sullivan, Harry Stack (1892-1949)**

believed that psychoanalysis needs to be supplemented by studying the impact of cultural forces on personality. Contributed to the understanding of schizophrenia and obsessional states.

■ **summum bonum**

Latin, 'the greatest good'.

■ **superego**

in Freud's tripartite division of the personality, the part that represents the internalisation of the values and morals of society, the conscience that controls the expression of the id's impulses through moral scruples.

■ **supererogatory actions**

over and beyond what is required by morality, deeds of extraordinary goodness that are saint-like.

■ **superordinate goal**

a mutually shared goal that can be achieved only through intergroup cooperation.

■ **superposition**

in perception, a monocular cue for depth. If an object has contours that cut through those of another, obstructing the other object's view, the overlapping object is perceived as being nearer.

■ **supervenience**

a one-to-one dependence between things at two different levels, such that one cannot have a list of things at one level, A, and not have the corresponding list of things at level B. Used in philosophy of mind to explain how mental states can depend on brain states and yet have different qualia.

■ supervised living

setting is a home which is like other homes in the neighbourhood in terms of size and number of residents. Consumers are provided individualised care, supervision, support and training services to maximise and/or maintain function and self-direction. Staff is present at night and other times when the consumer is present.

■ supine

lying on one's back.

■ supplication

advertising one's weaknesses or one's dependence upon others in order to solicit help or sympathy.

■ supported independent living

setting is a home chosen by the consumer who is primarily independent. Program offers support to assist the resident in maximising and/or maintaining independence and self-direction. Staff is available as needed and at planned intervals to offer assistance and support but not to provide supervision.

■ suppository

medicine contained in a capsule which is inserted into the rectum so that the medicine can be absorbed into the blood stream.

■ suppression

a process of self-control in which impulses, tendencies to action, and wishes to perform disapproved acts are in awareness but not overtly revealed.

■ survey method

a method of obtaining information by questioning a large sample of people.

■ syllogism

classical style of deductive argument that contains two premises and a conclusion. For example: all cats are felines, all felines are mammals, therefore all cats are mammals.

■ syllogism, disjunctive

a syllogism where one of the premises is a disjunctive statement. For example: to graduate, Mary must choose physics or advanced biology, she did not choose physics, therefore she chose advanced biology.

■ symbol

anything that stands for or refers to something other than itself.

■ symbolic interaction theory

a contemporary sociological theory, inspired by Mead's insights and based on the premise that the self and social reality emerge due to the meaningful communication among people.

■ **symbols**

arbitrary signs of objects that stand in the place of those objects.

■ **sympathetic division**

the subdivision of the autonomic nervous system that deals with emergency response and the mobilisation of energy.

■ **Sympathetic Nervous System (SNS)**

a branch of the ANS (autonomic nervous system) responsible for mobilizing the body's energy when stressed or aroused.

■ **sympathetic system**

a division of the autonomic nervous system, characterised by a chain of ganglia on either side of the spinal cord, with nerve fibres originating in the thoracic and lumbar portions of the spinal cord. Active in emotional excitement and to some extent antagonistic to the parasympathetic division.

■ **synapse**

the specialised junction between a neuron and another neuron or muscle cell for transfer of information such as brain signals, sensory inputs, etc., along the nervous system. One neuron may have many synapses with other neurons. As an impulse travelling along a nerve fibres arrives at the pre-synaptic area, it releases a neurotransmitter. The transmitter travels across the synapse and binds with a receptor on the post-synaptic membrane of the other cell.

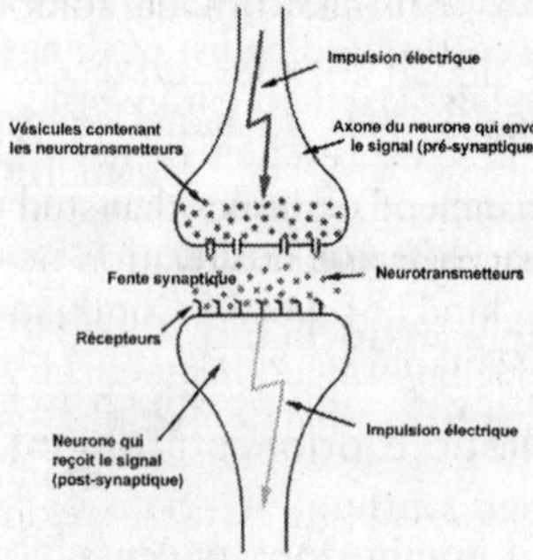

■ **synaptic gap**

the space between the presynaptic cell membrane and the postsynaptic cell membrane, the space across a synapse.

■ **synaptic terminals**

small swellings at the end of axon branches that enclose synaptic vesicles containing neurotransmitters.

■ **synaptic transmission**

the relaying of information from one neuron to another across the synaptic gap.

■ **synaptic vesicles**

small spherical or irregularly shaped structures within a synaptic terminal that contain neurotransmitters, when stimulated, they discharge the neurotransmitters.

■ **syncope**

fainting.

■ **syntactic analysis**

in language, an analysis that divides a sentence into noun phrases and verb phrases, and then divides these phrases into smaller units like nouns, adjectives, and verbs.

■ syntax

the branch of semiotics that studies grammar and the relation between kinds of words. Contrasts with semantics.

■ synthetic a priori statement

a truth about the natural world that can be known through reason alone, independent of sensory experience.

■ system (ANS)

the part of the nervous system that controls involuntary activities, including heart muscle, glands, and smooth muscle tissue. The autonomic nervous system is subdivided into the sympathetic and parasympathetic systems. Sympathetic activities are marked by the flight or fight emergency response, initiated by way of the transmitter norepinephrine (adrenaline). Parasympathetic activities are known by lowered blood pressure, pupil contradiction and slowing of the heart.

■ systematic desensitisation

a behaviour therapy technique in which hierarchies of anxiety-producing situations are imagined (or sometimes confronted in reality) while the person is in a state of deep relaxation. Gradually the situations become dissociated from the anxiety response.

■ systematic reinforcement

a method for modifying behaviour by reinforcing desirable responses (with praise or tangible rewards) and ignoring undesirable ones. Used in behaviour therapy.

■ tabula rasa

latin, meaning 'blank slate'. The term refers to the view that human beings are born without any innate knowledge or ideas, all knowledge is acquired through learning and experience. Proposed by the 17th- and 18th-century British empiricists (Locke, Hume, Berkeley, Hartley).

■ tachistoscope

an instrument for the brief exposure of words, symbols, pictures, or other visually presented material, sometimes called a T-scope.

■ tactile defensiveness

being overly sensitive to touch, withdrawing, crying, yelling or striking when one is touched.

■ task analysis

breakdown of a particular job into its component parts, information gained from task analysis can be utilized to develop training curricula or to price a product or service.

■ **taste buds**

receptors for taste located in clusters on the tongue and around the mouth.

■ **taste-aversion learning**

a biological constraint on learning in which an organism learns in one trial to avoid a food whose ingestion is followed by illness.

■ **tautology**

a statement that is necessarily true by virtue of logic, and which says nothing because it provides no information. For example, the statement, 'She is either dead or she is alive' is a tautology.

■ **t-cell (thymus-dependent cell)**

a type of lymphocyte that recognises and destroys foreign antigens (enzymes, toxins, or other substances) and thus plays an important role in the body's immune response.

■ **telegraphic speech**

a stage in the development of speech in which the child preserves only the most meaningful and perceptually salient elements of adult speech. The child tends to omit prepositions, articles, prefixes, suffixes, and auxiliary words.

■ **teleological argument**

see design argument.

■ **teleological ethics**

see consequentialism.

■ **teleology**

the study of the purpose or goal of all things.

■ **telepathy**

thought transference from one person to another without the mediation of any known channel of sensory communication (for example, identifying a playing card merely being thought of by another person).

■ **telos**

Greek, 'end, or final purpose'.

■ **temperament**

an individual's characteristic mood, sensitivity to stimulation, and energy level. Temperament is usually conceptualised as a genetic predisposition because striking differences in reactivity to stimulation, general mood, and activity level can be observed in newborns.

■ **temperature regulation**

the process by which an organism keeps its body temperature relatively constant.

■ **temporal lobes**

there are two temporal lobes, one on each side of the brain located at about the level of the ears. These lobes allow a person to tell one smell from another and one sound from another. They also help in sorting new information and are believed to be responsible for short-term memory. The right lobe predominately is involved with visual memory (i.e., memory for pictures and faces), and the left lobe delegates verbal memory (i.e., memory for words and names).

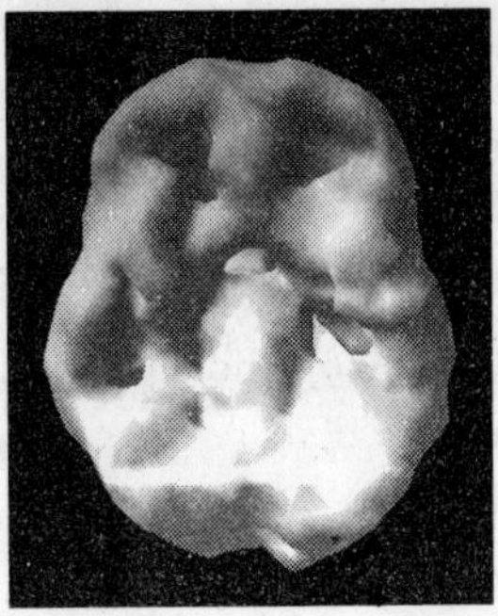

■ **temporal theory of pitch**

a theory of pitch perception which assumes that the frequency of neural impulses travelling up the auditory nerve correspond to the frequency of a tone.

■ **tend-and-befriend response**

a response to stressors that is hypothesised to be typical for females. Stressors prompt females to protect their offspring and join social groups to reduce vulnerability.

■ **tendon lengthening**

a procedure, usually involving the Achilles tendon, to treat contractures caused by spasms.

■ **tenodesis (hand splint)**

metal or plastic support for hand, wrist and/or fingers. Used to facilitate grater function to a disabled hand by transferring wrist extension into grip and finger control.

■ **terminal buttons**

the bulblike structures at the branched endings of axons that contain vesicles filled with neurotransmitters.

■ **test battery**

a collection of tests whose composite scores are used to appraise individual differences.

■ **test profile**

a chart plotting scores from a number of tests given to the same individual (or group of individuals) in parallel rows on a common scale, with the scores connected by lines, so that high and low scores can be readily perceived.

■ **testosterone**

a kind of androgen that is responsible during puberty for the sudden growth of facial, underarm, and pubic hair, it also causes a

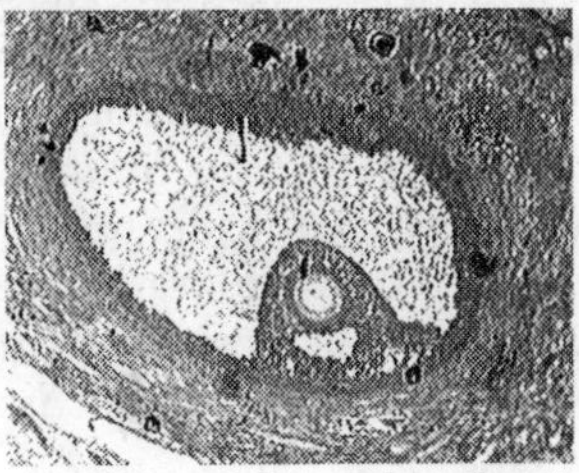

deepening of the voice, the development of muscles that lead to a more masculine form, and the growth of the external genitals.

■ **test-retest reliability**

the consistency of a test when given over successive occasions to the same person (syn. temporal stability).

■ **texture gradient**

a cue for perceiving depth directly. When viewing a surface in perspective, the elements that make up the surface appear to be packed closer and closer together, giving an impression of depth.

■ **thalamus**

an area of the brain that relays impulses along the sensory pathway.

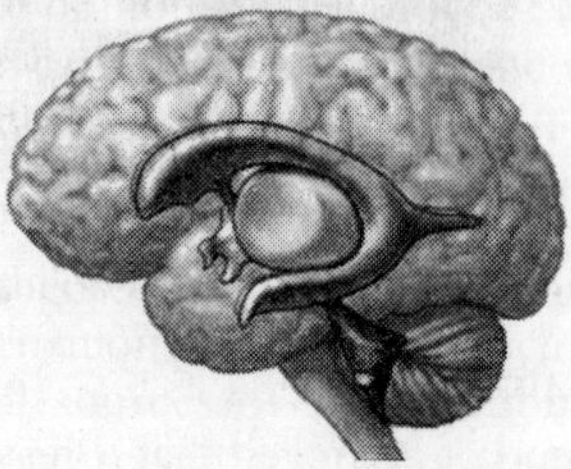

■ **thalamus**

two groups of nerve cell nuclei located just above the brain stem and inside the cerebral hemispheres. Considered a part of the central core of the brain. One area acts as a sensory relay station, the other plays a role in sleep and waking, this portion is considered part of the limbic system.

■ **that's-not-all strategy**

a two-step compliance technique in which the influencer makes a large request, then immediately offers a discount or bonus before the initial request is refused.

■ **the standard deviation**

the true standard deviation of the population often estimated by using the sample standard deviation.

■ **theism, theist**

the belief that a personal God exists who is involved in human affairs. A theist is one who believes in theism.

■ **Thematic Apperception Test (TAT)**

a projective test in which pictures of ambiguous scenes are presented to an individual, who is encouraged to generate stories about them.

■ **theodicy**

from ancient Greek, 'theo' (God) and 'dike' (justice); a branch of theology which attempts to defend the existence of an omnipotent and benevolent God, given the existence of evil and suffering in the world. It is an effort to reconcile the existence of evil with the existence of a good God. See also **evil, problem of.**

■ **theory**

a set of assumptions advanced to explain existing data and predict new events, usually applicable to a wide array of phenomena.

■ **theory of ecological optics**

a theory of perception that emphasises the richness of stimulus information and views the perceiver as an active explorer of the environment.

■ **theory of planned behaviour**

the theory that people's conscious decisions to engage in specific actions are determined by their attitudes toward the behaviour in question, the relevant subjective norms, and their perceived behavioural control.

Theory of Planned Behaviour

The theory has been found to predict:

condom use
sunbathing and sunscreen use
use of oral contraceptives
breast self-examination
mammography participation
testicular self-examination
exercise
mother's restriction of children's sugar intake
participation in cancer screening programmes
AIDS risk-related behaviours
Amount of sleep
Taking vitamins
Health care provider behaviour

■ theory of psychological reactance

the theory that people believe they possess specific behavioural freedoms, and that they will react against and resent attempts to limit this sense of freedom.

■ therapy

treatment and care of someone to combat disease, injury, or mental disorder.

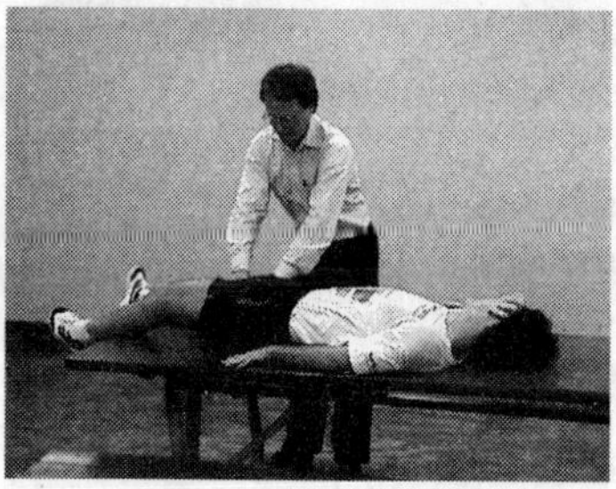

■ think-aloud protocols

reports made by experimental participants of the mental processes and strategies they use while working on a task.

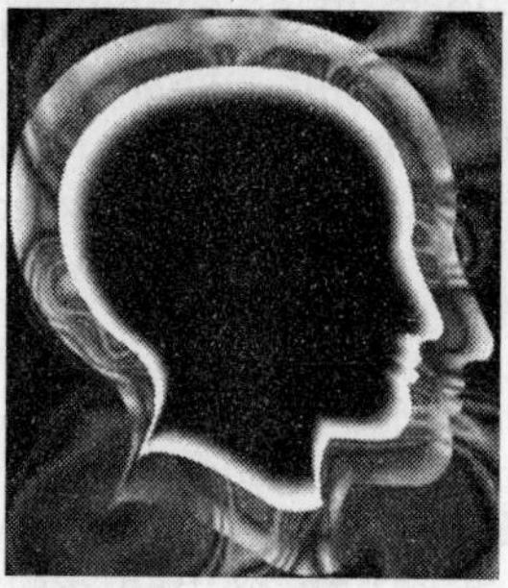

■ thinking

the ability to imagine or represent objects or events in memory and to operate on these representations.

■ Thomism

the philosophy of Thomas Aquinas.

■ thoracic

pertaining to the chest, vertebrae or spinal cord segments between the cervical and lumbar areas.

■ threat-to-self-esteem model

a theory stating that if receiving help contains negative self-messages, recipients are likely to feel threatened and respond negatively.

■ three primaries law

a basic law about colour vision. Three wavelengths of light can be combined to match almost any colour of light, as long as one light is drawn from the long-wave end of the spectrum, another light is drawn from the middle, and the third light is drawn from the short end.

■ **three-term contingency**

the means by which organisms learn that, in the presence of some stimuli but not others, their behaviour is likely to have a particular effect on the environment.

■ **threshold**

the transitional point at which an increasing stimulus or an increasing difference not previously perceived becomes perceptible (or at which a decreasing stimulus or previously perceived difference becomes imperceptible). The value obtained depends in part on the methods used in determining it.

■ **thrombophlebitis**

a clot in a vein due to diminished blood flow which can occur in a paralysed leg. Symptoms include swelling and redness.

■ **thyroid gland**

an endocrine gland located in the neck, whose hormone thyroxin is important in determining metabolic rate.

■ **tic**

an involuntary muscle spasm.

■ **tilt table**

a motorised table which is used to gradually increase patients tolerance to being in a standing position. Also used to teach partial weight bearing and to give prolonged stretch in each position.

■ **timbre**

the quality distinguishing a tone of a given pitch sounded by one instrument from that sounded by another. The differences are due to overtones and other impurities.

■ **tip-of-the-tongue phenomenon**

the experience of failing to recall a word or a name when we are quite certain we know it.

■ **token/type distinction**

types are kinds and tokens are examples or instances of types. There are thousands of types of mammals (defined as species), and millions of tokens of these types.

■ **tolerance**

the need to take more and more of a drug to achieve the same effect. An important factor in drug dependence.

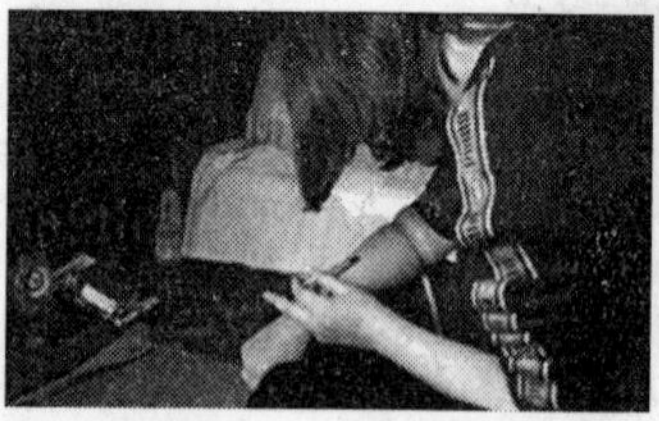

■ **tonic pain**

the kind of steady, long-lasting pain experienced after an injury has occurred, usually produced by swelling and tissue damage. In contrast to phasic pain.

■ **top-down processes**

processes in perception, learning, memory, and comprehension that are driven by the organism's prior knowledge and expectations, rather than by the input.

topographic model
freud's model of the human mind, containing the conscious, preconscious, and the unconscious.

trace conditioning
a classical conditioning procedure in which the CS terminates before the onset of the UCS.

tracheostomy
a temporary surgical opening at the front of the throat providing access to the trachea or windpipe to assist in breathing.

tracking, visual
visually following an object as it moves through space.

trait
a relatively stable way in which individuals differ from one another.

tranquilliser
a drug that reduces anxiety and agitation.

transactional analysis
focuses on an individual's interactions ('transactions') with others, analyses them for insight into the client. The goal is to help clients respond more consciously and intentionally to situations and people.

transactive memory
a collectively shared memory system for encoding, storing, and retrieving information that is greater than any individual memories.

transcendence
the state of being outside ordinary experience or understanding.

transducer
a device such as an electrode or gauge that, in psychophysiology, converts physiological indicators into other forms of energy that can be recorded and measured.

transduction
the translation of a physical energy into electrical signals by specialised receptor cells.

transfer-appropriate processing
the perspective that suggests that memory is best when the type of processing carried out at encoding matches the processes carried out at retrieval.

transference
in psychoanalysis, the patient's unconsciously making the therapist the object of emotional response, transferring to the therapist responses appropriate to other persons important in the patient's life history.

transformational leader
a leader who changes (transforms) the outlook and behaviour of followers (also referred to as a charismatic leader).

transitional living
non-medical residential program providing training for living in a setting of greater independence. The primary focus is on teaching functional skills and compen-

sating for abilities that cannot be restored.

■ **transpersonal**

emphasises spiritual growth. Eastern philosophy often informs this discipline.

■ **transsexual**

an individual who is physically one sex but psychologically the other. Transsexuals sometimes resort to surgery and hormonal treatment to change their physical appearance. They do not, however, consider themselves to be homosexual.

■ **transtheoretical**

uses a combination of orientations and techniques, 'tailoring' therapeutic method to the client.

■ **transvaluation of values**

term originated by Nietzsche, it describes the process by which the values attributed to egoism (considered evil), and selflessness (considered good) would be reversed, therefore celebrating egoism and condemning selflessness.

■ **treatment group**

experimental participants who are exposed to nonzero levels of the independent variable.

■ **tremor, intention**

course, rhythmical movements of a body part that become intensified the harder one tries to control them.

■ **tremor, resting**

rhythmical movements present at rest and may be diminished during voluntary movement.

■ **trichromatic theory**

a theory of colour perception that postulates three basic colour receptors (cones), a 'red' receptor, a 'green' receptor, and a 'blue' receptor. The theory explains colour blindness by the absence of one or more receptor types (syn. Young-Helmholtz theory).

■ **trichromatism**

normal colour vision, based on the classification of colour vision according to three colour systems: black-white, blue-yellow, and red-green. The normal eye sees all three, the colour-blind eye is defective in one or two of the three systems.

■ **tricyclic antidepressant**

a class of antidepressants that relieve the symptoms of depression by preventing the reuptake of the neurotransmitters serotonin and norepinephrine, thereby prolonging their action. Imipramine (brand names, Tofranil and Elavil) is one drug commonly prescribed.

■ **trigeminal nerve**

a nerve that delivers sensory impulses to the brain from the teeth, tongue and face.

■ **truth**

a condition in which a statement accurately reflects the world. Truth refers to statements, validity to arguments. In other words, truth refers to content and validity to good form in arguments. An argument may have good form, like a bottle of wine, but have false premises (bad wine).

■ **Turing machine**

a machine designed by Alan Turing in the mid-twentieth century to simulate human cognition.

■ **two-factor theory of emotions**

a theory that emotional experience is based on two factors: physiological arousal and cognitive labelling of the cause of that arousal.

■ **two-point threshold**

a kind of pressure threshold, it is the minimum distance by which two thin rods touching the skin must be separated before they are felt as two points rather than one.

■ **two-stage colour theory**

a theory of colour vision that postulates three types of cones (in agreement with trichromatic theory) followed by red-green and yellow-blue opponent processes (in agreement with opponent-colour theory). This theory accounts for much of what is known about colour vision, and serves as a prototype for the analysis of other sensory systems. See also opponent-colour theory, trichromatic theory.

■ **type a and type b**

two contrasting behaviour patterns found in studies of coronary heart disease. Type A people are rushed, competitive, aggressive, and overcommitted to achieving, type Bs are more relaxed and feel less pressure. Type As are at risk for heart disease.

■ **type a behaviour pattern**

a complex pattern of behaviour and emotions that includes excessive emphasis on competition, aggression, impatience, and hostility. Hostility increases the risk of coronary heart disease.

■ **type A personality**

characterised by impatience, concern with time, punctuality, anger, perfectionism.

■ **type B behaviour pattern**

as compared to Type A behaviour pattern, a less competitive, less aggressive, less hostile pattern of behaviour and emotion.

■ **type B personality**

personality profile that is relaxed, unhurried, and cooperative.

■ **type C behaviour pattern**

a constellation of behaviour patterns that may predict which individuals are more likely to develop cancer or to have their cancer progress quickly, include passive acceptance and self-sacrifice.

■ **ubermensch**

German, 'overlord, superman', Nietzsche's term for the superior man who overcomes the mediocrity of ordinary people, who determines for himself what is right and wrong, and who thus places himself above prevailing moral values.

unconditional positive regard

complete love and acceptance of an individual by another person, such as a parent for a child, with no conditions attached.

Unconditioned Response (UCR)

in classical conditioning, the response given originally to the unconditioned stimulus used as the basis for establishing a conditioned response to a previously neutral stimulus.

Unconditioned Stimulus (UCS)

in classical conditioning, a stimulus that automatically elicits a response, typically via a reflex, without prior conditioning.

unconscious

in Freud's topographic model, that part of the mind containing repressed thoughts and memories of which the individual is unaware.

unconscious inference

a term used by the German scientist Hermann von Helmholtz to describe the process by which the perceiver progresses from experiencing sensations evoked by an object to recognizing the properties of the object. We make this inference automatically and unconsciously, and eventually we do not even notice the sensations on which it is based. Helmholtz argued that unconscious inference is the basis of many perceptual phenomena, including distance and object perception.

unconscious motive

a motive of which the subject is unaware or aware of in distorted form. Because there is no sharp dividing line between conscious and unconscious, many motives have both conscious and unconscious aspects.

unconscious processes

memories, impulses, and desires that are not available to consciousness. According to the psychoanalytic theories of Sigmund Freud, painful memories and wishes are sometimes repressed that is, diverted to the unconscious where they continue to influence our actions even though we are not aware of them.

unilateral neglect

paying little or no attention to things on one side of the body. This usually occurs on the side opposite from the location of the injury to the brain because nerve fibres from the brain typically cross before innervating body structures. In extreme cases, the patient may not bathe, dress or acknowledge one side of the body.

■ **universal**

a statement that refers to all the members of the same group and describes that which all the members have in common.

■ **universalisability**

the feature of a maxim or principle that makes it capable of being consistently applied to everyone.

■ **unmoved mover, doctrine of**

see **prime mover**.

■ **upper motor neurons**

long nerve cells that originate in the brain and travel in tracts through the spinal cord. Any injury to these nerves cuts off contact with brain control. Reflex activity is still intact, however resulting in spasticity. For men with upper motor neuron injuries, reflex erections are possible.

■ **urinary tract infection**

when bacteria have reproduced to a large number in the bladder. This can cause fever, chills, burning on urination, urgency, frequency, incontinence or foul smelling urine.

■ **use/mention**

see **mention/use**.

■ **utilitariansim**

ethical theory founded by Jeremy Bentham, James Mill and John Stuart Mill in England in the 19th century that holds that acts are right which produce the greatest amount of happiness for the greatest number of beings affected, and second, that the particular act or rule being considered should produce more such good than any other possible act or rule. Act utilitarianism contrasts with rule utilitarianism, in that the act (rather than the rule) is the subject of what produces the greatest good. Utilitarianism is hence a theory about: (1) what is right (good consequences, not motives), (2) maximisation (the number of beings affected counts morally), and (3) what creates a good consequence. Hedonic utilitarianism holds that good consequences should be understood in terms of tangible pleasures.

■ **utility calculus**

the notion held by some utilitarians, especially Bentham, that the value of certain rules or acts in bringing about the greatest good for the greatest number can actually be measured in happiness units.

■ **utopia**

the term used to refer to an imaginary, ideal world.

■ **vagueness**

a term describing the imprecision or 'fuzziness' of classifying statements, which leads to borderline or 'unable to say' cases. For example, baldness is a vague concept: when is a man definitely bald?

■ **vagus nerve**

the nerve that helps to control function of the larynx, stomach, esophagus, heart, lungs and intestines.

■ **valid argument**

'invalid' and 'false', as well as 'true' and 'valid' are synonyms in ordinary language but not in philosophy, where only premises or statements are 'true' or 'false', and only arguments are 'valid' or 'invalid'. The difficult thing for people to grasp is that validity and truth, as used in philosophy, are two different kinds of relationships: 'validity' refers to the logical form of an argument whereas 'truth' refers to the relationship of a statement to the objects it describes in the world. So an argument can be valid with false premises and an invalid argument can have all true premises. An invalid argument, then, has some problem with its logical form, such as an ambiguous key term. A valid argument with true premises is called sound.

■ **validity**

the predictive significance of a test for its intended purposes. Validity can be measured by a coefficient of correlation between scores on the test and the scores that the test seeks to predict, in other words, scores on some criterion.

■ **validity coefficient**

the correlation between a test score and some criterion to which the test is supposed to predict.

■ **value judgement**

an evaluative statement.

■ **values**

enduring beliefs about important life goals that transcend specific situations.

■ **variable**

one of the conditions measured or controlled in an experiment.

■ **variable-interval schedule**

a schedule of reinforcement in which a reinforcer is delivered for the first response made after a variable period of time whose average is predetermined.

■ **variable-ratio schedule**

a schedule of reinforcement in which a reinforcer is delivered for the first response made after a variable number of responses whose average is predetermined.

■ **variance**

the square of a standard deviation.

■ **vegetative state**

a condition in which the person utters no words and does not follow commands or make any response that is psychologically meaningful.

■ **veil of ignorance**

a concept essential to the theory of justice of John Rawls, who asks us to choose in a social contract the structure of a just society without knowing what our sex, race, age, or health will be. When the veil lifts, we will discover who we really are, and as such, John Rawls thinks we will choose to make the worst position as good as possible. It is a theoretical device for forcing us to choose the basic principles of justice through the Golden Rule.

■ ventilator

mechanical device to facilitate breathing in persons with impaired diaphragm function. Also known as respirator.

■ ventricles, brain

four natural cavities in the brain which are filled with cerebrospinal fluid (CSF). The outline of one or more of these cavities may change if a haemorrhage or tumour has consumed space in a lobe of the brain.

■ ventromedial hypothalamus (VMH)

area of the hypothalamus important to the regulation of food intake. Electrical stimulation of this area will make an experimental animal stop eating, destruction of brain tissue here produces voracious eating, eventually leading to obesity.

■ verbal apraxia

impaired control of proper sequencing of muscles used in speech (tongue, lips, jaw muscles, vocal cords). These muscles are not weak but their control is defective. Speech is laboured and characterised by sound reversals, additions and word approximations.

■ verbosity

the tendency to be excessively wordy in conversation.

■ veridical

that which is literally true and presents things as they really are.

■ verification

the process of ascertaining, either through logical argument or empirical demonstration, the truth of a proposition.

■ vertebrae

the bones that make up the spinal column.

■ vestibular

pertaining to the vestibular system in the middle ear and the brain which senses movements of the head. Disorders of the vestibular system can lead to dizziness, poor regulation of postural muscle tone and inability to detect quick movements of the head.

■ vestibular apparatus

an organ in the inner ear that contains receptors for body movement and kinesthesis.

■ vestibular nerve

a main division of the auditory nerve. Arises in the ganglion and is concerned with equilibrium.

■ vestibular sacs

two sacs in the labyrinth of the inner ear, called the saccule and utricle, which contain the otoliths ('ear stones'). Pressure of the otoliths on the hair cells in the gelatinous material of the utricle and saccule gives us the sense of body tilt or linear acceleration.

vestibular sense

the sense that tells how one's own body is oriented in the world with respect to gravity.

vicarious learning

learning by observing the behaviour of others and noting the consequences of that behaviour (syn. observational learning).

virtue

from Latin, 'virtu', righteous conduct. Virtue has a Christianised connotation that the ancient Greek virtues lacks, whereby a man of virtue does a right thing because it is right or it pleases God (such a sense is not conveyed by the virtues of Ancient Greece).

virtue ethics

the theory of ethics that values virtue, or virtues, rather than duty or the utilitarian greatest good, as the answer to the question, "What makes an act right?"

virtues

as a plural, the term refers to excellences of character that include (as the cardinal virtues) courage, wisdom, self-control, and justice, as well as other admirable traits such as loyalty and compassion. 'Virtues' refers to excellences of character identified in ancient Greece, whereas 'virtue' is broader and also includes humility and charity.

vision therapy

specific therapies and corrective lenses designed to treat visual disorders resulting from brain injury or defect.

visual acuity

the ability to detect visual detail.

visual area

a projection area lying in the occipital lobe. In humans, damage to this area produces blindness in portions of the visual field corresponding to the amount and location of the damage.

visual buffer

in short-term memory, a hypothesised component of the encoding process that briefly stores information in a visual code (i.e., a visual representation of verbal and nonverbal items).

visual cliff

an experimental apparatus with glass over a patterned surface, one half of which is just below the glass and the other half, several feet below. Used to test the depth perception of animals and human infants.

visual cortex

the region of the occipital lobes in which visual information is processed.

visual field

the total visual array acting on the eye when it is directed toward a fixation point.

visual-evoked potentials

a method of studying perception using electrodes placed on the back of the head over the visual cortex. The electrodes record electrical responses related to how well the observer can discriminate a presented stimulus.

■ vocational evaluation

an organised and comprehensive service staffed by specialists who systematically and comprehensively utilise work activities (real or simulated) and/or educational services as the focal point for educational and vocational assessment and exploration. In addition, psychological testing, counselling, social summaries, occupational information, etc., are other evaluation tools that are used. It incorporates the medical, psychological, social, vocational, educational, cultural, and economic data for establishment and attainment of individual goals.

■ voice stress analyser

a device that graphically represents changes in a person's voice associated with emotion. Used in lie detection.

■ volley principle

an extension of frequency theory which proposes that when peaks in a sound wave come too frequently for a single neuron to fire at each peak, several neurons fire as a group at the frequency of the stimulus tone.

■ volumetric receptors

hypothesised receptors that regulate water intake by responding to the volume of blood and body fluids. Renin, a substance secreted by the kidneys into the bloodstream, may be one volumetric receptor, it constricts the blood vessels and stimulates the release of the hormone, angiotensin, which acts on cells in the hypothalamus to produce thirst.

■ voluntary processes

activities selected by choice and controlled or monitored according to intention or plan.

■ vulnerability-stress model

an interactive model of physical or mental disorders that proposes that an individual will develop a disorder only when he or she has both some constitutional vulnerability (predisposition) and experiences stressful circumstances. Same as diathesis-stress model.

■ warranted assertibility

term associated with Dewey whereby knowledge is a process, the end product of which allows us to have such good reason to accept its truth, that it is exempt from criticism.

■ Watson, J. B. (1878-1958)

originated behaviourism, where behaviour is described in terms of physiological responses to stimuli. It rejects concept of conscious or unconscious mental activity.

weak methods

general problem-solving strategies that do not depend on specific knowledge of a problem. Examples are difference reduction, means-ends analysis, and working backwards.

Weber's law

the observation that the difference threshold is a fixed proportion of the stimulus magnitude at which it is measured. The proportion is constant over a wide range of stimulus magnitudes, and is called Weber's constant. The value of Weber's constant depends on the sensory modality, the smaller the constant, the more sensitive the modality.

wellness

optimal health, incorporating the ability to function fully and actively

over the physical, intellectual, emotional, spiritual, social, and environmental domains of health.

weltanschauung

German, 'world view'.

wernicke's area

a portion of the left cerebral hemisphere involved in language understanding. Individuals with damage in this area are not able to comprehend words, they can hear words, but they do not know their meanings.

will-to-believe argument

term associated with William James, it describes the act of believing not just because there is evidence to believe, but because it is efficacious to do so.

will-to-power

an idea central to Nietzsche's philosophy. First, as a factual claim, it is the view that all people seek control over each other, and hence, that traditional Christian ethics and religion are just one way of doing so, and it is an ethical claim, where the ubermensch transcends the conventional morality of the masses and engages in life-affirming egoism.

wisdom

expertise in the fundamental pragmatics of life.

withdrawal symptoms

unpleasant physiological and psychological reactions that occur when a person suddenly stops taking an addictive drug, these range from nausea, anxiety, mild tremors, and difficulty sleeping at low levels of dependence to vomiting, cramps, hallucinations, agitation, and severe tremors or seizures at higher levels.

within-subjects design

a research design that uses each participant as his or her own control; for example, the behaviour of an experimental participant before receiving treatment might be compared to his or her behaviour after receiving treatment.

■ **working backwards**

a problem-solving strategy in which one works backwards from the goal towards the current state.

■ **working memory**

a memory resource that is used to accomplish tasks such as reasoning and language comprehension. It consists of the phonological loop, visuo-spatial sketchpad, and central executive.

■ **working through**

in psychoanalytic therapy, the process of re-education by having patients face the same conflicts over and over in the consultation room, until they can independently face and master the conflicts in ordinary life.

■ **X chromosome**

a chromosome that, if paired with another X chromosome, determines that the individual will be a female. If it is combined with a Y chromosome, the individual will be a male. The X chromosome transmits sex-linked traits.

■ **XYY syndrome**

an abnormal condition in which a male has an extra Y sex chromosome some, reputedly associated with unusual aggressiveness, although the evidence is not conclusive.

■ **Y chromosome**

the chromosome that, combined with an X chromosome, determines maleness.

■ **yerkes-dodson law**

1. theory arguing that for performance to be optimal, the amount of arousal required must be optimised. Too much or too little stimulation will result in a poorer performance.
2. a correlation between task performance and optimal level of arousal.

■ **zeitgeist**

German, 'the spirit of the times'.

■ **zeno's paradoxes**

paradoxes devised by the ancient Greek, Zeno of Elea, to demonstrate the impossibility of motion. See also paradox.

■ **zero correlation**

the absence of a relationship between two or more variables as determined by a correlation statistic. Often abbreviated as 'r=0.'

■ **zoroastrianism**

a dualistic religion dominant in ancient Persia in the sixth century B. C. that emphasised the struggle between the god of light, and the god of darkness. The meaning of life for each person consists in a struggle between giving allegiance to either, and world history is determined by how many souls support which god. The belief of some Christians in the ongoing battle between Satan and God reflects the continuing appeal of this view.

■ **z-score**

a standard score that sets the mean to zero and standard deviation to one.

■ **z-test**

the statistical formula to determine the z-score of a particular raw score.

■ **zygote**

a fertilized ovum or egg.

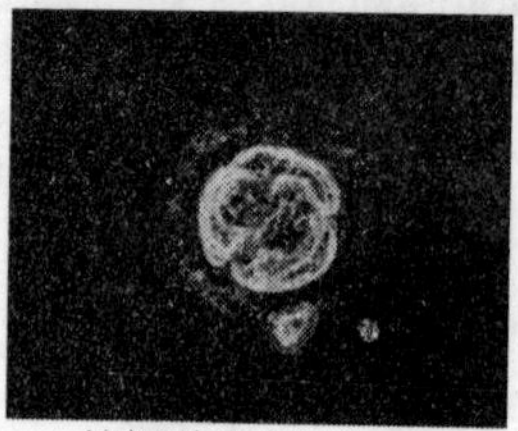

A developing eight-cell egg that resulted in pregnancy

Notes

Notes

34. Genetic Engineering 125/-
35. Health & Nutrition 125/-
36. History 125/-
37. Import and Export 125/-
38. Information System Management 125/-
39. Internet 125/-
40. IT 125/-
41. Inorganic Chemistry 125/-
42. Law 125/-
43. Library & Information Science 125/-
44. Literature 125/-
45. Management 125/-
46. Mathematics 125/-
47. Marketing & Sales 125/-
48. Mass Communication 125/-
49. Mechanical Engg. 125/-
50. Medical 125/-
51. Music 125/-
52. Organic Chemistry 125/-
53. Philosophy 125/-
54. Physical Education 125/-
55. Physics 125/-
56. Psychology 125/-
57. Science 125/-
58. Sex 125/-
59. Sociology 125/-
60. Sports 125/-
61. Textile 125/-
62. Zoology 125/-

Lotus PRESS

Unit No. 220, Second Floor, 4735/22,
Prakash Deep Building, Ansari Road, Darya Ganj,
New Delhi - 110002, Ph.: 32903912, 23280047, 09811594448
E-mail: lotuspress1984@gmail.com, www.lotuspress.co.in